ENCOUNTERS cultural histories

Series editors:
Roger Cooter
Harriet Ritvo
Carolyn Steedman
Bertrand Taithe

Over the past few decades cultural history has become the discipline of encounters. Beyond the issues raised by the 'linguistic turn', the work of theorists such as Norbert Elias, Pierre Bourdieu, Michel Foucault or Jacques Derrida has contributed to the emergence of cultural history as a forum for bold and creative exchange. This series proposes to place encounters – human, intellectual and disciplinary – at the heart of historical thinking. *Encounters* will include short, innovative and theoretically informed books from all fields of history. The series will provide an arena for exploring new and reassembled historical subjects, stimulating perceptions and re-perceptions of the past, and methodological challenges and innovations; it will publish at history's cutting edge. The *Encounters* series will demonstrate that history is the hidden narrative of modernity.

Already published

Plants, patients and the historian   Paolo Palladino

Mourning becomes ...: Post/memory, commemoration and the concentration camps of the South African War   Liz Stanley

Dust   Carolyn Steedman

Benjamin's *Arcades*

An unGuided tour

PETER BUSE, KEN HIRSCHKOP,
SCOTT MCCRACKEN AND BERTRAND TAITHE

Manchester University Press
Manchester and New York
Distributed exclusively in the USA by Palgrave

Published by Manchester University Press
Oxford Road, Manchester M13 9NR, UK
and Room 400, 175 Fifth Avenue, New York, NY 10010, USA
www.manchesteruniversitypress.co.uk

Distributed exclusively in the USA by
Palgrave, 175 Fifth Avenue, New York, NY 10010, USA
Distributed exclusively in Canada by
UBC Press, University of British Columbia, 2029 West Mall, Vancouver, BC,
Canada V6T 1Z2

British Library Cataloguing-in-Publication data
A catalogue record for this book is available from the British Library
Library of Congress Cataloging-in-Publication Data applied for

ISBN   0 7190 6988 2   hardback
EAN   978 0 7190 6988 8
ISBN   0 7190 6989 0   paperback
EAN   978 0 7190 6989 5

First published 2005

14 13 12 11 10 09 08 07 06 05   10 9 8 7 6 5 4 3 2 1

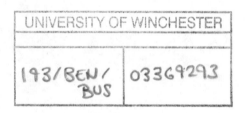
Typeset
by Northern Phototypesetting Co. Ltd., Bolton
Printed in Great Britain
by Bell and Bain Ltd, Glasgow

Contents

Preface: beginnings

These notes devoted to the Paris arcades were begun under an open sky of cloudless blue that arched above the foliage. (N1, 5)

This book was not. The sky remained cloudy, the trees devoid of foliage and the horizon grey: we worked in Manchester, that other capital of the nineteenth century. It began as a reading group that focused on the newly translated *Arcades Project*, for it is not a book one can read entirely by oneself and it is not a book one can read in one sitting. Its mass and complexity, its accumulative wealth of citations and allusions, make it an enigmatic and elusive text. Moreover, we came at it from different disciplinary contexts, each with our individual baggage of differences and critical perspectives, from which we each devised our own tactics, inroads and tangential takes on its thousand or more pages. Both the work and its readers called for discussion and debate. When it came to writing about it we wanted to preserve some of that form.

From the beginning, we recognized that, as a work, the *Arcades Project* invites raiding rather than reading. One starts from the Exposés, from the sketches, from the list of Convolutes, from the index, from the cross-references, the notes and bibliography. One dives in rather than swims through. But as a collection of individuals brought together by locality rather than discipline or institution, we chose the slow way: the long labour of reading through the entire text, negotiating along the way with its opacity and with each other. On countless evenings, we took our time to begin, investing in idleness, before we began to ask each other, alighting on a dense and impenetrable passage – what is this about? – expressing both frustration and admiration at the incomplete work.

Only towards the end, as the object that had brought us together began to recede, when excuses for evenings and 'working' lunches diminished, did we think of writing. But what? To continue the pleasure of our dis-

cussions, the same mode had to be perpetuated. Nothing like an argument would do. We didn't have a theory of Benjamin. We had to seize on
the topics that had animated us, the passages that had perplexed, then
enthused. Yet we wanted to increase the ambit of our conversations. With
Dorothy Richardson's damning definition of the realist novel as a 'guided
tour' in mind, we decided to offer the opposite: an unguided tour of the
arcades.

The result is seventeen short entries on topics that reflect our collective
sense of what needed to be discussed, but which are, at the same time,
topics chosen because they reflect the interests of the individuals who made
up the group. In one sense they are all co-authored, in that each stems from
the original discussions of the reading group. But most are, at least initially,
the product of an individual author, which has then been subject to comments, criticism, suggestions and revisions by the other three.

We wanted to write a book that, like the *Arcades Project* itself, could be
read in more than one way, not just cover to cover. We also wanted to
engage with certain parts of the *Arcades* from different perspectives in
parallel, rather than suggesting that a comprehensive understanding of,
say, the figure of the collector or the Angel of History can be defined or
summarized at one time or in one way. To do otherwise would be to do
violence to Benjamin's principle of constellative work. Consequently, we
return to certain passages and ideas under different headings, but each
time from a new perspective.

None the less, the order of entries is not random. 'Encounters' situates
the book in relation to the *Encounters* series and gives an outline of the
Arcades Project's intellectual encounters with cultural history. The four
entries that follow give some of the *Arcades*' contexts. 'Arcades' provides
valuable historical background on the spaces that gave the work its title.
'Method' begins, but certainly doesn't exhaust, the discussions of Benjamin's methodologies that run through the book. 'Judaism' engages with
Benjamin's relationship with theology, and 'Modernity/modernism' with
his relationship to social, political and aesthetic theory. The following ten
entries offer different ways into the *Project*. Many take their titles from the
headings of the convolutes, but, just as no one convolute can be read outside its relation to the other convolutes, no entry confines itself to a single
convolute, either in theme or in theoretical scope. The penultimate entry,
'Nazis', returns the focus with force to the politics of Benjamin's moment,
but it is not, in any sense, meant to be read as an ending.

So, this is an analytical kaleidoscope, which should not be read from
cover to cover, but which might be of use to anyone who wants to

negotiate the *Arcades Project* itself. With Benjamin's *Passagen-Werk*, we don't deny the ruptures and discontinuities. This book is wilfully conceived as a series of entries which can be read either as self-standing thematic explorations or as interrelated chapters which cross-reference each other. We do not pretend to complete an uncompleted work, to write the book Benjamin did not write. As with the *Arcades Project* itself, this book is like a wind-up toy that can only go so far without fresh input. It does not summarize the unsummarizable. It awaits the fresh conversations it hopes to provoke.

Acknowledgements

We owe many thanks to our partners and families, who regarded us sceptically whenever we announced we were about to meet for an evening, a day or a weekend to 'work on the *Arcades*'. We hope the appearance of the book allays their worst suspicions. The fact that we also wish to thank innumberable cafés, restaurants, and, God forbid, hotels, for their hospitality (particularly warm thanks for the patient staff at the Fat Cat Café in Llandudno) will no doubt stoke those suspicions yet again. On a more sober note, we want to acknowledge the support of the Universities of Manchester, Salford and Sheffield Hallam, and their libraries in particular. Projects like this are possible only because of continued and in many respects generous public support for what is often quite recondite and esoteric research. Thanks to Keya Ganguly, who commented on earlier versions of 'Method' and 'Modernity/modernism' and to David Glover, Mandy Merck and Jenny Bourne Taylor, who commented on an earlier version of 'Idleness'. Finally, thanks to the staff of Manchester University Press and to our patient editors.

References and abbreviations

All references to the text of the *Arcades Project* itself (as opposed to the exposés, commentaries and additional materials which have been included with the publication of the English translation) are provided in the text and refer to the convolute and sheet number. The following abbreviations for works by Benjamin are used in the notes:

Adorno–Benjamin Correspondence	Benjamin, Walter and Theodor Adorno, *The Complete Correspondence 1928–1940*, ed. Henri Lonitz, trans. Nicholas Walker (Cambridge: Polity Press, 1999)
AP	*The Arcades Project*, ed. Rolf Tiedemann, trans. Howard Eiland and Kevin McLaughlin (Cambridge, Mass. and London: Belknap Press, 1999).
Correspondence	*The Correspondence of Walter Benjamin*, ed. Theodor Adorno and Gershom Scholem, trans. Manfred R. Jacobson and Evelyn M. Jacobson (Chicago and London: University of Chicago Press, 1994)
Scholem–Benjamin Correspondence	Benjamin, Walter and Gershom Scholem, *The Correspondence of Walter Benjamin and Gershom Scholem, 1932–1940*, ed. Gershom Scholem, trans. Gary Smith and Andre Lefevere (Cambridge, Mass.: Harvard University Press, 1992)

SW 1   *Selected Writings, Vol. 1, 1913–1926,* ed. Marcus Bullock and Michael W. Jennings (Cambridge, Mass. and London: Belknap Press, 1996)

SW 2   *Selected Writings, Vol. 2, 1927–1934,* ed. Michael W. Jennings, Howard Eiland and Gary Smith, trans. Rodney Livingstone and others (Cambridge, Mass. and London: Belknap Press, 1999)

SW 3   *Selected Writings, Vol. 3, 1935–1938,* ed. Howard Eiland and Michael W. Jennings, trans. Edmund Jephcott, Howard Eiland and others (Cambridge, Mass. and London: Belknap Press, 2002)

SW 4   *Selected Writings, Vol. 4, 1938–1940,* ed. Howard Eiland and Michael W. Jennings, trans. Howard Eiland and Michael W. Jennings (Cambridge, Mass. and London: Belknap Press, 2003)

Encounters

Introductory notes and historical perspectives

Encountering the Arcades Project: composition and timeline

The *Arcades Project* has been published in book form, but anyone who reads it cover to cover will struggle to find a single book in it. For a long time the work enjoyed a quasi-mythical status, filtered down to an Anglophone audience through such crucial intermediaries as Susan Buck-Morss in *The Dialectics of Seeing*.[1] First published in 1982 as volume 5 of the *Gesammelte Schriften*, then translated into French in 1989, its interest for Benjamin scholars has passed its height, and non-experts now have the opportunity to assess its wider importance and usefulness. With the recent publication of the four-volume *Selected Writings*, those of us who have known Benjamin mainly from the essays in *Illuminations*, *One-Way Street* and *Understanding Brecht* are suddenly faced with the bewildering range and complexity of his *oeuvre*. Given the content of the *Arcades Project* – just over a thousand pages of citations, commentary, fragments and notes, with little in the way of overarching explanatory apparatus – it seems more than likely that the work will baffle most readers. Either that, or it will be plundered for the precious aphorisms amongst the thickets of citations that make up the bulk of the work. For the dedicated, there are certainly more than a few gems here: Adorno, custodian of the manuscript for many years, particularly liked 'The eternal is in any case far more the ruffle on a dress than some idea' (B3, 7; N3, 2). It has become received wisdom that the *Arcades* should be approached selectively, in non-linear fashion: unsuitable for reading cover to cover, it is better dipped into here and there, or even read as a kind of primitive hyper-text, with a citation or comment in one 'convolute' leading through a cross-reference to related material in a distant part of the book. Benjamin would undoubtedly have approved of such a 'rag-picking' approach to his work, but it is important not to overlook some of its wider ambitions and achievements. In his attempt to come to terms with the cultures of consumption in the arcades and *magasins de nouveautés* of the nineteenth century, Benjamin anticipates concerns of much later cultural theorists and historians, while rethinking the origins and nature of contemporary capitalism and the formation and workings of the modern metropolis. The *Arcades Project* is perhaps most notable for its extraordinary historical method, with its emphasis on residues and collecting, dialectical image and citation. For those willing to work through the *Arcades*, it becomes clear that this monstrous thing is something like the historical practice for which the endlessly quoted 'On the concept of history' gave a glimpse of the theory.

Benjamin began work on the *Arcades* in 1927, thinking he was preparing a short essay ('a project that will take just a few weeks', he confidently predicted) that combined the 'profane motifs of *One-Way Street* . . . hellishly intensified' with material he had drawn in equal parts from the surrealists and the streets of Paris.[2] Although the material was enthusiastically received by Max Horkheimer and the Adornos (Theodor and Gretel) in a reading in 1929, Benjamin was forced to put it to one side in 1930, probably from the pressure of having to focus his efforts on the reviews, journal essays, feuilletons and radio work that earned him a living. When he was forced to flee Germany for Paris in 1934, he resumed work on the project, which assumed the convoluted form that is now its signature. As is well known, Benjamin continued working on the *Arcades* until the end of his life, leaving the manuscript – if that is the right word for hundreds of pages of notes arranged by topic – with his friend Georges Bataille, who squirreled it away for the duration of the war in the Bibliothèque Nationale, from which it was taken in 1947 and delivered to Adorno, then living in New York. Adorno eventually passed on the unenviable task of editing the papers to his doctoral student Rolf Tiedemann.

The English publication of the *Arcades Project* incorporates Tiedemann's exegetical essay 'Dialectics at a standstill', but eliminates a good deal – although by no means all – of his scholarly apparatus. The volume opens with two versions of 'Paris, capital of the nineteenth century', an essay already familiar to English-language readers, which Benjamin prepared as 'exposés' for the Institute of Social Research, underwriters of the project from 1934. The end of the published volume consists of 'First sketches' and 'Early drafts', an assortment of incomplete essays, collected fragments and outlines. The real substance of the *Arcades Project*, however, consists of 36 'convolutes', each one a bundle or sheaf of notes and quotations on a specific theme or topic relating to nineteenth-century Paris, labelled with an upper-case or lower-case letter of the alphabet. (For instance, Convolute B is 'Fashion', D 'Boredom, eternal return',

M 'The flâneur', W 'Fourier', d 'Literary history, Hugo', and m 'Idleness'.) The shortest one, 'Reproduction technology, lithography', takes up only two pages, while the longest, 'Baudelaire', extends to 160. Each one consists of a series of numbered entries – made up of Benjamin's own prose, quotations with commentary, and most often, quotations without commentary – with a system of cross-referencing to other convolutes. It is hard to dispute with those who can find no coherent whole in such a system, but to those who scoff that this is no more than an elaborate card catalogue, one can reply, yes, but *what* a card catalogue.

One productive way of looking at the convolutes is as a sort of workshop for Benjamin's writings in the 1930s. In Convolute H, 'The collector', one can find the outlines of 'Unpacking my library'; Convolute J, 'Baudelaire', provides the elements for 'On some motifs in Baudelaire' and *Charles Baudelaire: A Lyric Poet in the Era of High Capitalism*; and 'On the concept of history' is to a great extent a distillation of ideas explored in Convolute N, 'On the theory of knowledge, theory of progress'. In fact, the entire *Arcades Project* is inseparable from all Benjamin's work of the 1930s, which is known collectively as his 'Paris production cycle'. Paris, of course, is where Benjamin spent the last years of his life in exile, and, along with Berlin, Naples and Moscow, is one of the constellation of cities that formed his understanding of the urban. Paris, in this scheme, was the model of the modern capitalist city and the arcades marked its pre-history:

> today arcades dot the metropolitan landscape like caves containing the fossil remains of a vanished monster: the consumer of the pre-imperial era of capitalism, the last dinosaur of Europe. On the walls of these caverns their immemorial fauna, the commodity, luxuriates and enters, like cancerous tissue, into the most irregular combinations. A world of secret affinities opens up within: palm tree and feather duster, hairdryer and Venus de Milo, prostheses and letter-writing manuals. The odalisque lies in wait next to the inkwell, and priestesses raise high the vessels into which we drop cigarettes as incense offerings. (R2, 3)

This approach to the arcades of course owes a considerable debt to the surrealists. Louis Aragon's dream-like passage through the Passage de l'Opéra just before its demolition in *Paysan de Paris*, and Breton's *Nadja* first taught Benjamin about 'the revolutionary energies that appear in the "outmoded"'.[3] And if surrealism gave him his early schooling in arcade-work, he soon found other *practices* that embodied or mimicked his own historical method: the volume does not come equipped with a user's guide, but inscribed within its pages we find characters from whose habits we might learn to read the *Arcades*. Foremost among the figures who populate the text and suggest to us models for encountering it are the flâneur and the collector.

Fortuitous encounters: 'of a space, of moments and discontinuities'[4]

Among the many literary encounters of the *Arcades Project*, Baudelaire figures most prominently. In Baudelaire Benjamin found the archetypal flâneur strolling through the arcades in decline (and the archetype is always male). The term *flâneur* was coined around 1806 and refers to an individual whose state of heightened individuality and interiority spurs him to romantic journeying in the infinity of the self. In the nineteenth century and in the work of Baudelaire it acquired another layer of meanings, being associated with the notion of stimuli.[5] The flâneur is open to stimuli and walks the streets of the modern city at a slow and leisurely pace, an observer and recorder of modernity, the archetypal modern subject, passive and open, restrained and appreciative, a customer of the world. In French there is another term for the purposeless idler, also walking the streets in search of sensation but lacking any aesthetic intent: the *badaud*.[6] *Badaud* (a Norman dialect term accepted in French) is a much older term than flâneur, but it is significantly tainted with notions of stupidity. To place both the flâneur and the *badaud* in context is to admit that the flâneur will remain an isolated individual crossing through the crowd while the *badaud* is the atom of a crowd or a mob.[7] The class connotations are obvious once again but they primarily refer to propriety and social distance. The flâneur is searching, at least in a superficial and random way, while the *badaud* is devoid of aesthetics, impressionable and passive. These cultural stereotypes remain vital in modern debates.

To give two famous examples: Stendhal, the first French flâneur of London, walked the streets of the English capital in 1821 as a romantic 'egotist' in search of peace of mind:

> London affected me deeply because of the walks alongside the river Thames towards Little Chelsea. There were there some little houses covered with roses that were for me truly elegiac. It was the first time that this bland [literary] genre touched me. I understand now how sick my soul was. I had an almost hydrophobic hatred of the sight of anyone coarse[8]

The small houses evoked an inaccessible intimacy made of quiet and delicately balanced feelings. The spectacle of the streets was paradoxically that of the intimate and homely,[9] inviting in the dandy who cannot stand the coarse and vulgar.[10] While these feelings would have been shared by that dandy of the third generation, Baudelaire, his definition of the flâneur had a substantially different connotation of historical quest which has fed the historiography of the flâneur ever since:

> Thus he goes, he runs, he seeks. What is he looking for? To be sure this man, such as I have described him, this loner gifted with an active imagination, always travelling through the *great human desert* has a grander aim than that of a pure flâneur, a more general aim than the fugitive pleasures of circumstances. He seeks what we will be allowed to call *modernity*; for there is no better word to express the idea in question. For him it is about discovering what fashion contains of poetics in history, of extracting what is eternal from the transient.[11]

What is striking in this often-quoted definition of the flâneur is precisely that it is not the definition of any flâneur but rather of a transcendental flâneur involved in an aesthetic quest immersed in history and historicism. The flâneur investigator is thus an elaboration on the concept of the man who enjoys the spectacle of the streets because he will make aesthetic and intellectual sense of this spectacle. Even when possessed with a rabid hatred of vulgarity, the flâneur haunts the streets in search of material with which to make sense of time and space. Whether there is method in this search is not made explicit in Baudelaire. Benjamin undoubtedly identified with Baudelaire, but he attempted to add method and ideological coherence to the flâneur's quest. Benjamin saw in Baudelaire the individualist on the edge of the abyss, the solipsistic soul facing the world of capitalist alienation, the dreamer lost in a world of phantasmagoria. Everything in the arcades was shaped to invoke this dream: they were sheltered from time and weather, the windows faced on to a passage looking into them, the hotels to be found in them thus opened on a closed world, the people looking out looked in instead, and mirrors and gaslight multiplied the detachment from anything like a construction of the real; all this is in the name of the commodity fetish luring herds of consumers and spectators into a space built using the material and the social and intellectual tools of Utopian socialism.[12]

Details, time and materiality: the collector

The historiography of memory and the literature of detail which have recently acquired such tremendous currency through the work of Nora[13] and Raphael Samuel[14] and through a return to the work of Husserl[15] or, in literary terms, Proust,[16] has much to learn from the *Arcades Project* (see N2, 6), even though, until now, this literature has remained mainly oblivious of

Benjamin. The issues of time and consciousness are central in Benjamin's work not only because he was reacting against the dominant historicist paradigm of his time, but also because these issues dominated many of his sources. Julia Kristeva, who does not refer to Benjamin, remarks in *Le Temps sensible* on the correspondence between Proust and the authors who had marked Benjamin's philosophical youth and on the correspondence or 'echoing' between Proust and Freudian free associations, and by extension, also, surrealist writings.[17] Kristeva notes the parallels between Bergson and Proust, but this is a parallel that Benjamin had observed before her in his preliminary sketches and in a more elaborate manner in Convolute H:[18]

> At the conclusion of *Matière et mémoire,* Bergson develops the idea that perception is a function of time. If, let us say, we were to live vis-à-vis some things more calmly and vis-à-vis others more rapidly, according to a different rhythm, there would be nothing 'subsistent' for us, but instead everything would happen right before our eyes; everything would strike us. But this is the way things are for the great collector. They strike him. How he himself pursues and encounters them, what changes in the ensemble of items are effected by a newly supervening item – all this shows him his affairs in constant flux. Here, the Paris arcades are examined as though they were properties in the hand of a collector. (At bottom, we may say, the collector lives a piece of dream life) (H1a, 5)

This appropriation of the figure of the collector (for more on the collector see 'Method'; see also the discussion of the flâneur and the gambler in '*Jeux/joie/jouissance*') as a path to the understanding of the material forces of modernity is perhaps the one that intimates most clearly Benjamin's historical sensibility and his apprehension of time and perception. This adds to the notion of 'dialectics at a standstill' as a material encounter between the collector and the object of collection as well as a process specific to the arcades themselves.

Benjamin's emphasis on how meanings emerge retrospectively from the rearrangement of material objects leads to a more complex and challenging phenomenology which, while opposing equally cheap forms of empathy and disincarnated analyses, allows for a poetic form of history that embraces concrete and abstract traces. It is precisely the objects of Benjamin's investigations that historians are now confronting. 'He was drawn to the petrified, frozen or obsolete elements of civilization, to everything in it devoid of domestic vitality', just as historians today seek to understand through dust or rag rugs the cultural and social interactions to which these remainders were central.[19]

Historical encounters: appropriating Benjamin and academic politics

A sceptical historian faced with the *Arcades* might well argue that a flâneur is no more than a privileged idler and a collector nothing but an amateur crank. While the endless spare time of the former and the obsessive nature of the latter may be essential prerequisites for tackling Benjamin's text, as role models for the sober historian they leave much to be desired. It is one thing to quote selectively from 'On the concept of history', quite another to extract from it a workable way of doing history. Almost inevitably, given the history of Benjamin's reception, it is first and foremost cultural theorists who have been drawn to the *Arcades*. But are they the best equipped to assess what is above all an historical undertaking? More to the point, do historians of nineteenth-century Paris have anything to gain from reading the *Arcades*, and to what extent has this encounter already begun?

Historians of nineteenth-century France and Paris have only recently begun to come to terms with the work of Benjamin, and his influence is yet to be fully felt. Only a few, mostly young, historians have shown an interest in the *Arcades Project* and its textual siblings. On the whole this reflects the evolution of the historiography on consumer culture, with its emphasis on spectacle and the spectacular politics of everyday life and historiographical developments such as Nora's *Lieux de mémoire* which look again at space and memory using Husserl and the early *Annales* work. The first French encounter with Benjamin took place in 1947 among literary critics in the review *Les Temps Modernes* edited by Jean-Paul Sartre through an article by Pierre Missac on Benjamin's historical method.[20] This article was later to have an impact on the historical scholarship on Blanqui, and Missac's translation was reprinted among Blanqui's collected works.[21] In spite of some considerable overlap of interests, notably over Baudelaire,[22] Sartre himself did not pay much attention to Benjamin, and one has to wait until 1959 to see a volume of Benjamin's works appear translated in France by the specialist of Nietzsche and medieval philosophy Maurice de Gandillac.[23] The first major critical reception in France followed the conference organized by Heinz Wismann in 1983, whose proceedings were published in 1986.[24] This path-breaking compilation of forty-nine translations and original contributions to Benjaminian studies did not contain the work of a single historian.

During these years the recurring story in historical circles is the limited and often partial readings of Benjamin. Benjamin was appropriated as the theoretician of literature, of visual culture, of technology, but his work had a limited impact on historians.[25] Turning its back on Adorno's systematic and systemic understanding of Benjamin, French interpreters such as Heinz Wismann summarized the dominant French interpretation: 'Benjamin is at his most stimulating for his reader when the reader does not attempt to reconstruct his thought in a fictitious continuity . . . Towards him some have very unpleasant servile attitudes [*suivisme*]. To honour him truly, to be up to his own standards, one needs to have a critical mind.'[26] This is welcome advice to historians who could not, even if they wished to, follow Benjamin to the letter. To write history in a messianic style is well nigh impossible without doing damage to one's academic credentials. Yet there is much that historians can take from Benjamin simply by plundering his footnotes and fragments, such is the richness of his materials in the *Arcades Project*, and so self-knowing and playful the ways in which he appropriates historical data. Benjamin collated these quotations and pasted them in a unique palimpsest, which reveals an enormous breadth of reading (one will need to refer to the German edition to find the whole bibliography) and a genius for distilling revealing associations of ideas and views. In terms of breadth of reading, Benjamin for instance uses Eugène Buret (a6a, 3) and Denis Poulot (a7, 4) decades before historians considered these authors again.[27] His focus on urban space, not simply as a backdrop to important events such as a revolution but also as an actor, predated historians by nearly two generations since the earliest works that echoed, unknowingly, Benjamin's interests and sources were by Louis Chevalier and Jeanne Gaillard in 1958 and 1976 respectively.[28] The British and American historical reception of Benjamin focused predictably enough on the thesis of the 'aura' in arts to begin with, opening up fractionally more in the 1980s, particularly as the history of consumerism found that some of its central themes had already been developed in Benjamin's work.[29] But one is hard pressed to find many instances of Benjaminian history until the mid- to late 1990s, when the *Arcades* begins to be engaged with more fully – particularly in the work of Vanessa Schwartz in *Spectacular Reality* and *Early Mass Culture in Fin-de-Siecle Paris*. This is a reflection of a series of new directions given to an increasingly polyphonic field. The 'linguistic turn', which so agitated historians with the promises and threats of postmodernity, was an important factor in the late 1980s and early 1990s for a reconsideration of historical narrative forms.[30] This debate opened the way for more experimental engagements with historical prose, which, associated with an autobiographical turn dating from the mid-1980s, has enabled the rediscovery of pre-Rankian and Annaliste narrative voices.[31] Furthermore the collapse of socialist regimes and of Communism as an intellectual force in Western Europe led many to reconsider the object of their study through the history of the body or of material culture, both ancient avenues that historians had failed to frequent since the 1930s.[32] To simplify greatly, the novelty of the old and the rediscovery of intellectual forms dating from the 1930s has meant that Benjamin reappears now as an important cultural historian through his work on Paris.

To illustrate this growing influence one could consider epoch-making studies of Paris such as David Harvey's *Consciousness and Urban Experience*, which originally ignored Benjamin's *Arcades Project* in favour of a more strictly Marxist analysis of the economic forces shaping the city.[33] In a new edition, Harvey took stock, at least at a superficial level, of the discredit of over-deterministic structuralism and of the rise of cultural paradigms based on Benjamin: the title of this re-issue itself could not have been more Benjaminian: *Paris, Capital of Modernity.*[34] This is not to say that a Benjaminian model exists with the clarity of a template or that his methodology is always clear (on which see 'Method' below). For instance, Benjamin emphasizes the collaborative nature of the management of a newspaper, *L'Autographe* (U2a, 3), probably to make a point about the influence of Saint-Simonian ideas over the press, but he does not comment on the fact that *L'Autographe* was a fascinating mid-nineteenth century attempt to reprint the facsimile of historical manuscripts in order to contextualize history and make possible graphological and psychological readings of its main actors. Yet Benjamin himself was an amateur graphologist and was interested in this quintessentially nineteenth-century system of psychological exploration (see also 'Magic').[35] In this particular instance as in many others, Benjamin felt obliged to privilege the 'high politics' of proto-socialism rather than root his form of historical materialism entirely in these fragments of self-exploration. The final result or effect is Benjamin's and this accretion of quotations might very well, as Adorno suggested, be an attempt at surreal historical writing. One can imagine that they might serve as a 'quarry, to be worked surreptitiously for doctoral advancement' while 'the stones lifted from it end up by adding only to the featureless sprawl of academic suburbia'.[36] For the time being, what is perhaps most troubling is how cultural theorists on the one hand and historians on the other go about their explorations of Benjamin entirely independently of each other. In an excellent recent edition of *boundary 2* devoted to the English translation of the *Arcades Project*, the contributors hail from departments of German, French, English,

Comparative Literature and Art History, but not a single one from a History department.³⁷ The present volume is the fruit of the collaboration of three cultural theorists and one historian of nineteenth-century France; it may very well find its audience among cultural theorists, but Benjamin's work also has an urgency for historians.

Notes

1 Susan Buck-Morss, *The Dialectics of Seeing: Walter Benjamin and the Arcades Project* (Cambridge, Mass. and London: MIT Press, 1989).
2 Letter 168, from Benjamin to Gerhard Scholem, 30 January 1928, in *Correspondence*, pp. 321–5 (p. 322). It is interesting to note that, in a letter to Jula Radt (née Cohn) two years earlier, Benjamin enthused about the Parisian fairs that 'drop like bombs on one or another quarter of the city'. There he found the incongruous juxtapositions that would later loom so large in his descriptions of the arcades: 'shooting galleries, silk canopies, butcher's stalls, antique stores, art dealers, waffle stands'; Letter 154, 8 April 1926, in *Correspondence*, pp. 295–7 (p. 297).
3 Walter Benjamin, 'Surrealism: the last snapshot of the European intelligentsia' [1929], in *SW 2*, pp. 207–21 (p. 210).
4 Walter Benjamin, 'A Berlin chronicle' [1932], in *SW 2*, pp. 595–637 (p. 612).
5 See Roger Smith, *Inhibition: History and Meaning in the Science of Mind and Brain* (Berkeley: University of California Press, 1992), pp. 57–66.
6 Richard D.E. Burton, *The Flaneur and his City: Patterns of Daily Life in Paris, 1815–1851* (Durham: University of Durham, 1994), pp. 1–6.
7 Benjamin himself emphasizes the distinction in 'The Paris of the Second Empire in Baudelaire' [1938], in *SW 4*, pp. 3–92 (pp. 41, 83 n189). On the nineteenth-century crowd see Gustave Le Bon, *The Crowd: A Study of the Popular Mind* (London: T. Fisher Unwin, 1896); Robert Nye, *Crime, Madness and Politics in Modern France: The Medical Concept of National Decline* (Princeton, NJ: Princeton University Press, 1984); Susanna Barrows, *Distorting Mirrors: Visions of the Crowd in Late Nineteenth-Century France* (New Haven: Yale University Press, 1981).
8 Stendhal, *Souvenirs d'egotisme* (Paris: Le Divan, 1927). These memoirs were written in 1832 but referred to a journey made in 1817.
9 As pointed out by Sharon Marcus, the contrast between the homely and the tenement flats of Paris was a cliché of any comparative perspective. Sharon Marcus, *Apartment Stories: City and Home in Nineteenth-century Paris and London* (Berkeley: University of California Press, 1999), pp. 27–8.
10 Doris Gunnell, *Stendhal et l'Angleterre* (Paris: Charles Bosse, 1909), p. 12.
11 Charles Baudelaire, *Oeuvres complètes* (Paris: Robert Laffont, 1980), p. 797.
12 Vanessa Schwartz, *Early Mass Culture in Fin-de-Siècle Paris* (Berkeley: University of California Press, 1998).

13 Pierre Nora (ed.), *Realms of Memory,* 3 vols (New York: Columbia University Press, 1996–8).

14 Raphael Samuel, *Theatres of Memory: Past and Present in Contemporary Culture* (London: Verso, 1992) and *Island Stories: Unravelling Britain* (London: Verso, 1998); Bertrand Taithe, '*Monuments aux Morts?* Reading Nora's *Realms of Memory* and Samuel's *Theatres of Memory*', *History of the Human Sciences,* 12: 2 (1999), 123–39.

15 Benjamin placed Husserl as the third most important influence of his youth, after Plato and Kant. See Walter Benjamin, 'Curriculum vitae III' [1928], in *SW 2*, pp. 77–9 (p. 77).

16 The entire work of Proust deals fundamentally with memory and recovered involuntary memory. See in this regard Benjamin, 'On the image of Proust' [1929], in *SW 2*, pp. 237–47 (p. 238).

17 Julia Kristeva, *Le Temps sensible: Proust et l'expérience littéraire* (Paris: Gallimard, 1994), pp. 520–2.

18 Walter Benjamin, 'First sketches: Paris arcades <I>', in *AP*, pp. 827–68 (p. 841), Convolute F° 34.

19 Theodor W. Adorno, 'A portrait of Walter Benjamin', in *Prisms*, trans. Samuel and Shierry Weber (Cambridge, Mass.: MIT Press, 1981), pp. 227–41 (p. 233).

20 25 octobre 1947.

21 Auguste Blanqui, *Instructions pour une prise d'armes [Texte imprimé]; L'Éternité par les astres, hypothèse astronomique et autres texts,* ed. Miguel Abensour and Valentin Pelosse (Paris: Société Encyclopédique Française, Éditions de la Tête de Feuilles, 1973).

22 Jean-Paul Sartre, *Baudelaire* (Paris: Gallimard, 1947)

23 Walter Benjamin, *Œuvres de Walter Benjamin,* 2 vols, ed. Maurice de Gandillac (Paris: Les Lettres Nouvelles, Denoël, 1971).

24 Heinz Wismann, *Walter Benjamin et Paris* (Paris: CERF, 1986). For the early reception in Italy see Riccardo Gavagna, *Benjamin in Italia, bibliographica italiana, 1956–1980* (Florence: Sansoni, 1982). In Spain, inter alia, the short text by Hans Mayer was reprinted in *El Pais* of 1990 for the fiftieth anniversary of Walter Benjamin's death: *Der Zeitgenosse Walter Benjamin* (Frankfurt am Main: Jüdischer Verlag, 1992).

25 With some notable exceptions of sub-disciplines such as architectural history.

26 Heinz Wismann, interview by Lionel Richard, *Magazine Littéraire,* 408 (April 2002), 25.

27 Adrian Rifkin and Roger Thomas (eds), *Voices of the People: The Politics and Life of 'La Sociale' at the End of the Second Empire* (London: Routledge & Kegan Paul, 1987).

28 Louis Chevalier, *Classes laborieuses et classes dangereuses* (Paris: Plon, 1958) and *Montmartre des plaisirs et du crime* (Paris: Robert Laffont, 1980); Jeanne Gaillard, *Paris, la Ville 1852–1870* (Lille: Champion, 1976).

29 Peter Gurney, *Cooperative Culture and the Politics of Consumption in England, 1870–1930* (Manchester: Manchester University Press, 1996).

30 Raphael Samuel, 'Reading the signs', I and II, *History Workshop Journal*, 32 (1991), 88–109; 33 (1992), 220–51.

31 Carolyn Steedman, *Dust* (Manchester: Manchester University Press, 2001).

32 Mark Jenner and Bertrand Taithe, 'The historiographical body', in John Pickstone and Roger Cooter (eds), *History of Medicine in the Twentieth Century* (New York: Harwood Publishing, 1999), pp. 187–200.

33 David Harvey, *Consciousness and the Urban Experience: Studies in the History and Theory of Capitalist Urbanization* (Oxford: Blackwell, 1985).

34 David Harvey, *Paris: Capital of Modernity* (London: Routledge, 2003).

35 See 'Graphology old and new' [1930], in *SW 2*, pp. 398–9.

36 These are E. P. Thompson's words on his own *William Morris* (New York: Pantheon Books, 1976), p. 768.

37 Kevin McLaughlin and Philip Rosen (eds), *Benjamin Now: Critical Encounters with* The Arcades Project, *boundary 2*, 30: 1 (2003).

Arcades

'Arcades' is not an ideal translation of the French *passages couverts* or the German *Passagen*. The French term 'passages' insisted on its original purpose, which was to provide a short-cut through one of the large Parisian blocks and, in so doing, to offer a new space for pedestrians. From their origins the arcades received more than their share of investment, architectural innovation and literary appropriation. At their inception they endeavoured to enclose and merge spaces of consumerism and of leisure. While the authors of *physiologies*[1] located in the arcades insisted on the ubiquity of the flâneurs and their expectant gaze, always seeking serendipitous encounters, the arcades also framed the half-woman, half-counter creatures seen through the windows or the absent-looking shopkeeper gazing through the windows at the mirrors in the shop opposite.[2] Ultimately, the arcades – spaces of exclusivity – were constantly losing ground to each other; transiently fashionable, they precipitated their own decline by enabling customers to pass through without stopping.

Birth of a new architectural form

When was the first 'passage' built? Architectural historians agree the first was the late eighteenth-century urban, commercial and social experiment known as the Palais Royal. What is now the quietest public garden and most elegant set of archways in Paris was then a beehive harbouring dens of iniquity and providing refuge to a multitude of sins.[3] Towards the Louvre end of the gardens was a great wooden gallery covered by window frames making a passage between two rows of shops, which could thus claim the title of the first covered passage of the world. As buildings, the arcades represent a transitional set of structures using pre-existing courtyards and open passages to create a new physical environment for consumerist practices. The use of plated glass, iron and mirrors from the

1820s onwards prefigured the Crystal Palace and many of the exhibition spaces of the nineteenth century. The new term 'arcade' reflected the renewal of the building type and, in Paris at least, reflected a desire to differentiate the new attractions from mere decayed 'passages'.[4] The use of courtyards and the linking of private spaces to create a network of alleyways was not specific to Paris: the best examples of it are the *traboules* in Lyon, which made the working-class quarters of the Croix-Rousse a maze and fortress.[5] But these products of wild urbanization were essentially different from structures created to maximize profits in a crowded urban environment.

The arcades were also interesting for a geometrical reason: built within a pre-existing Parisian cityscape, they produced regular and relatively straightforward lines in highly intricate and irregularly shaped building blocks of different eras.[6] The entrepreneurs, who were obviously speculators maximizing their investment in an age when the revolutionary paper money had plummeted, unwittingly conveyed a sense of revolutionary order and regularity in their commercial planning. This insistence on regularity and order matched that developed by the state for its own uniform series of archways lining the rue de Rivoli (1802–1855).[7]

In their pursuit of lucre the *passages couverts*, opened by entrepreneurs wishing to create a new attraction and to maximize the use of space by making fruitful use of courtyards, drew from the beginning on the technical resources of modern industry. Plated glass, iron and industrial-size mirrors appeared there first as did public gas lighting, floor heating and the cheap ornaments of fake gold and plated metals. The butchers Dodat and Véro represented in an exemplary manner how these ventures began when two entrepreneurs joined forces and their private spaces to create a public space held in private, a confusion between a street and a shop.[8]

The architectural historian Johann Friedrich Geist, in his often-imitated master compendium of all the world's arcades, has identified the main characteristics of this fleeting moment in urban architecture.[9] The main point of a passage is to provide a convenient space protecting passers-by from the rain, the mud and the cold while offering the possibility of finding decorous entertainment and shopping opportunities. What unites the massive arcades built at the end of the nineteenth century with the modest 10-feet-wide passages built at the end of the French revolution (for instance the passage Feydeau opened in 1791 or the Passage des Panoramas in 1800) is their use of natural and artificial light, their confusion between internal and external space and their systematic use of modern materials, particularly plated glass. Many wooden structures, such as the Passage des Panoramas, were later 'modernized' by the use of cast iron. This has led many architecture specialists to pay particular attention to the ironwork, which relates the roofing of these passages to the masterpieces of civic and capitalistic architecture: bridges, railway stations and the Statue of Liberty or Eiffel Tower. This modernity in design and the competitive dimension of the enterprise whereby each arcade attempted to improve on the competition (to the point of making the venture a poor investment) means that most historians now see the then common parallel between the arcades and the Arabian and Iranian bazaar (Ispahan's was the key model with Cairo's bazaar) as an Orientalist fantasy.[10] Only the Passage du Caire, which opportunistically celebrated Bonaparte's Egyptian adventure, really maintained this fiction in its decorations. This Orientalist myth of the arcades was important, however, in that it presented the shopping activities and social movements of the arcades as novel and culturally alien. The arcades did not invite a comparison with the narrow alleyways of street markets, which still exist as semi-permanent fixtures on the Parisian boulevards and squares. They called on the exoticism of a world of luxury, decorum and leisure. They often included Turkish baths and hammams, where the skin of the customer could be exfoliated and massaged; theatres and amusements for which the arcades and their cafés served as a backroom providing refreshments at the *entracte*.[11]

Originally conceived as places where light flowed, the Parisian arcades declined into sordid and miserly alleyways where the air stagnated in obscure recesses. Only the great arcades constructed abroad, such as the Galeries St Hubert in Brussels or the Pariser Hof in Budapest, became enduring monuments to an imperial project, on a scale very dissimilar to the original arcades. The *Arcades Project* is undoubtedly more concerned with the smaller Parisian arcades than with the shopping malls of Berlin, Milan or Moscow, like the GUM built in 1888.[12] Benjamin chose to limit himself to an early type. This choice is probably linked to the fact that the 'passages' structures did not experience a revival on such a bloated scale in Paris and that in Paris alone they presented early signs of decay, making them ripe for the kind of dialectical recuperation Benjamin practised on the city's ruins. In spite of major dissimilarities in scale, all arcades share the same confusion between private and public space. This confusion is accentuated by the fact that some shops in the Paris arcades consist of deep display cabinets hanging on the wall of the passage with the shop attendants standing in the passage itself. Restaurants serve inside and out and the *terrasses* are nothing but encroachments on the passage's public space itself. Beyond the shops, in the back passages (passages behind the passages) and above the shops were a number of as yet unstudied flats and apartments, even hotels.[13]

The literature of the arcades

Among the more famous literary residents of this city under a glass roof were the novel character Thérèse Raquin and the novelist Céline, who grew up in a passage he later evoked in *Mort à crédit*.[14] Émile Zola's Nana, who epitomized the social climbing of a *goutte d'or* slum beauty, constantly frequented the passages that lead to the Bourse neighbourhoods and the easy money of the gambling bourgeois. Of Zola, Benjamin retained only *Thérèse Raquin*: 'If this book really expounds something scientifically, then it's the death of the Paris arcades, the decay of a type of architecture. The book's atmosphere is saturated with the poisons of this process: its people drop like flies' (H1, 3). Yet Zola locates many of the scenes of seduction, corruption and louche sexual desire in the arcades. In his novel on speculation, *l'Argent*, money and sex meet in the Passage Verdeau and in the Passage des Panoramas.[15] The Passage des Panoramas recurs in *Nana* as a site of consumerist pleasure for the seductress and disappointed love for her admirers.[16] The contrast between the passages in decline and the large-scale department stores, which shared, on a very different scale, elements of the same demotic architecture, was also to be found in Zola's *Au bonheur des dames* in which the shops of the arcades face ruin while attempting to compete with the department store.[17] Perhaps because Zola was exclusively interested in the positivist narrative of the displacement of one sort of capitalist enterprise by another and probably because naturalism lacked metaphysical depth, Benjamin rarely used the naturalist novelist.

The scientific pretensions of Zola's experimental novels might have also been off-putting for Benjamin at more than one level: 'The nineteenth century did not reveal itself to Zola or Anatole France, but to the young Proust, the insignificant snob, the playboy and socialite who snatched in passing the most astounding confidences from a declining age.'[18] Yet Zola was observing the dying days of the arcades, comparing them to cellars, and he clearly perceived them as the poisonous confined settings for cosmic conflicts. The fact that for Benjamin Zola was perhaps too obvious and intellectually dated does not diminish the long literary tradition which used the passages in order to make a critical commentary on modernity and on the competing tensions of sexual and material desire in the modern city.[19] The arcades have had a long and continuous association with notions of modernity and their decay is one of the most documented tropes of literary history. In this sense, and probably against his wish, the arcades were an obvious locus for Benjamin's synoptic book; in the nineteenth century they were not the 'marginal and despised everyday structure' (M21a) Benjamin described.

Decay and rehabilitation

Walter Benjamin encountered the arcades in the work of early surrealists such as Aragon, precisely at the moment when one of the most famous of the early arcades, the Passage de l'Opéra, was destroyed to make way for the last major boulevard in the Haussmannian style. Little could indicate then that Paris was going to survive the twentieth century essentially in its nineteenth-century guise, as if preserved in aspic, and that there would be arcades left even today. The emphasis of Aragon's *Paysan de Paris* was on the dreamworld of the decaying bric-a-brac of these badly lit (by twentieth-century standards) shopping alleyways meandering through the apartment blocks of Balzacian Paris. The passages were the first embodiment of a consuming culture emphasizing novelty products, textiles and artefacts of fashion. They offered socially segregated and relatively warm avenues for shopping or *lèche vitrine* (shop window gazing). As an architectural and commercial undertaking, the Parisian arcades were often imitated, from most small French provincial cities to Budapest or Brussels; and they are now being rehabilitated, with the small shops, second-hand book dealers and odd shops giving way to designer clothes shop, couturiers and coffee shops. Redeveloped and rescued by Parisian authorities who seek to make them into tourist attractions[20] using all the tropes of 'retrochic' to use Raphael Samuel's phrase, they are now once again the emporia of the modish.[21] In fact they are now closer to their origins than they were in the 1920s or even the 1860s. Little is left of the decayed appearance which so struck Aragon and after him Benjamin in the 1920s and 1930s.[22] Only a few examples such as the less frequented Passage du Caire taken over by a specific community or trade retain some of this poetic dereliction. One of their more striking particularities is that these passages often lead to another passage or to nothing at all. More often than not they open on to a bleak street, often devoid of shops, where lodgings have long been converted into offices. They are like forgotten threads running through the city, linking parts that have no longer any purpose for being connected. They are now more isolated than connecting, more dead-ends than passages. Of all the monuments of modernity in Paris there are still mysteries and hidden pleasures to be found in the passages of the *rive droite*. Their particular atmosphere – often compared to the glow of an aquarium – is eminently photogenic.[23] In due time the efforts to preserve these monuments to bourgeois life will eventually kill what they seek to rescue.

Bric-a-brac consumerism, alternative sociability

In the historiography of consumerism the arcades fit with the appearance of ready-made objects, 'articles de Paris', clothes, boots, and with the development of the publishing trade, which often had its bookshops or headquarters in the arcades. One of the most important publishers of poetry, *libraire*-publisher, was set in the arcades, as was the printer of *Le Charivari*, the pioneering caricature magazine of Philipon.[24] The caricatures exhibited in the windows of the arcades merged publishing and spectacle and made them entertainment, less passages than destinations themselves. Since their inception the second-hand book dealers perpetuate the memory of this trade by returning these books to the site of their original conception.

The multitude of shops in today's arcades perpetuate another specific consumerist tradition: that of very small shops specializing in a wide range of specific but ultimately pointless objects. Paris in the nineteenth century had become the capital of small-craftwork and decorative objects exported around the world under the title of *article de Paris*. In 1851 French bourgeois taste had dominated the section of the Great Exhibition devoted to the decorative arts.[25] The arcades presented a wide array of plasterworks, statuettes, bibelots and trinkets. This bric-a-brac was the novelty of these shopping spaces and made possible a kind of low-key consumerism. Unlike most pre-modern consumer artefacts, the objects purchased were devalued by the act of purchasing. The jewels were intrinsically valueless, the novelty bibelots made of plaster, their attractiveness depending on fashion and context. The arcades opened up the world of conspicuous consumption to those whose consuming powers were negligible: servant women or even children. The forms of consuming leisure afforded in the arcades were not significantly different from those offered by the boulevards, but they tended to precede the fuller development of the latter and they offered a significantly more compact and abbreviated experience. The aggregation of shops of a similar nature contributed further to the specialization of the arcades as sites of specific consumerism. There were other shops lending themselves to the pursuit of 'curiosités'

1 Passage du Grand Cerf (1925)

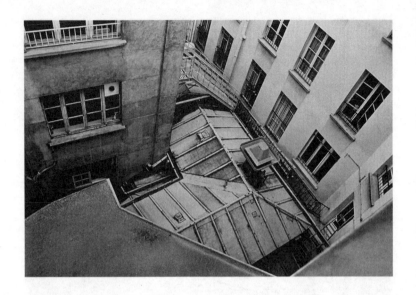

2 The roof of the arcades – view from Hôtel Chopin

3 Entrance to Passage Verdeau

4 Galerie Véro-Dodat (1826)

5 The Hôtel Chopin in the Passage Jauffroy (1846)

6 Passage Verdeau (1846)

and more valuable bibelots, but their eclecticism made the pursuit of desirable objects a quest rather than a straightforward shopping experience.[26]

Crucial to the commercial success of the passages was the need to lead on to something other than themselves. Most led to busy thoroughfares or were near important sites of arrival, such as the *messageries* headquarters in what is now rue Jean-Jacques Rousseau.[27] Others were linked up with sites of spectacle such as the Panoramas, but most contained at least a mime or even a small theatre. During the nineteenth century both mime and children's theatres were used to convey satirical and political undertones free of the censorship imposed on fully developed plays. The public of these theatres was thus little different from that of the 'Boulevard du Crime' immortalized in the Marcel Carné film *Les Enfants du paradis* (1943). Central to the development of one of the most famous passages, the Panoramas developed in the early nineteenth century lived on until the end of the century to convey on a circular canvas the enormity of landscapes and events which only a panoptic gaze could cover.[28] The Alps could thus be conveyed as well as the Detaille representations of the great battles of the Franco-Prussian war.[29] Panoramas could then be cut off and sold on as separate artworks, because they were a compilation of anecdotes: through their profusion the Panoramas conveyed the confusion of warfare or romantic landscape. The perspective and the scale of the spectacle intimated a sense of awe and humility while allowing a circumspect and detailed inspection. The successors of the Panoramas were the dioramas, which subsisted well into the twentieth century and, by offering three-dimensional representations of space and history, resisted for longer the competition of cinema. The First World War could thus be represented in dioramas with the possibility of exploring each plan separately: *premier plan, second plan, fond du tableau* (forefront, middle ground, background) as well as the more complex relationship between these layers of signification.[30] Simultaneously flat and deep, the diorama offered different norms of narrative. The ultimate collection of such tableaux was to be found in the wax Musée Grévin, building on the same tradition of wax figuration as Madame Tussaud.[31]

Still within the arcades, the cafés, Balzac's '*parlements du peuple*', offered, within and without, the heavily policed forms of sociability specific to Parisian thoroughfares.[32] With the café the arcades acquired an additional layer of homeliness, of 'intimate anonymity' reinforced in the baths where individuals and groups could experience levels of great intimacy in public.[33] Historians of governmentality claim that these baths represented ways of shaping the body. The bath thus promoted ideals and routines of cleanliness which were as many self-reformatory regimens. The arcades, open and closed, public and private, represented spaces of intimate sociability, of decorum and *laissez aller* which Benjamin picked on as exemplifying the making of modern 'man'. Much of this behaviour now eludes us: the cafés and public baths are in decline and the transient pleasures of the arcades where only a handful of sources of entertainment subsist tend to be nostalgic rather than futuristic. Even though they have lost their Utopian lustre, the fact that the arcades hinted at a different sort of society is still palpable.

Arcadian dreams

The reformatory dimensions of the arcades did not elude Benjamin, who noted repeatedly how congruent this architecture of leisure and life, sheltered from the elements and the forces of history, was with the Utopian architectures of Fourierist communities. From Gaston Ledoux to Le Corbusier, architects have debated the zoning of leisure and work, in turn arguing for clear zoning or for them to be associated together under a common roof. The architecture of sheltered space has dreamt of societies of order and fulfilment. Some of the Utopian plans for the rebuilding of Glasgow also stated the desire to shelter and thus create a common space (the shelter) where communities might thrive without excessive promiscuity. The arcades represented the glorification of the street as public and communal space, but improved by being made interior and safe, lit and heated. Unlike most Utopian fantasies, the arcades at first sight do not seem to include much in the way of spaces of production. Apart from publishing houses, tailor shops, cobblers and small craftworks, the windows of the arcades' shops open on to a world of retailing rather than a world of production. The adding of value to labour has taken place elsewhere and the arcades represent a site of exchange, trading and exploitation. If one considers the whole setting of the arcades and the back alleyways and the other courtyards nearby, which provided some of the goods, the arcades appear to be fronting an urban landscape devoted to the production of precisely the world of goods sold in the novelty and clothes shops. The modes of being in the arcades – warm, desultory, idle, pleasure-grabbing, but also clean and safe – were idyllic and represented the possibility of social and physical reformation through a reshaping of the cityscape. That the Parisian arcades remained strictly circumscribed in space and time and that eventually they lost their shine, acquiring the patina of antiquity and obsolescence, did not diminish their accidental Utopian nature. Quite the contrary. According to Benjamin, only a faded modernity was ready to release its Utopian energies.

Arcades in context

But can one draw a message for modernity out of a Parisian phenomenon? The arcades were exported throughout Europe, but with some significant delays. The arcades of Leeds, Budapest, Manchester or Huddersfield date from the 1880s, 1890s or 1900s, when the Paris arcades were in full decline and had acquired the decayed appearance that made them a propitious site of surrealist encounters. Some of the *Arcades Project*'s universal message depends on the ubiquity of this physical structure, but the diffusion of this mode of consumerism was complex. For instance, it is obvious that many of the meanings of the Paris arcades were altered by their physical translation in foreign cities. As a space of dream, pleasure and consumerism, the arcades represented one model of modernity, interwoven with the 'grand boulevards', department stores and the *Montmartre of pleasures* described by Louis Chevalier.[34] Translated into other urban settings, they acquired different meanings and became the attraction in their own right. Their rhizome-like quality became less important than the material and style in which they were constructed. In Leeds, for instance, the buildings are built around the arcades rather than the reverse. The arcades no longer creep into blocks to make an opening, they are channels around which blocks are built with communications between the street, the shop and the arcade. In Paris, most arcades penetrated without communicating much with the rest of the block. The shops opening on the arcades were often courtyard-deep, if not simple windows and stalls attached to a wall.

Later arcades prefigured the shopping malls of the twentieth century, in so far as they were constructed around a central 'atrium', but in a fully integrated manner so that one could move from an arcade space to a department store. The confusion between outdoor and indoor space was diminished even as the scale of these domes and glass-roofed spaces grew. In these inflated volumes the intimacy of the arcade declined as their anonymity increased.

Notes

1 *Physiologies* used a medical metaphor to establish a nomenclature and stereo-typical description of characters and fashions in the modern world of 1830s and 1840s Paris.

2 Priscilla Parkhurst Ferguson, *Paris as Revolution: Writing the Nineteenth Century City* (Berkeley: University of California Press, 1994).

3 Victoria E. Thompson, *The Virtuous Marketplace: Money and Politics in Paris, 1830–1870* (Baltimore and London: Johns Hopkins University Press, 2000), pp. 86–130; P. Sabatier, *Histoire de la législation sur les femmes publiques et les lieux de débauches* (Paris, 1828); C. Béraud, *Les Filles publiques de Paris et la police qui les régit* (Paris, 1839); 1830 saw the impositiuon of stricter rules on prostitution and contributed to the decline of Palais Royal, *Circulaire*, 7 Sept, 1830. Archives de la Préfecture de Police de Paris (ApdP) Da 223, a detailed regulation of authorized streets and hours.

4 Patrice de Moncan, *Les Passages en Europe* (Paris, Edn du Mécène, 1993), pp. 14–15.

5 Josette Barre, *La Colline de la Croix Rousse, histoire et géographie urbaine* (Lyons: Privat, 1993), pp. 176–8.

6 Bertrand Lemoine, *Les Passages couverts en France* (Paris: Délégation à l'Action Artistique de la Ville de Paris, 1989), p. 43.

7 François Loyer, *Paris XIXe siècle: L'Immeuble et l'espace urbain* (Paris: Imprimerie de l'APUR, 1982).

8 This confusion between spaces was reflected in the ordinances regulating these spaces: *Ordonnance concernant les passages ouverts au public sur des propriétés particulières, 30 mars 1847*, Paris, Imp. de Boucquin, 1847.

9 Johann Friedrich Geist, *Arcades: The History of a Building Type* (Cambridge, Mass.: MIT Press, 1983); among the imitators and followers: Patrice de Moncan, *Les passages de Paris* (Paris: Seesan, 1990); *Le Guide des passages de Paris* (Paris: Seesan, 1991); *Les Passages couverts de Paris* (Paris: Edn du Mécène, 1995); *Guide littéraire des passages de Paris* (Paris: Hermé, 1996); Jean-Claude Delorme and Anne-Marie Dubois, *Les Passages couverts parisiens* (Paris: Parigramme, 1996).

10 Lemoine, *Les Passages couverts*, pp. 8–21.

11 Hydrotherapeutics and heat treatment reached their apex in the first half of the nineteenth century and were thus gradually integrated to pre-existing passages or to the new ones of the 1840s. John Fife (ed.), *Manual of the Turkish Bath: Heat a Mode of Cure and a Source of Strength for Men and Animals* (London: Mr. Urquhart, 1865).

12 Delorme and Dubois, *Les Passages couverts*, p. 62.

13 Delorme and Dubois, *Les Passages couverts*, p. 64.

14 De Moncan, *Les Passages en Europe*, p. 59; Geist, *Arcades*, p. 354.

15 E. Zola, *L'Argent* (Paris: Bibliopolis,[1891] 1999) pp. 160–1, 406.

16 E. Zola, *Nana* (Paris: Bibliopolis, [1880] 1999), pp. 47, 42, 116, 268, 277.

17 E. Zola, *Au bonheur des dames* (Paris: Bibliopolis, [1883] 1999), pp. 36, 339.

18 Walter Benjamin, 'On the image of Proust', *SW2*, p. 240.

19 T. W. Laqueur, 'Sexual desire and the market economy during the industrial revolution', in D. C. Stanton (ed.), *Discourses of Sexuality: From Aristotle to AIDS* (Ann Arbor: University of Michigan Press, 1992), pp. 185–215.

20 Lemoine worked for the City of Paris.

21 See Samuel, *Theatres of Memory*.

22 See 'Passages de Paris', Geo, 274 (Juin 2001), 48.

23 Robert Doisneau, *Passages et galleries du xixème siècle*, texte Bernard Delveille (Paris: ACE, 1981).

24 Robert Justin Goldstein, *Censorship of Political Caricature in Nineteenth Century France* (Kent, Ohio: Kent State University Press, 1989), pp. 160–1.

25 Whitney Walton, *France at the Crystal Palace: Bourgeois Taste and Artisan Manufacture in the Nineteenth Century* (Berkeley: University of California Press, 1992).

26 For this obsession reminiscent of *Cousin Pons* see Ernest Bosc, *Dictionnaire de l'art, de la curiosité et du bibelot* (Paris, 1883).

27 The Galerie Véro-Dodat was thus the first sight of the passengers arriving by the coaches of the messageries Laffite et Caillard. When they closed in 1880 the passage ceased to have a natural feeder and survived only by presenting a useful shortcut through a very long block. Lemoine, *Les Passages couverts en France*, p. 180.

28 Stephan Oettermann, *The Panorama: History of a Mass Medium* (New York: Zone Books, 1997).

29 Alphonse de Neuville and Edouard Detaille, *Panorama of the Battle of Champigny*, 1882, was followed by another *Panorama of the Battle of Rezonville*, 1883. Both were later cut to pieces and sold as individual paintings. John Milner, *Art, War and Revolution in France 1870–1871, Myth Reportage and Reality* (New Haven and London: Yale University Press, 2000), p. 215.

30 *Visions de guerre, dioramas et scènes de tranchées* au sous sol du Modern Cinema, 1917.

31 Pam Pilbeam, *Madame Tussaud and the History of Waxworks* (London: Hambledon, 2002).

32 W. Scott Haine, *The World of the Paris Café: Sociability among the French Working Class, 1789–1914* (Baltimore and London: Johns Hopkins University Press, 1996), pp. 10, 27.

33 Haine, *Paris Café*, pp. 150–70.

34 Louis Chevalier, *Montmartre du plaisir et du crime*; Gabriel P. Weisberg (ed.), *Montmartre and the Making of Mass Culture* (New Brunswick, NJ: Rutgers University Press, 2001).

Method

The main task of Benjamin's late work is how to rescue the cultural heritage of the past. Such an act of rescue must include history's forgotten and discarded objects as well as its cultural treasures, because, he argues, it is only through the recognition of such discarded objects that a history might be written from a perspective other than the victor's. Consider two statements on the subject – the first, well-known from 'On the concept of history', the second, less well-known, but also the subject of debate amongst Benjamin scholars, from 'Literary history and the study of literature':[1]

> no state of affairs having causal significance is for that very reason historical. It became historical posthumously, as it were, through events that may be separated from it by thousands of years. The historian who proceeds from this consideration ceases to tell the sequence of events like the beads of a rosary. He grasps the constellation into which his own era has entered, along with a very specific earlier one. Thus, he establishes a conception of the present as now-time shot through with splinters of messianic time.[2]

> It is not a question of representing works of literature in the context of their time, but to bring to representation, in the time when they were produced, the time which recognises them – that is, our time.[3]

Both statements are problematic in their application. Neither yields easily anything that might be described as a Benjaminian approach. One of the advantages of having the *Arcades Project* available in English at last is that it begins to help us to understand what Benjamin means in practice by such statements of intent.

What remains

Perhaps the *Project*'s most complex theoretical term is the 'dialectical image'. The aim of the dialectical image is to retrieve an object, practice or figure from obscurity. Its rearrangement in a new constellation offers the possibility of its transfiguration. In Convolute O, 'Prostitution, gambling', for example, gambling is represented as a dialectical *concept*, but a full understanding of it as a dialectical *image* requires that it be understood in relation to other concepts, as part of a constellation akin to that described in *The Origin of the German Mourning Play*:

> For ideas are not represented in themselves, but solely and exclusively in an arrangement of concrete elements in the concept: as the configuration of these elements.
>
> The set of concepts which assist in the representation of an idea lend it actuality as such a configuration. For phenomena are not incorporated in ideas. They are not contained in them. Ideas are, rather, their objective virtual arrangement, their objective interpretation . . . Ideas are to objects as constellations are to stars.[4]

Thus gambling in Convolute O understood as a dialectical concept is a self-destructive, short-sighted practice, which none the less involves a temporality that gives rise to Utopian possibilities only dimly intimated by its superstitious and fateful trappings. The anticipatory moment before the bet is laid is pregnant with possibility, which is why the gambler delays the laying of the bet to the last possible moment (O12a, 2). The prospect of the win (although not the win itself, which is always a disappointment) conjures up whole new worlds, far more enticing in possibility than they could be in actuality. Gambling as a dialectical image, however, can be understood only in relation to the other dialectical concepts in Convolute O, the most important of which is prostitution, and to the rest of the *Arcades Project* as a whole.

Before considering the complex and overlapping dialectical images thrown up by the different constellations that emerge from the *Project* it is necessary to return to Benjamin's interest in the discarded objects of the nineteenth century, its 'residues',[5] whose reality was the dream-world of commodity fetishism. As historical relics they have lost even the logic of their original place in the market. In a draft of an early essay on the arcades, Benjamin lists a melancholy litany of goods on sale in a contemporary arcade, one which exemplifies the decline of arcades in the twentieth century: '"Souvenirs" and bibelots take on a hideous aspect; the odalisque lies in wait next to the inkwell'. Perhaps the most satisfying of these, in its sense of loss and, at the same time, its promise of some future redemption, are the 'types of collar studs for which we no longer know the corresponding collars and shirts'.[6] In that sad and comic image we are given both the proper material of the historian – the orphaned object – and the promise of its restoration: that, at some future date, stud, collar and shirt will be reunited. The prospect of sartorial salvation may seem mundane in comparison with the theological language of Benjamin's more abstract writings. But we can grasp his more abstruse formulations only if we understand how the detritus of the past might be redeemed.

If the experience of the nineteenth century was that of a dream, then the dialectical image for historical recovery in the *Arcades Project* is awakening:

> the arcades . . . are the residues of a dream world. The realization of dream elements, in the course of waking up, is the paradigm of dialectical thinking. Thus dialectical thinking is the organ of historical awakening. Every epoch, in fact, not only dreams the one to follow but, in dreaming, precipitates its awakening. It bears the end within itself and unfolds it – as Hegel already noticed – by cunning.[7]

Despite Benjamin's invocation of Hegel here, the methodology he elaborates is materialist, owing more to Marx, to Ernst Bloch and to Proust than to idealist philosophy. His emphasis on the object-world opens not just Hegel but Marxism itself to a form of materialist interrogation. A key reference point is Marx's letter to Arnold Ruge:

> Our motto must be: the reform of consciousness not through dogmas but by analysing mystical consciousness obscure to itself, whether it appear in religious or political form. It will become plain that the world has long since possessed the dream of a matter, of which it must only possess the consciousness in order to possess it in reality. It will become plain that our task is not to draw a sharp mental line between past and future but to *complete* the thought of the past. Lastly, it will become plain that mankind will not begin any *new* work, but will consciously bring about the completion of its old work.[8]

The 'old work' that Marx argued it was the task of humanity to complete is found by Benjamin in its unfinished form in the ruins and discarded objects of the everyday. In Marx's formulation past and present are in a dialectical relationship: hope for the future is already present in humanity's 'old work'. In dialogue with Ernst Bloch's concept of 'anticipatory consciousness',[9] Benjamin develops the possibility of old work's completion through the opening chapter of Proust's *In Search of Lost Time*, where an account of awakening precedes the first instance of involuntary memory (*mémoire involuntaire*) brought about by the object, the madeleine.

Arrangement/organization

The dialectical moment of awakening is one of preservation through recovery, but, once acquired, the re-constellation of the lost objects of the everyday requires distance and reflection. In Benjamin's dialectic of the everyday, habit, Proust's 'skilful but slow-moving arranger', is broken by involuntary memories, which then need to be rearranged to become something other than what is. The point of awakening is the point of rupture at which past and present may recognize each other, not through a spurious theory of causation or progress but in a moment in which the totality of the past is recognized in the present. The dialectical image is about spatial as well as temporal rearrangements. As Benjamin put it in the thesis from 'On the concept of history' quoted above: the historian 'grasps the constellation into which his own era has entered, along with a very specific earlier one'.

The *Arcades Project*'s frequent references to Poe's 'Philosophy of furniture' and to Proust's interest in the arrangement of the room take us back to Benjamin's concern with the bourgeois interior as microcosm of the city, but here also refers to the actual constellation of objects that forms the mental structure within which the remembrance of the constellation of an earlier era can take place. Benjamin uses the same trope himself at the end of his autobiographical 'Berlin chronicle': 'I must have memorized my room and my bed, the way you observe with great precision a place where you feel dimly that you'll later have to search for something you've forgotten there.'[10]

The construction of that constellation can begin through involuntary memory with the most everyday object. Traces of the forgotten or only dimly remembered dream are to be found in the most transitory elements of modernity. In fact, the more transitory, the more likely they are to evoke that which has been lost to consciousness. Thus, a whole convolute, B, is devoted to fashion because fashion is modernity's response to what it has obliterated: 'Fashions are a collective medicament for the ravages of oblivion. The more short-lived a period, the more susceptible it is to fashion' (B9a, 1). A period that is quickly forgotten can be redeemed only by studying the expressions of its transitoriness, summed up in that already-quoted aphorism: 'the eternal . . . is far more the ruffle on a dress than some idea' (N3, 2). Proust, at least, was able to remember the nineteenth century. We, the students of the nineteenth century, have to experience it indirectly and as a group:

> Every current of fashion or of worldview derives its force from what is forgotten. This downstream flow is ordinarily so strong that only the group can give itself up to it; the individual – the precursor – is liable to collapse in the face of such violence, as happened with Proust. In other words: what Proust, as an individual, directly experienced in the phenomenon of remembrance, we have to experience indirectly (with regard to the nineteenth century) in studying 'current', 'fashion,' 'tendency' – as punishment, if you will, for the sluggishness [*Trägheit*] which keeps us from taking it [the phenomenon of remembrance] up ourselves. (K2a, 3)

The need for a group response to history means, for Benjamin, a political response. The sluggishness we exhibit as a group is our reluctance to awake from the dream. A sluggishness, which in the German *Trägheit* from *tragen* to carry, suggests the burden of the past we carry whether we recognize it or not.

This burden includes not just the nineteenth century but *Urgeschichte* or prehistory: periods or forgotten moments that predate or elude historical consciousness.[11] Prehistory is resurrected in Benjamin's historiography as the possibility that the whole of the past can be redeemed from its ruins: 'fashion . . . triumphs over death. It brings the departed into the present. Fashion is contemporary with every past.'[12] The whole of history is present in the fragment that is the object of study. But, in order to gain access to that history, a methodology of arrangement, or what Baudelaire called 'correspondences', is required that will allow past and present to recognize one another. The form of the *Arcades Project* was to be 'to develop to the highest degree the art of citing without quotation marks. Its theory is intimately related to that of montage' (N1, 10). Borrowing from modernist form, the *Arcades Project* would be 'literary montage': 'I needn't *say* anything. Merely show. I shall purloin no valuables, appropriate no ingenious formulations. But show the rags, the refuse – these I will not inventory but allow, in the only way possible, to come into their own: by making use of them' (N1a, 6). Benjamin wanted to reproduce in historical methodology the aesthetic call-to-arms found in Eisenstein's cinema or Brecht's theatre. The form of the work would produce the dialectical images that might represent both shock and reflection: the difference between two types of experience, *Erlebnis* and *Erfahrung*.

As historical method, the images work to allow the representation of the past in 'now-time' and, crucially, offer the promise of a better future:

'the splinters of messianic time'. Some convolutes seem to represent a final arrangement more than others. 'Idleness' (Convolute m), for example, is exemplary in its structure, in that it attempts to bring the concept of idleness to consciousness through its form. Slight changes in entries that almost repeat earlier entries subtly reinterpret them. The entries gesture to other parts of the *Arcades Project* and to other parts of Benjamin's work. If this seems to propose that every part of the *Arcades Project* needs to be read in relation to every other part, that suggests too systematic a conception of the text, which itself requires a sauntering pace and an idle sensibility to allow the correspondences to emerge. Idleness can be read alongside M, 'The flâneur', J, 'Baudelaire', and X, 'Marx'. It has correspondences with, at least, H, 'The collector', I, 'The interior, the trace', O, 'Prostitution, gambling' and a, 'Social movements'. The idler has relationships with Benjamin's other urban types: the gambler, the flâneur, the collector, the brooder and the student, but these types are not distinct. Gamblers, flâneurs and students are all idle, but idlers have tendencies towards gambling, flânerie and studiousness. Idleness, like gambling, is a dialectical concept, which cannot be understood except in terms of this broader arrangement or constellation.

Collecting

One of the most potent, because most practical, of Benjamin's offered methods of reconfiguration is collecting.[13] The collector

> makes his concern the transfiguration of things. To him falls the Sisyphean task of divesting things of their commodity character by taking possession of them. But he bestows upon them only a connoisseur value, rather than use value. The collector dreams his way not only into a distant or bygone world but also into a better one – one which, to be sure, human beings are no better provided with what they need than in the everyday world, but in which things are freed from the drudgery of being useful.[14]

In this passage, which brings together the concepts of space, dreaming and reconfiguration, there is a striking similarity between the language used and that employed in Marx's letter to Ruge. Marx writes that the world has 'possessed the dream of a matter' ('den Traum von einer Sache besitzt', where *Sache* means matter as in 'concern' but also material 'thing', or 'object'), 'of which it needs only to "possess the consciousness in order to possess it in reality"' ('von dem sie nur das Bewußtsein besitzen muß, um sie wirklich zu besitzen').[15] For Benjamin's collector the concern or matter ('Sache') in hand is also transfiguration; but the collector first possesses things ('durch seinen Besitz an den Dingen')[16] then reconfigures them; and it is in the process of that reconfiguration that he is able to possess a new consciousness.[17] Bloch's dialectic of hope is operating here from two directions. Where Marx urges the materialization of the dream, Benjamin urges an assembly of materials to provoke the moment of awakening that brings the dream to consciousness.

In Convolute H ('The collector'), Benjamin seems to be suggesting that the arcades themselves are, if not collections, then vast reserves of historical memory. The role of the collector is to 'live a piece of dream life' (H1a, 5); but collecting is also a 'form of practical memory'. Benjamin's aim is to take that element of practical consciousness and to 'construct here an alarm clock that rouses the kitsch of the previous century to "assembly"' (H1a, 2). The German word for 'assembly', *Versammlung* (derived from *sammeln*, to collect), is picked out here for its double sense of arrangement and organization: assembly, but also a 'muster' or 'rally'. With some poetic licence, T. J. Clark renders the passage as 'an uprising of the overlooked',[18] a version which at least gets closer to the strong affinity between the collector's organization of things and the activist's organization of people. This, as Clark points out, is an indication of the central importance of Convolute a, 'Social movements', to the *Arcades Project* – a section which is likely to be of less interest to the merely aesthetic or philosophical critic, but which makes sense of montage and re-assembly as a process that is in itself political. Benjamin's most graphic example of the dialectic between the politics of form and the form of politics is given in the image of Blanqui watching his secret army parade before him on the Champs-Élysées, its presence unnoticed in the city crowd of which it is, simultaneously, a part (V9, 2).

Thus, the collector gives a practical political dimension to the abstract statements quoted earlier from 'On the concept of history' – 'the historian . . . grasps the constellation which his own era has formed with a definite earlier one' – and from 'Literary history and the study of literature': 'It is not a question of representing works of literature in the context of their time, but to bring to representation, in the time when they were produced, the time which recognises them – that is, our time'. In Convolute H, temporal abstraction is materialized through spatial practicality: 'The true method of making things present is to represent them in our space (not to represent ourselves in their space). (The collector does this and so does the anecdote.)' (H2, 3). Time is redeemed through space. The reorganization of objects brings the potential of the past into the present and makes it a living actuality. This is because, 'for the collector, the world is present, and indeed ordered, in each of his objects' (H2, 7; H2a, 1). If use value is not the objective of the collector, stripping things of their commodity value opens up the possibility of politics.

Politics

If this approach seems to prioritize the aesthetic over the political, it is misleading to say, as Peter Osborne does, that the political is 'the black hole at the centre of Benjamin's work'.[19] Osborne's judgement rests on his reading of Thesis III of 'On the concept of history': 'only for a redeemed mankind has its past become citable in all its moments. Each moment it has lived becomes a *citation à l'ordre du jour*. And that day is Judgement Day.'[20] This he reads to mean that redemption 'does not come until Judgement Day: the end of time'.[21] It could be read to mean not that redemption is outside history but that the moment in history when the past becomes citable in all its moments will be Judgement Day.[22] That moment is the moment of revolution. If Benjamin were resorting to the theological at this crucial moment in his argument on history then neither his preoccupation with thresholds (which we discuss in 'Modernity/modernism' below), his engagement with Marx nor the sheaves of notes on the material culture of the everyday would make sense. Only by ignoring much of the *Arcades Project* and the figure of the collector, for whom new constellations are spatial phenomena, is it possible to argue, as Osborne does, that 'there is no historico-philosophical consideration of the spatial side of the "now", no geo-politics of the European "here", no sociological breakdown of the "dreaming collective"'.[23]

The collector, like the allegorist, the gambler or the flâneur, offers one route to practical consciousness. When Benjamin compares the collector with the allegorist the relationship is at root to do with the dialectical relationship between *Erlebnis* and *Erfahrung* (see section on *Erlebnis/ Erfahrung* in 'Modernity/modernism'). Both collector and allegorist are in shock at 'the confusion . . . the scatter, in which the things of the world are found'. In one sense, 'the allegorist is the polar opposite of the collector'. Each reacts to the shock of modernity (*Erlebnis*) in different ways. But in their desire to reconstruct a full and complete experience (*Erfahrung*), to achieve the completion of old work, they are similar: 'As far as the collector is concerned his collection is never complete; for let him discover just a single piece missing, and everything he's collected remains a patchwork, which is what things are for allegory from the beginning' (H4a, 1). If neither the allegorist nor the collector can achieve their desire for completion, they prefigure the conditions of possibility for what might. As so often, Benjamin returns to Proust: 'A sort of productive disorder is the canon of the *mémoire involuntaire*, as it is the canon of the collector' (H5, 1). The spaces of the city provide the most advanced form of productive disorder, which is in fact one aspect of the disorganized nature of capitalism itself. Its transformation, however, requires not an individual but a collective political response. This is expressed most clearly in the following passage, where the 'interest taken in the [historical] object' describes the way in which the 'world is present, and indeed ordered' in each of the collector's objects:

> It is said that the dialectical method consists in doing justice each time to the concrete historical situation of its object. But that is not enough. For it is just as much a question of doing justice to the concrete historical situation of the *interest* taken in the object. And *this* situation is always so constituted that the interest is itself preformed in that object and, above all, feels this object concretized in itself and upraised from its former being into a higher concretion of now-being <*Jetztsein*> (waking being!). In what way this now-being (which is nothing less than the now-being of 'the time of now' <*Jetztzeit*>, but punctuated and intermittent) already signifies, in itself, a higher concretion – this question, of course, can be entertained by the dialectical method only within the purview of a historical perception that at all points has overcome the ideology of progress. In regard to such a perception, one could speak of the increasing concentration (integration) of reality, such that everything past (in its time) can acquire a higher grade of actuality than it had in the moment of its existing. How it marks itself as higher actuality is determined by the image as which and in which it is comprehended. And this dialectical penetration and actualization of former contexts puts the truth of all present action to the test. Or rather, it serves to ignite the explosive materials that are latent in what has been (the authentic figure of which is *fashion*). To approach, in this way, 'what has been' means to treat it not historiographically, as heretofore, but politically, in political categories. (K2, 3)

Jetztzeit, the 'now-time shot through with splinters of messianic time', is the time the historian has to establish when grasping the constellation the present era forms with an earlier one. The effect is one of distancing, a true, Brechtian *Verfremdungseffekt*, in which the 'naturalness' of 'what actually happened' is defamiliarized and rendered available to political critique and practice.

The dialectical personalities that populate the *Arcades Project*, of which the flâneur is only the best known, each prefigure a new set of constellations and each proffer flashes of illumination; but ultimately the project that interested the author was not *Sammlung* (collection), but *Versamm-*

lung: a collective assembly. Benjamin's idea of the collective is also one in which the joins, the disagreements, are allowed to show. As such, it is thoroughly up-to-date, pertinent to the new alliances that have to be made. His theory of the everyday acts as a corrective to abstract ideas of the collective or of revolution. Critical engagement with the *Arcades Project* suggests that only through an imagining of such a workable and everyday collective is it possible to glimpse how the work of the past, Marx's 'old work', might be completed.

Notes

1 See Brook Thomas, *The New Historicism: And Other Old-fashioned Topics* (Princeton, NJ: Princeton University Press, 1991).
2 Walter Benjamin, 'On the concept of history' [1940], in *SW* 4, pp. 389–400 (p. 397; supplemental Thesis A).
3 Walter Benjamin, 'Literary history and the study of literature' [1931], in *SW* 2, pp. 459–65 (p. 464; translation modified).
4 Walter Benjamin, *The Origin of German Tragic Drama*, trans. John Osborne (London: New Left Books, 1977), p. 34 (usually translated now as *The Origin of the German Mourning Play*). On constellations see Esther Leslie, 'Stars, phosphor and chemical colours: extraterrestiality in *The Arcades*', *new formations*, 54 (2004/5), 13–27.
5 Walter Benjamin, 'Paris, the capital of the nineteenth century (Exposé of 1935)', in *AP*, pp. 3–13 (p. 13).
6 Walter Benjamin, 'Arcades' [1927], in *AP*, pp. 871–2 (p. 872).
7 Benjamin, 'Exposé of 1935', p. 13.
8 Karl Marx, Letter to Arnold Ruge, September 1843, in *Early Writings* (Harmondsworth: Penguin, 1975), pp. 206–9 (p. 209; translation modified).
9 For Bloch's elaboration of anticipatory consciousness through the same passage see *The Principle of Hope* (Oxford: Blackwell, [1959] 1986), pp. 155–6, 1363–4.
10 Benjamin, 'A Berlin chronicle', p. 635.
11 The English version of *The Arcades Project* translates this as 'primal history' and Susan Buck-Morss gives it as the 'history of origins', but we are grateful to Graeme Gilloch for steering us towards the correct and Marxist term.
12 Walter Benjamin, 'Exposé of 1935, early version', in *AP*, pp. 893–8 (p. 894).
13 As Esther Leslie has shown, the original collector, like the keenest observer of thresholds, is the child: see her 'Telescoping the microscopic object: Benjamin the collector', in Alex Coles (ed.), *The Optic of Walter Benjamin* (London: Black Dog, 1999), pp. 58–93 (pp. 64–5).
14 Benjamin, 'Exposé of 1935', p. 9.
15 Karl Marx, *Die Frühschriften* (Stuttgart: Alfred Kröner, 1953), p. 171.
16 Walter Benjamin, *Das Passagen-Werk*, vol. 1, ed. Rolf Tiedemann (Frankfurt

am Main: Suhrkamp, 1982), p. 53.

17 Benjamin's collector is always male.

18 T. J. Clark, 'Reservations of the marvellous', *London Review of Books*, 22 June 2000, 3–9 (p. 7).

19 Peter Osborne, 'Small-scale victories, large-scale defeats: Walter Benjamin's politics of time', in Andrew Benjamin and Peter Osborne (eds), *Walter Benjamin's Philosophy: Destruction and Experience*, 2nd edn (Manchester: Clinamen Press, 2000), pp. 55–107 (p. 93). On the move to disavow Benjamin's politics see Esther Leslie, *Walter Benjamin: Overpowering Conformism* (London: Pluto, 2000), pp. 225–8.

20 Benjamin, 'On the concept of history', p. 390 (Thesis III).

21 Osborne, 'Small-scale victories', p. 86.

22 *Citation à l'ordre du jour* is a military designation equivalent to 'mentioned in dispatches'. Here it means that moments otherwise lost become visible and even heroic in the act of being remembered.

23 Osborne, 'Small-scale victories', p. 90.

Judaism

Benjamin alludes to 'theology' occasionally in the *Arcades*, and in virtually every case the allusion is to Jewish theology in particular. But the most significant mention of the Jewish tradition is a comment Benjamin lifts from handwritten addenda he had made to his *Trauerspiel* book in 1928, in which he noted that the concept of 'origin' he had pioneered in that text was 'in effect, the concept of *Ur*-phenomenon extracted from the pagan context of nature and brought into the Jewish contexts of history' (N2a, 4).[1] The contrast of nature and history is standard fare for Benjamin, but only here does he identify his concept of history as such with Jewish tradition. History 'shot through with splinters of messianic time' constituted the very centre of Judaism, the central observance of which is the reading of sacred texts recounting the history of the Jewish people.[2] It therefore demanded a distinctive kind of retelling: 'the Jews were prohibited from inquiring into the future: the Torah and the prayers instructed them in remembrance'.[3] History as memory and remembrance would provide the alternative to the positivist aspirations of contemporary historicism.

The issue of Benjamin's relationship with Jewish tradition has, however, a stormy tradition of its own. No one doubts that Benjamin was interested in Judaism, or that he used some of its vocabulary for his critical work. But for the most part discussion of this topic has assumed that his interest in Judaism must be put in the scales against his interest in Marxism, as if the two were engaged in some zero-sum game. Benjamin himself chose to address the matter by means of a characteristically enigmatic analogy: 'My thinking is related to theology as blotting pad is related to ink. It is saturated with it. Were one to go by the blotter, however, nothing of what is written would remain' (N7a, 7). If this was meant to imply that his writing was infused by, but not reducible to Jewish theology, the message was clearly lost both to his contemporaries and to the numerous critical friends he acquired posthumously. In life, he must have felt torn between Gershom Scholem, who made no effort to mask his disappointment when Benjamin swung towards Marxism, accusing him of an 'an unusually intent kind of self-deception' which varnished metaphysical insight with a Marxist coating, and Brecht, whose *plumpes Denken* didn't really stretch to theology. In death, he's been caught in the same field of fire: between Marxists who insist that the Judaism is colourful but ultimately dispensable, at best scaffolding for a superior materialism, and Jewish writers who think that the Marxism is poorly digested and doesn't really add much to his most brilliant insights. At a time when synergy and interdisciplinarity are supposed to be the *sine qua non* of successful work in the human sciences, there are some boundaries which apparently are still uncrossable.

Yet curiously, it appears that in Benjamin's mind the theological stance and the political one were, if not identical, either proximate or parallel. 'The change in fashions, the eternally up-to-date, escapes "historical" consideration; it is truly overcome only through a consideration that is political (theological)' (S1, 3). His friend Scholem, the principal conduit for his knowledge and experience of Judaism ('I have come to know living Judaism in absolutely no form other than you', he wrote to him in 1930), was careful to separate these two, in the interest of maintaining the transcendence of the divine.[4] Benjamin, however, seemed to regard theology and politics as two paths to the same goal, so much so that, when he was considering learning Hebrew and moving to Palestine, the only other conceivable option was immersion in 'pure party politics'.[5]

Given the expansiveness of the Jewish tradition, the multiple possibilities of influence and the constitutive ambiguity of much of Benjamin's writing, pinpointing lines of connection is often at best a speculative affair. There is, of course, one exception: Benjamin's messianism, which draws directly on Jewish messianic teaching, no doubt mediated by Scholem, who had researched and written extensively on this theme.[6] (We treat that theme in our discussion of 'The Angel of History'). It has been argued, however, that too much emphasis is placed on Scholem's interest in the Kabbalah, when Benjamin was open to other Jewish thinkers as well, and when Scholem himself had knowledge and interests beyond the field he made uniquely his own.[7]

Politics can be rendered equivalent to theology, but only when the politics in question takes the past as well as the present as its field of action. In that case, politics and theology find themselves united by a redemptive impulse and a distinctive constituency: the victims of history. Benjamin liked to point out that the winners and losers of history's myriad struggles did not occupy symmetrical positions, for while the victors carried forward the fruits of their victory ('cultural treasures' as he called them in 'On the concept of history'), for the vanquished defeat was the end of the line. Only a redemptive criticism could rescue the defeated, not just from defeat itself and its consequences but from the fate of being lost to history altogether.

But could it? The issue was posed in the sharpest possible manner within the *Arcades Project* itself. Wishing to take on the strongest possible opposing argument, Benjamin included in his materials the following excerpt from a letter by Max Horkheimer, together with his response:

> On the question of the incompleteness of history, Horkheimer's letter of March 16, 1937: 'The determination of incompleteness is idealistic if completeness is not comprised within it. Past injustice has occurred and is completed. The slain are really slain ... If one takes the lack of closure entirely seriously, one must believe in the Last Judgement ... Perhaps, with regard to incompleteness, there is a difference between the positive and the negative, so that only the injustice, the horror, the sufferings of the past are irreparable. The justice practiced, the joys, the works, have a different relation to time, for their positive character is largely negated by the transience of things. This holds first and foremost for individual existence, in which it is not the happiness but the unhappiness that is sealed by death.' The corrective to this line of thinking may be found in the consideration that history is not simply a science but also and not least a form of remembrance <*Eingedenken*>. What science has 'determined', remembrance can modify. Such mindfulness can make the incomplete (happiness) into something complete, and the complete (suffering) into something incomplete. That is theology; but in remembrance we have an experience that forbids us to conceive of history as fundamentally atheological, little as it may be granted us to try to write it with immediately theological concepts. (N8, 1)

This have-your-cake-and-eat-it argument depends, in the final instance, on the practice and experience of remembrance, which makes no sense if the past is truly dead and buried.

Remembrance, in the sense of commemoration, was a frequent enough experience in modern societies. But the general ethos of public commemoration was an appreciation of what the past had passed on to the present (typically, the fruits of military victory). In no sense did the affairs of the past remain unfinished or incomplete, and one could therefore not claim here that 'politics attains primacy over history' (K1, 2). In Jewish commemoration, however, the past was unfinished business and would remain so until the Jews were redeemed as a people and given a home in the Promised Land. Although the central element of weekly Jewish religious ritual is the reading of Torah, which recounts the history and law of the Jewish people, the *locus classicus* of Jewish remembrance is undoubtedly the Feast of Passover, in which the Exodus story, that of the Jews' exile in Egypt and their eventual liberation, is communally recounted. As Bram Mertens has pointed out, in the Passover service 'everyone is reminded "they are slaves in Egypt"', because the recounting of the story itself places the tellers of it in a direct relationship to past suffering and is the very means through which it might finally be made good.[8]

The 'Jewish contexts of history' therefore refers not merely to the history of the Jewish people but to the peculiar form of their historiography, which was bound up with a distinctive philosophy of history. To call the Jews a historical people was to call attention to the facts that their sacred texts were narrative histories and their religious observance was meant to recall that history and complete it. Remembrance was the medium in which the Jewish people established their identity; it modified the past by ensuring the movement of that people towards their historical goals. The exile in Egypt was a distinct historical event, but it was also the creation of a historical task, for it served as the model for exile after it and the spur to return and repair the broken world of the Jews. The Messiah eagerly anticipated in the Jewish apocalyptic tradition did not just do battle with evil and lead the people to a utopian future: it made whole, repaired (*tikkun*) a historically fractured existence.

Of course, not every Jewish intellectual endowed historical contexts with the same meaning. The most dramatic dividing line, or, rather, spray of lines, separated the Zionist movement from those outside it, and separated Zionists among themselves. Benjamin's first recorded intensive encounter with Judaism took place in the summer of 1912, in the shape of discussion on Zionist topics with his friend Kurt Tuchler.[9] Although Benjamin would discuss Zionism with Scholem on many occasions, and lead Scholem on a merry dance when he flirted with emigration to Palestine in the late 1920s, the Zionist interpretation on Jewish history did not seem to compel him. Whatever the cost – and the price turned out to be the highest imaginable – Benjamin chose to be a Jew in Europe. 'For me', he wrote to Ludwig Strauss in 1912, 'Jewishness is not in any sense an end in itself, but the most noble bearer and representative of the intellect'.[10] Benjamin aspired to be a European Jew, above all else.

The date of Benjamin's encounter with Jewish questions, 1912, was not a coincidence: it was the moment at which Jews across central Europe were reacting to Martin Buber's dramatic intervention, the 'Three

Speeches on Judaism' delivered to the Bar Kochba Union in Prague in 1909 and 1911 and printed in 1911.[11] Buber's lectures were aimed squarely at the liberal rationalism that sought to 'normalize' Judaism within Europe, turning its theology into a precursor of Kantian ethics and reducing its aspirations to political emancipation within the framework of the European nation-state. Buber's interpretation of the condition of exile, however, abstracted Jewish religiosity from every worldly aspiration, turning Jewishness into an existential drama or condition that every Jewish individual had to confront on his or her own. Remarking on the fact that Jewish identity depended on the chain of generations (substance) and not a shared way of life, he condemned the Jew to isolation:

> Whoever, faced with the choice between environment and substance, decides for substance, will henceforth have to be a Jew truly from within, to live as a Jew with all the contradiction, all the tragedy, and all the future promise of his blood.[12]

Benjamin and Scholem would have none of this: private ridicule of Buber's positions became a bonding experience. At stake was Buber's definition of Jewishness as a substance devoid of tradition, in which sudden epiphanies were the order of the day. Benjamin 'said derisively that if Buber had his way, first of all one would have to ask every Jew "Have you experienced Jewishness yet?"'[13] For Scholem, who believed that study of the Talmud was the defining Jewish experience, the crux of the matter was Buber's worship of incommunicable contact with the sacred, when all around it was clear that Judaism was inextricably bound to the task of commentary. Even Jewish mysticism, Scholem pointed out, consisted not of wordless mystical experiences but mystical commentary on sacred texts. The Kabbalah, for all its drama, required philology, not existentialism.

But Scholem did not limit himself to the inherited tradition of scriptural study; he had a modernizing project of his own. According to David Biale: 'Scholem's transformation of the traditional Jewish notion of commentary into historiography suggests that he views historical science, no matter how secular or "radical" as the modern form of Judaism.'[14] In which case the *Arcades Project* is the most Jewish of texts, as Benjamin seems well aware:

> Bear in mind that commentary on a reality (for it is a question here of commentary, of interpretation in detail) calls for a method completely different from that required by commentary on a text. In the one case, the scientific mainstay is theology; in the other case, philology. (N2, 1)

Instead of strange words in need of decipherment, strange objects; instead of symbols indicating the divine, inconspicuous details with a messianic spark. Benjamin's commentary approaches its objects with the hope that it can get them to surrender their secrets. And just as study in the Orthodox tradition means studying the Hebrew scripture *and* Talmudic glosses at the same time, Benjamin examines objects that are themselves swathed in commentary, liberally presented in the notes themselves.

For 'the place where one encounters' dialectical images 'is language' (N2a, 3). In keeping with the philosophy of language Benjamin first set out in 'On language as such and the language of man', human language exists not in its raw positivity but as a task consequent on Creation and the Fall. Human language lacks the creative power of the Divine Word, but it has is own peculiar job to do: to cognize the world and name it. In this context remembering the past means bringing its language back to life, fanning the embers of divinity sedimented in profane symbols. If remembrance is commentary, it modifies its objects by drawing out of them the dream content that points to the future. This weak messianic power, as Benjamin called it in 'On the concept of history', endows every object with an afterlife, for which commentary is the necessary spark.

But just as the Torah demands study and commentary for its completion, so the objects of the nineteenth century now compel the commentary that will realize their substance. Remembrance is not wilful or voluntaristic; it resembles, instead, an acknowledgement of the past's claims on the present. Benjamin called 'awakening . . . the dialectical, Copernican turn of remembrance'. For in remembering the dream 'we pass through and carry out *what has been*' (K1, 3). Which is to say that remembering is not a way of rendering the complete incomplete, as Horkheimer would have it, but completing, in the only way possible, something the past could not finish off itself. In an echo of the old joke about the psychiatrist and the light bulb ('How many psychiatrists does it take to change a light bulb? One, but the light bulb has to want to change'), remembrance can modify the past, but only if the past wants to be modified.

In his 'Theological-political fragment', Benjamin takes care to distinguish between the messianic completion of history, which can be accomplished only by an irruption from outside it, and the legitimate aims of a secular order. 'The secular order', he writes, 'should be erected on the idea of happiness'.[15] In pursuing this happiness, the secular order 'promotes the coming of the Messianic Kingdom'. In the *Arcades Project* the detritus of the previous century speaks of a happiness dreamed of but never grasped. Remembering it cannot change the factual content of the past, for that could only be accomplished by the actual Messiah. Benjamin's more modest claim is that the secular order can redeem these objects in the same way that a commentary redeems a text – not by changing its letters but by making it a luminous symbol that points to better days.

Notes

1 Gershom Scholem, *Walter Benjamin: The Story of a Friendship* (London: Faber & Faber, 1982), p. 149.
2 Benjamin, 'On the concept of history', p. 397 (supplemental Thesis A).
3 Benjamin, 'On the concept of history', p. 397 (supplemental Thesis B).
4 Letter 196, from Benjamin to Scholem, 25 April 1930, in *Correspondence*, p. 364.
5 Letter 195, from Scholem to Benjamin, 20 February 1930, in *Correspondence*, p. 363.
6 See Gershom Scholem, *The Messianic Idea in Judaism* (London: Allen & Unwin, 1971), in particular the opening essay, 'Towards an understanding of the messianic idea in Judaism'.
7 Anson Rabinach has pointed out that Benjamin was involved in Jewish debates on Zionism and the reception of Martin Buber's 1909 and 1911 speeches in Prague before he had even met Scholem. See his 'Between enlightenment and apocalypse: Benjamin, Bloch and modern Jewish messianism', *New German Critique*, 34 (1985), 78–124. Bram Mertens has recently emphasized that Benjamin's closest contact with Scholem dates from the time before Scholem had embarked on the Kabbalah; see '*The Arcades Project*: a Talmud for our time', *new formations*, 54 (2005), 60–73.
8 Mertens, 'A Talmud for our time', p. 60.
9 See Rabinach, 'Between enlightenment and apocalypse', p. 90.
10 Quoted in Rabinach, 'Between enlightenment and apocalypse', p. 97.
11 Published as *Drei Reden über das Judentum* (Frankfurt am Main: Rütten and Loening, 1911).
12 Martin Buber, 'Judaism and the Jews', in *On Judaism* (New York: Schocken, 1967), p. 19.
13 Scholem, *Walter Benjamin: The Story of a Friendship*, p. 29.
14 David Biale, *Gershom Scholem: Kabbalah and Counter-History*, 2nd edn (Cambridge, Mass. and London: Harvard University Press, 1982), p. 135.
15 Walter Benjamin, 'Theological-political fragment', in *SW 4*, pp. 305–6 (p. 305).

Modernity/modernism

Karl Marx, Max Weber, Georg Simmel and Georg Lukács all contributed to Benjamin's understanding of modernity.[1] But for Benjamin it was the aesthetic dimension of modernity that was his primary object of study. He was as influenced by literature – Baudelaire, Proust, Kafka, Brecht, and the French surrealists – as by philosophy, political theory or sociology. None the less, there is much to be gained in tracing the influence of social theory on Benjamin's development. In a letter to Gershom Scholem Benjamin wrote that Lukács's *History and Class Consciousness* was a book that was 'very important, especially for me'; and in this he wasn't alone: Lukács's book was a key influence on all the scholars connected to the Frankfurt School.[2] The most cited section was 'Reification and the consciousness of the proletariat', which incorporated a development of both Marx's theory of commodity fetishism and Weber's theory of rationalization. It is probable that Benjamin's knowledge of Marx's theory was largely through Lukács and secondary sources until the 1930s. Although there is no reference to him in the *Arcades Project*, Weber's ideas had also permeated the thinking of Benjamin and his circle.[3] Simmel, on the other hand, appears frequently. Benjamin had attended his seminar in 1912 and Fredric Jameson has argued that Simmel was a greater, if again indirect, influence on Benjamin than has usually been acknowledged.[4] Certainly, Simmel's *Philosophy of Money* had been an early influence on Lukács, and Jameson sees his ideas in Lukács's 'climactic outcry in *History and Class Consciousness*: "history is the history of the unceasing overthrow of the objective forms that shape the life of man"'.[5] Whether from Lukács or more directly, Benjamin's understanding of urban modernity could not, to borrow Jameson's phrase, 'escape the force-field' of Simmel's famous essay 'The metropolis and mental life'.

What Benjamin took from these philosophers of modernity, directly or indirectly, were key concepts: commodity fetishism; rationalization; the overstimulation to which the urban dweller is subjected; and reification. But he tended to draw aesthetic as much as sociological conclusions when he put them to work. Marx's theory of commodity fetishism, for example, describes how social relations between people 'assumes in the eyes of those people, the phantasmagorical form of a relation between things' (G5, 1).[6] The 'mysterious' manifestation of commodity culture is explained through an analogy with 'the mist-enveloped regions of the religious world', where

> the products of the human brain appear as autonomous figures endowed with a life of their own, which enter into relations both with each other and with the human race. So it is in the world of commodities with the products of men's hands. I call this the fetishism that attaches itself to the products of labour as soon as they are produced as commodities.[7]

In the *Arcades Project*, the concept of 'phantasmagoria' refers to the aesthetics of the mysterious world of commodities as they appear in exhibitions, advertising and the arcades.

If commodity fetishism describes how things become abstractions, Lukács's concept of reification describes how, in the (Weberian) rationalized world of modern production, abstract ideas 'based on what can and cannot be calculated' become a reality for the modern worker, who becomes nothing but 'reified, mechanically objectified "performance" . . . wholly separated from . . . total human personality'.[8] In Benjamin's work this experience becomes *Erlebnis*, the shock or trauma of modernity that is the subject of modernist artists and writers, and is the particular interest of Baudelaire.

Aesthetic modernity

More than just a philosopher of the modern, Benjamin followed writers such as Baudelaire who thought that a modernist aesthetic was the only appropriate response to the modern. Many of Benjamin's methods, including of course montage, are borrowed from art. For example, in his poem 'Le Crépuscle du matin' Baudelaire describes the dispersal of the 'clouds of myth', uncovering human life as it is lived. Benjamin argues that the structure of the poem mimics an arcade:

> The central portion of this poem is composed of nine couplets which, while chiming one with another, remain well sealed off from the preceding as well as the following pairs of lines. The reader moves through this poem as through a gallery lined with showcases. In each one, the immaculate image of naked misery is on display. The poem closes with two quatrains that, in

their presentation of things earthly and celestial, match each other like pilasters. (J88a, 2)

Baudelaire's use of mimesis is part of an attempt to grasp the most elusive elements of the modern, which he described elsewhere as 'the ephemeral, the fleeting forms of beauty in the life of our day'.[9] Benjamin, in Baudelaire, finds an understanding of modernity's dynamic relationship with the past: 'the modern, with Baudelaire, appears not only as the signature of an epoch but as an energy by which this epoch immediately transforms and appropriates antiquity. Among all the relations into which modernity enters, its relation to antiquity is critical' (J5, 1). The aesthetic means by which Baudelaire represents that relationship is allegory: 'the stamp of time that imprints itself on antiquity presses out of it the allegorical configuration' (J6a, 2). But, while Baudelaire's method opened up the possibility of the dialectical relationship between past and present that might unleash the full potential of the modern, Benjamin found his understanding of the relationship between the present and the past too rigid: 'The correspondence between antiquity and modernity is the sole constructive conception of history in Baudelaire. With its rigid armature, it excludes every dialectical conception' (J59a, 4).

Benjamin's more 'dialectical conception' interprets the Baudelairean account of modernity as itself a kind of historical remnant or ruin: 'The experience of allegory, which holds fast to ruins, is properly the experience of eternal transience.' Faced with the difficulty of grasping the transience of the modern, Benjamin follows his friend Bertolt Brecht's delight in things that have been used.[10] From ruins, things in use, and the uncompleted (in short, the detritus of modern life), Benjamin begins to build his own account of the modern as dialectical process. If capitalism's creative destruction leaves wreckage, a 'scatter' (H4a, 1; Benjamin's term is *Zerstreutheit*, which also means 'absentmindedness'), Benjamin's modernism aims both to mimic and to reflect upon modernity's ruins. To reflect upon the distracted, dreamlike quality of this process, Benjamin developed the concept of remembrance, *Eingedenken*: a concept that has clear links to Proust's *In Search of Lost Time*, where the term *désagrégé*, usually translated as 'scattered', is also used to describe the narrator's state before involuntary memory recaptures the past and can be reconsidered.[11]

Erlebnis/Erfahrung

The relationship between reflection (mimesis) and reflecting upon is elaborated through the twin concepts of *Erlebnis* and *Erfahrung*, already raised in 'Method'. *Erlebnis*, a concept derived equally from social and aesthetic theory, describes the alienated subjectivity of the worker bound to routine attendance on a machine or the anaesthesia brought on by constant stimulation in the city. It is discussed at greatest length in 'On some motifs in Baudelaire':

> The greater the shock factor in particular impressions, the more vigilant consciousness has to be in screening against stimuli; the more efficiently it does so, the less these impressions enter long experience [*Erfahrung*] and the more they correspond to the concept of isolated experience [*Erlebnis*]. Perhaps the special achievement of shock defense is the way it assigns an incident a precise point in time in consciousness, at the cost of the integrity of the incident's contents. This would be a peak achievement of the intellect; it would turn the incident into an isolated experience [*Erlebnis*]. Without reflection, there would be nothing but the sudden start, occasionally pleasant but usually distasteful, which, according to Freud, confirms the failure of the shock defense.[12]

Miriam Hansen describes *Erfahrung*, on the other hand, as not having

> as much of an empiricist connotation as 'experience', which links to 'expert' and 'experiment' and tends to assume a basically unmediated, stable relationship between subject and object. The German root of *fahren* (to ride, to travel) [. . .] conveys a sense of mobility, of journeying, wandering, cruising, implying both a temporal dimension, that is, duration, habit, repetition, and return, and a degree of risk to the experiencing subject.[13]

The dialectic between *Erlebnis* and *Erfahrung* offers the possibility that modern experience can be preserved and then transformed. In Benjamin's view, Baudelaire's poetry does this more successfully than his undialectical theory of modernism: Baudelaire's poems turned *Erlebnis* into *Erfahrung*.[14] The *Erlebnis/Erfahrung* dialectic was not merely conceptual for Benjamin: his experience of it was a factor in the very birth of the *Arcades Project*. The first seeds of the *Arcades* were sown when Benjamin read Louis Aragon's surrealist work *Le Paysan de Paris*, and his immediate and then more considered response to that text played out the dialectic. The initial effect was corporeal shock: 'I could never read more than two or three pages in bed at night [*abends*] before my heart started to beat so strongly that I had to lay the book aside.'[15] Of his bodily response to Aragon's surrealism, Benjamin wrote: 'What a warning! What an indication of the many years which had to be spent between myself and such a reading.' Those years constituted the time necessary to reconfigure the shock of the text as *Erfahrung*. Only through relating the shock defence – the conditioned and habitual response to modernity – to reflective experience can the experience of modernity be properly understood. Benjamin's modernism is therefore a *considered* response to modernity. 'Literary montage', the modernist technique he first deployed in the earlier *One-Way Street*, reconfigures the impressions and comments that make up the matter of the *Arcades*. The unfinished project is almost certainly not the ordering Benjamin would have wished,[16] but in the suggestions about allegory, correspondences and collecting (amongst others) Benjamin leaves us clues as to how the experience of the nineteenth-century city might be reflected upon.

Urban modernity

After Simmel, when Benjamin discusses modernity, it is urban modernity that is his subject matter. He wrote, 'every city is beautiful to me'. The *Arcades Project* is, above all else, a history of a city – Paris, the capital of the nineteenth century, whose system of streets is 'a vascular network of imagination'.[17] As Benjamin's study of Paris progressed, the image of the city started to operate as an alternative to individualist models of consciousness, notably that of psychoanalysis. The *Arcades* expands on an insight Benjamin finds in the Swiss art historian Sigfried Giedion: 'In the nineteenth century construction plays the role of the subconscious.' The technologies of the industrial city should henceforth be seen as its '"artistic" architectures', gathering around 'bodily processes' (which would include the new engagements with technology) 'like dreams around the framework of physiological processes' (K1a, 7). The most explicit suggestion of a spatial model of the self is proffered at the beginning of his memoir, 'A Berlin chronicle', when Benjamin confesses that he had 'long, indeed for years, played with the idea of setting out the sphere of life – *bios* – graphically on a map'.[18]

It is the material culture of the city, rather than the psyche, that provides the shared collective spaces where consciousness and the unconscious, past and present meet: 'We . . . are less on the trail of the psyche than on the track of things. We seek the totemic tree of objects within the thicket of prehistory' (I1, 3). In the *Arcades Project* the relationships between things, the thresholds and invisible boundaries of Paris are therefore the prime object of scrutiny. This follows logically from

Benjamin's earlier city essays: 'Naples', 'Moscow', 'Marseilles', in which the presence and/or permeability of borders was a notable theme.[19]

In the *Arcades Project*, the city's 'porosity' becomes a characteristic feature of capitalist modernity, the familiar aspects of which are permeated with unfamiliar and unconscious elements. To focus on the immediately familiar is to limit our experience to *Erlebnis* – the alienated experience of city life – without recognizing the wider urban context that conditions that choice and offers alternative possibilities. When Benjamin writes that 'immediate experience [*Erlebnis*] is the phantasmagoria of the idler' (m1a, 3),[20] he suggests that the familiar or everyday has a wider dimension: 'What distinguishes *Erfahrung* from *Erlebnis* is that the former is inseparable from the representation of a continuity, a sequence' (m2a, 4).

The problem of modernity then becomes to understand the dialectic of urban *Erlebnis* and urban *Erfahrung*. The first task for the critic of the modern must be to investigate the nature of shock experience: the points of rupture in the everyday experience of modernity, its cracks and fissures. Hence the importance in the *Arcades* of the threshold as the point of transition between one state of consciousness and another.[21] For Benjamin, the everyday is not just *what is*, because what exists is made up of the complex social relations that constitute collective living. It is at the fractures and joins of the everyday that the possibilities of *what might be* emerge, and these fractures and joins relate to space, time and the relationship between dreamworlds and awakening.

Thresholds

To elaborate a theory of threshold, to establish a 'mythological topography' of Paris, Benjamin reaches back to the ancient world.[22] In the twentieth century, traditional 'threshold experiences', 'the ceremonies that attach to death and birth, to marriage, puberty, and so forth' (O2a, 1) are in abeyance. But although 'we have grown very poor' in such traditional experiences, Paris produces innumerable new thresholds in space and time: points of transition, passages from reason to myth, moments of magic that exist at the interstices of modernity.

The key to these new thresholds is the commodity, which, as understood by Marx, has both a use value and an exchange value. It might even be argued that the commodity form itself is kind of a threshold: it stands at the point where use and exchange value meet. According to Benjamin, the commodity form is only just emerging in the early nineteenth century. It is itself on the threshold: 'the forces of production shattered the wish symbols of the previous century'. Engineered construction as opposed to architecture, photography, commercial art and serialized fiction all 'are on the point of entering the market as commodities' and 'from this epoch derive the arcades and *intérieurs*, the exhibition halls and panoramas'.[23] Similarly, Benjamin believed that his own era also stood at a threshold, the end of the commodity form: 'With the destabilizing of the market economy, we begin to recognize the monuments of the bourgeoisie as ruins even before they have crumbled.'[24] By 1935, National Socialism was entrenched in Germany and Benjamin was already disillusioned with the Stalinist turn in the Soviet Union.[25] In the face of these political setbacks, he found hope in capitalism's inherent instabilities. Where some contemporary theories of postmodernism see commodification as a total experience, for Benjamin the threshold was a potent image for the possibilities opened up by capitalism's contradictions.

The relationship between the commodity form as threshold and the kinds of thresholds encountered in the modern city is complex. In the following passage, posters for aperitifs guard the entrances to the Paris Métro, facilitating the transition in states of spatial consciousness from streets to underground:

> at dusk glowing red lights point the way into the underworld of names . . . they have thrown off the humiliating fetters of street or square, and here in the lightening-scored, whistle resounding darkness are transformed into misshapen sewer gods, catacomb fairies . . . Here each name dwells alone; hell is its demesne. Amer, Picon, Dubonnet are guardians of the threshold. (C1a, 2)

'The advertisement', Benjamin writes, 'is the ruse by which the dream forces itself on industry' (G1, 1), mediating between the conscious world of city streets and the spatial unconscious of the Métro. In fact, the very borders and thresholds of the city may remain below the level of consciousness, because the transitoriness of commodity culture induces an active forgetting. Habit and the dream of the commodity (here in the shape of the advertisement) make points of entrance and departure invisible to the adult mind. Children, however, are less bound by routine. It is the 'Task of childhood: to bring the new world into symbolic space. The child . . . can do what the adult absolutely cannot: recognise the new once again' (K1a, 3). Infant joy in objects forgotten or ignored by the adult world reveals the symbolic function of the city's thresholds:

> Threshold magic. At the entrance to the skating rink, to the pub, to the tennis court, to resort locations: *penates*. The hen that lays the golden praline-eggs, the machine that stamps our name on nameplates, slot machines,

fortunetelling devices, and above all weighing devices (the Delphic *gnothi seaton* [know thyself] of our day) – these guard the threshold. Oddly, such machines don't flourish in the city, but rather are a component of excursion sites, of beer gardens in the suburbs. And when, in search of a little greenery, one heads for these places on a Sunday afternoon, one is turning as well to the mysterious thresholds. Of course this same magic prevails more covertly in the interior of the bourgeois dwelling. Chairs beside an entrance, photographs flanking a doorway, are fallen household deities, and the violence they must appease grips our hearts even today at each ringing of the doorbell. (IIa, 4)

Once identified, such points of transition provide the dialectical images that are the stellar points of Benjamin's re-presentation of modernity. The *Arcades Project* abounds in images of outsides that mirror insides and insides that are outsides: squares that are like rooms, parks enclosed by iron and glass. Benjamin delights in finding the violence of the city streets not only in the fear inspired by a doorbell, but in the imprints left in the plush of expensive furniture – the clues that furnish the evidence for the detective novel.[26] There is little room for Victorian moralism in Benjamin's work, but when one of his dialectical images strikes home, it dissolves the boundary between bourgeois interior and the exterior of the street, representing each as parts of the same urban totality: 'For what do we know of streetcorners, curb-stones, the architecture of the pavement – we who have never felt heat, filth, and the edges of the stone beneath our naked soles, and have never scrutinized the uneven placement of the paving stones with an eye toward bedding down on them' (P1, 10).

Peter Osborne argues that, for Benjamin, even as modernity impoverishes experience, it offers the temporal possibility of its redemption.[27] The same can be said of Benjamin's understanding of space (as discussed in 'Method'). Even as the everyday journey through the city develops into the familiarity of habit, so the thresholds between the city's different spatial orders offer the possibility of a collective transformation. Just as the threshold transformed the person who passed over it in the ancient world, so the modern city's boundaries offer fulfilment in the present of a promise of which the past has dreamed.[28]

Modernity as dreamworld

The city produces dreamscapes. Although the arcades provide the project's working title, they are not the only city spaces embodying the surreal dreamworld of the nineteenth century: 'arcades, winter gardens, panoramas, factories, wax museums, casinos, railroad stations' are all 'dream houses of the collective' (L1, 3). The concept of 'phantasmagoria' that describes these dream spaces is a product of the new commodity culture that emerged after the French revolution: 'Capitalism was a natural phenomenon with which a new dream-filled sleep came over Europe, and, through it, a reactivation of mythic forces' (K1a, 8). If the opening of the nineteenth century marks the threshold of this new era, its first and most enduring expression are the great exhibitions. These events – the beginnings of which Benjamin traces to the first public exhibitions in Paris in 1798 (G4, 1) – juxtaposed commodities from across the globe, wrenching them out of their original context and into a new arrangement or constellation. Torn from their cultural traditions, they were reassembled like the found objects of a surrealist work of art. In the unlikely, and perhaps still underestimated, culture of nineteenth-century commercialism, Benjamin rediscovers the poetics of the modern in a 'premature synthesis' (G2, 3). The experience closest to that of nineteenth-century urban life is the intoxication offered by drugs. By contrast, when he writes that the 'history that showed things "as they really are" was the strongest narcotic of the century', the distinction between lived experience and dependency is clear (N3, 4).

Despite offering the thresholds, juxtapositions and boundaries that make possible Benjamin's modernist rendering of Paris, the dominant tendency of nineteenth-century capitalism is still towards mystification. The new presents itself as the ever-the-same, rather than replete with possibility. The reactivation of mythic forces of which Benjamin writes describes the sense of eternal recurrence best illustrated by fashion. In a way that is not immediately obvious, historicism, which appears to offer the opposite of the ever-the-same in progress or linear development actually offers something very similar. The teleological nature of the 'Whig' version of history means that every stage of history is understood in relation to its arrival at an already decided endpoint, for example liberal democracy or free-market capitalism. Social transformation is reduced to these goals and the possibility of realising full human potential is limited to the version of humanism offered by current circumstances rather than what might be.

It would be wrong to suggest that Benjamin wants only to demystify the dreamworlds of the nineteenth century – through, for example, some kind of ideology critique. He is too interested in the imaginative power of such worlds to suggest that they should simply be seen through or awakened from. As discussed in 'Awakening', the point is not to be awake, but to be waking up. Instead, his counter-strategy is to turn his attention to the moment when the full power of a dreamworld has faded: its remains or 'residues'.[29] Benjamin's primary interest is in the ordinariness or everyday aspects of the modern, which can be rediscovered in the discarded objects of the nineteenth century. The *Arcades Project* looks to the ordinary modern as the threshold between the ordinary and the extraordinary, for while the extraordinary is never the 'truth' of the everyday, neither is it its untruth: 'boredom is a warm gray fabric lined on the inside with the most lustrous and colorful of silks' (D2a, 1). Benjamin's understanding of modernity suggests that to describe the everyday as what is, is as dangerous a narcotic as a rendering of history as 'what actually happened'. Both versions oversimplify the cultures of modernity, ignoring the thresholds and boundaries that fracture the space in which they are made and to which modern states of consciousness adhere. What is available to the cultural critic is never what exists but rather what remains. In the scatter and confusion that is modernity there is no act of description that is not also an act of interpretation, an act of re-assembly (as discussed in 'Method'). Just as Brecht inveighed against 'culinary' theatre as drama that hid the joins, so Benjamin wanted to write a history of modernity that foregrounded the process of putting together new constellations.

Notes

1 Max Weber, *The Protestant Ethic and the Spirit of Capitalism* (London: Allen and Unwin, 1930); Georg Lukács, *History and Class Consciousness* (Cambridge Mass.: MIT Press, 1971), particularly the chapter 'Reification and class consciousness', pp. 83–222, which is influenced by Weber; Georg Simmel, 'The metropolis and mental life', in D. Levine (ed.), *Individuality and Social Forms* (Chicago: Chicago University Press, 1974). See also David Frisby, *Fragments of Modernity: Social Theories of Modernity in the Works of Georg Simmel, Siegfried Kracauer and Walter Benjamin* (Cambridge: Polity Press, 1986).

2 Letter 134, from Benjamin to Scholem, 13 June 1924, in *Correspondence*, pp. 241–4 (p. 244).

3 See Momme Brodersen, *Walter Benjamin: A Biography*, trans. Malcolm R. Green and Ingrida Ligers (London: Verso, 1997), p. 182.

4 Fredric Jameson, 'The theoretical hesitation: Benjamin's sociological predecessor', *Critical Inquiry*, 25: 2 (1999), 267–88 (p. 269).

5 Jameson, 'The theoretical hesitation', p. 272.

6 In many translations, '*die phantasmagorische Form*' is rendered as 'the fantastic form', see e.g. Karl Marx, *Capital*, vol. 1, trans. Ben Fowkes (London: Lawrence and Wishart, 1977), p. 165.

7 Marx, *Capital*, vol. 1, p. 165.

8 Lukács, *History*, p. 90.

9 Charles Baudelaire, 'The painter of modern life', in *Selected Writings on Art and Artists* (Harmondsworth: Penguin, 1972), p. 435.

10 See Bertolt Brecht, 'Of all the works of man', in *Poems, Part 2, 1929–1938*, ed. John Willett and Ralph Manheim (London: Methuen, 1976).

11 Marcel Proust, *In Search of Lost Time* vol. 1, *Swann's Way*, trans. C. K. Scott Moncrieff and Terence Kilmartin, rev. D. J. Enright (London: Vintage, 1996), p. 54. For more on the relationship to Proust see 'Method'.

12 Walter Benjamin, 'On some motifs in Baudelaire' [1940], in *SW* 4, pp. 313–55 (p. 319). See also Andrew Benjamin, 'Tradition and experience: Walter Benjamin's "On some motifs in Baudelaire"', in Andrew Benjamin (ed.), *The Problems of Modernity: Adorno and Benjamin* (London: Routledge, 1989), pp. 129–39.

13 Miriam Hansen, 'Foreword', in Oskar Negt and Alexander Kluge, *Public Sphere and Experience: Towards an Analysis of the Bourgeois and Proletarian Public Sphere* [1972] (Minneapolis: University of Minnesota Press, 1993), pp. xvi–xvii.

14 Andrew Benjamin, 'Tradition and experience', p. 132.

15 Letter 32, from Benjamin to Theodor Adorno, 31 May 1935, in *Adorno-Benjamin Correspondence*, pp. 87–92 (p. 88).

16 See Leslie, 'Stars, phosphor and chemical colours' on the proposed structure.

17 Walter Benjamin, 'Materials for the exposé of 1935', in *AP*, pp. 899–918 (p. 901). The most developed account of Benjamin's relationship with the city is Graeme Gilloch's *Myth and Modernity* (Cambridge: Polity Press, 1996).

18 Benjamin, 'A Berlin chronicle', p. 596.

19 See Walter Benjamin and Asja Lacis, 'Naples' [1925], in *SW 1*, pp. 414–21; Walter Benjamin, 'Moscow' [1927] and 'Marseilles' [1929], in *SW 2*, pp. 22–46 and 232–6. On porosity see Gilloch, *Myth and Modernity*, pp. 25–36.

20 See 'Idleness'.

21 T. J. Clark argues that the 'The arcades were a vision of the city as one great threshold', 'Reservations of the marvellous', p. 6.

22 See the quotations from Ferdinand Noack's *Triumph und Triumphbogen* (C7a, 3, C8, 1).

23 Walter Benjamin, 'Exposé of 1935', p. 13.

24 Walter Benjamin, 'Exposé of 1935', p. 13.

25 Benjamin discussed his fears about Stalin with Brecht: see Walter Benjamin, 'Conversations with Brecht', in T. W. Adorno et al., *Aesthetics and Politics* (London: Verso, 1980), pp. 86–99 (pp. 95–8). For an account of the political situation in France see Leslie, *Overpowering Conformism*, pp. 123–9.

26 Walter Benjamin, 'Paris, capital of the nineteenth century, Exposé <of 1939>', in *AP*, pp. 14–26 (p. 20).

27 Peter Osborne argues that Benjamin derives this insight from Baudelaire: see 'Small-scale victories', pp. 79–80.

28 On Benjamin's concept of 'image-space' see Leslie, *Overpowering Conformism*, pp. 24–5.

29 Walter Benjamin, 'Exposé of 1935', p. 13.

~

Magic

What is the relation between capitalism and magic? The *Arcades Project* provides an unconventional answer. Historians tend to agree that sorcery in Europe has been in retreat since the Reformation and that capitalism, propelled by the Protestant ethic, relentlessly sweeps aside the magical world-view. For Max Weber, 'In the last resort the factor which produced capitalism is the rational permanent enterprise, rational accounting, rational technology and rational law . . . the rational spirit, the rationalization of the conduct of life in general, and a rationalistic economic ethic'.[1] Since magic insists that there is a realm beyond the calculable, it is 'one of the most serious obstructions to the rationalization of economic life'.[2] If the twentieth century saw the completion of this 'disenchantment of the world', the nineteenth century was its original crucible. Writing about the dominant aesthetic mode of that century, Fredric Jameson confirms Weber's thesis: 'realism – but also that desacralized, postmagical, common-sense, everyday, secular reality which is its object – is inseparable from the development of capitalism, the quantification of the market system of the older hierarchical or feudal or magical environment, and thus . . . both are intimately linked to the bourgeoisie and its commodity'.[3] The city, in particular, is generally considered inhospitable to magic, which, as Christopher Hill has argued, is largely 'agrarian', and therefore thrives in the isolated constituency of the village cunning man, but fails in the urban industrial milieu of capitalism.[4]

In contrast to this standard view, Benjamin's city of consumption teems with magical effects. Capitalism banishes the wizards, but they take up residence in the arcades as fortune-tellers. Artificial light extinguishes the stars and their astrological importance, but creates the 'black magic' of 'fairy grottoes' (T1a, 8). Organized religion may decline, but sects of Saint-Simonians – 'a salvation army in the midst of the bourgeoisie' (U13a, 1) – spring up in its place. And as for 'everyday, secular reality', in the *Arcades Project* nothing is more bewitched: the commodity-on-display, as Susan Buck-Morss has argued, is the ultimate apparition in Benjamin's phantasmagoric Paris.[5] Not only has capitalism failed to entirely desacralize the world, it generates more than its fair share of secular enchantment. In the challenge it poses to Weber's rationalization thesis, the *Arcades Project* is not without precedent. In seeking out the irrational and phantomatic elements in capitalism and the modern city, Benjamin in fact turns to *Capital* for support. In what Tiedemann claims is a fairly selective reading,[6] Benjamin seizes on some of the same passages which Jacques Derrida later isolates in *Spectres of Marx*, a text which analyses 'the counter-magic' Marxism 'still risks being'.[7] In particular, the first two sentences of 'The fetishism of the commodity and its secret' (part 1, chapter 1, section 4), are cited in whole or in part in the exposés of 1935 and 1939 and twice in the convolutes (G5, 1 and G13a, 2). Their attraction for Benjamin is obvious: 'A commodity appears at first sight an extremely obvious, trivial thing. But its analysis brings out that it is a very strange thing, abounding in metaphysical subtleties and theological niceties.'[8] Is not Benjamin's writing precisely the continuous extraction of metaphysical complexities from the trivial and ephemeral? Benjamin also cites (in d17a, 5) from the same paragraph of *Capital* a footnote added in the second German edition (1872) which remarks on the ghostly character of the 'dancing' table-commodity and alludes simultaneously to the spiritualist craze of the mid nineteenth century. In other words, he had ample authority to justify his view of the pseudo-magical nature of capitalist commodity culture.

This aspect of the *Arcades Project* has not gone unnoticed. According to Rolf Tiedemann, 'commodity fetishism was destined to form the central schema for the whole project', and 'The concept of phantasmagoria that Benjamin repeatedly employs seems to be merely another term for what Marx called commodity fetishism'.[9] Margaret Cohen claims that Benjamin is almost unique among Marxists of his generation in his 'valorization of the realm of culture's ghosts and phantasms as a significant and rich field of social production rather than a mirage to be dispelled'.[10] And Christina Britzolakis has argued that the phantasmagoria of commodity culture puts on hold Weber's disenchantment of the world.[11] While it would be wrong to underestimate the importance of 'phantasmagoria' as an organizing concept in the *Arcades*, the prominence it is given can overshadow some of the other magical features Benjamin analysed in the Paris of the nineteenth century. A full magical inventory of the *Arcades* would take in at least the following: (1) phantasmagoria, (2) technology,

(3) the astral and (4) language and naming. Across these four topics, a consistency of view emerges, summed up in a comment found in Convolute R ('Mirrors'): 'One may compare the pure magic of those walls of mirrors which we know from feudal times with the oppressive magic worked by the alluring mirror-walls of the arcades, which invite us into seductive bazaars' (R2a, 2). Just as the modern magician deals in trickery and deception rather than mystical powers, the spell cast by the modern city and its commodities is illusory, a prestidigitation of the market, although no less powerful for that. Benjamin is not content, however, with simply denouncing such illusions, and cannot help wondering whether obsolete 'pure magic' can still be put to work, an aspect of his thinking which should make us uneasy, but which cannot be dispensed with readily. Let us explore this with each of the forms of magic in turn:

Phantasmagoria

Cohen explains that in the nineteenth century this term referred in the first instance to magic lantern shows, but she emphasizes its polysemy in the *Arcades Project*, offering five separate meanings. The indications are that Benjamin adopted 'phantasmagoria' as a substitute for the set of associations around the 'dream collective', which had been his initial theoretical framework for the *Arcades*. This was done at the prompting of Adorno, who was highly critical of the latter formulation. In fact, Adorno's understanding of phantasmagoria is the only full definition of the term to be found in the *Arcades*. In an essay on Wagner (1939), Adorno calls it 'a consumer item in which there is no longer anything that is supposed to remind us how it came into being. It becomes a magical object, insofar as labor stored up in it comes to seem supernatural and sacred at the very moment when it can no longer be recognized as labor' (X13a). The surrealists were particularly sensitive to this process. For Louis Aragon, in the decaying Passage de l'Opéra the goods in shop windows take on an unearthly quality: standing intoxicated outside a cane shop in *Paris Peasant*, he cannot account for the 'supernatural gleam' of the items on display.[12] This sort of profane illumination, Benjamin says in his essay on the surrealists, is the first step to 'the true, creative overcoming of religious illumination', implying that it is necessary to first see the 'magic' of the commodity as 'satanic' rather than simply natural and inevitable.[13] The difference between the surrealists and Benjamin is that the latter resists being swept away by the enchantment of the dream logic. He even chastises surrealism for its detours into the 'humid backroom of spiritualism', a topic, along with occultism, which distracts him occasionally in the *Arcades*.[14]

There are references scattered throughout the *Arcades* to 'faery-plays', the gothic theatrical spectacles popular in Paris during the second Empire; indeed, the essay on the arcades that Benjamin first planned in 1927 was to be entitled 'Paris arcades: a dialectical fairy play'.[15] Benjamin clearly saw such plays as the aesthetic counterparts of the arcades, which were theatrical spaces for the *mise-en-scène* of the phantasmagoric commodity. It is for this reason that he places so much emphasis on the visual and spatial aspects of the arcades: lighting, windows, signs, displays, entrances and exits. It is no accident that the arcades reach the 'height of their magic' in the Passage des Panoramas, with its many painted scenes bringing to the domesticated interior of the arcade innumerable illusions visible by moonlight or the flicker of oil and gas lamps.[16] The phantom commodity requires a phantom stage, and the arcades were perfectly designed to provide it, as Johann Friedrich Geist, their historian, explains:

> In the time of its conception the arcade was home to luxury and fashion. It offered to the bourgeois public in all its various guises – the *flâneur*, the bohemian, the *boulevardier* – the opportunity to display itself to the world. It presented the myriad products of a blossoming luxury industry for gazing, buying, flaunting, and consuming. The public served by the arcade felt at home in the artificial lighting . . . It reveled in this illusionistic realm, this man-made jungle under glass, this urban reality which replaced nature.[17]

The notion that the bourgeois 'felt at home' in the arcades is crucial to Benjamin's conception of their magic. The displacement of public magic by private ritual can be seen in his analysis of the fate of bourgeois 'thresholds' in modernity. The mystical power of the 'Roman victory arch' which 'makes the returning general a conquering hero' cannot be matched by the Arc de Triomphe 'which today has become a traffic island' (C2a, 3), although it finds worthy competitors in its miniaturized bourgeois substitutes, 'Chairs beside an entrance, photographs flanking a doorway' which Benjamin calls 'fallen household deities' (I1a, 4; see the discussion of thresholds in 'Modernity'). It remains to the collector – the apotheosis of bourgeois acquisitiveness – to undo the spell of the commodity, by removing it from the circuit of exchange and introducing it into an 'historical system' (H1a, 2). Even then, Benjamin clearly considers the activity of the collector, whom he compares to an 'augur' (H2a, 1), as a form of counter-magic: 'It is the deepest enchantment of the collector to enclose the particular item within a magic circle, where, as a last

shudder runs through it (the shudder of being acquired), it turns to stone'
(H1a, 2). At moments like these it is difficult to assess the levels of irony
or detachment in Benjamin's prose, but his metaphorical attachment to
such matters betrays a reluctance to disavow entirely the magical effects
conjured up by phantasmagoria.

Technology

In one of his radio talks for children, Benjamin spoke about the Lisbon
earthquake, which devastated the Portuguese capital on 1 November
1755.[18] Apart from the familiar motif of the catastrophe, it is not immediately clear what draws Benjamin to this event. Lisbon was not among
the constellation of cities (Paris, Berlin, Naples, Moscow) that made up
his urban typology. He does not describe the earthquake itself, instead
explaining 'why this event affected people's minds so powerfully'
throughout Europe.[19] He leaves the description of the catastrophe to an
eyewitness account by an unnamed Englishman who 'would welcome
the opportunity to speak once again' and in due course this apocalyptic
pamphlet gets a hearing.[20] However, Benjamin playfully delays reading
out this account, mentioning Kant's 'slim book' on the earthquake – 'certainly the beginnings of seismology' – and giving a short lecture on the
movements of the earth's crusts.[21] While elegantly executing its pedagogic
aims, the piece is also a reflection on historical development and change
in the technologies of information. In the pamphlets circulated after the
event Benjamin finds precursors of mass print newspapers: 'Whoever
was able to do so obtained eyewitness descriptions in as much detail as
possible, and then printed and sold them.'[22] He also takes the opportunity
to consider the changes in the arts of prognostication which have come
about with the advances of science. In 1755, the forecasting of the disaster was retrospective, and on the very cusp of the Enlightenment, only
half rooted in superstition: 'people's imaginations brooded on the strange
phenomena of nature that had been observed in the weeks preceding the
earthquake and that subsequently – and probably not always without justification – were regarded as portents of the catastrophe to come'.[23] Now,
however, 'in Germany alone, there are thirteen earthquake monitoring
stations' whose 'sensitive instruments are never entirely still', thus turning
the divination of disaster from an occult skill into a precise science.[24] He
ends on an ambiguous note: 'The catastrophe it brought in its wake is one
of the very few that can render men as impotent now as they were 170
years ago. But here, too, technology will find ways to combat it, even if in

a roundabout way: by prediction.'[25] He wryly adds that a dog is often a helpful amanuensis to science, since its forecasting senses are more acute than the best instruments.

The conventional wisdom about technology is that it renders magic redundant. In a pre-technological era, the wizard manipulates the occult forces of an often destructive natural world. But as Keith Thomas argues, technology, with a different kind of manipulation of the physical world, is less haphazard than the superstition it displaces: 'the stronger man's control of his environment, the less his recourse to magical remedies'.[26] The sieve and shears of sixteenth-century thief-magic are imprecise tools of detection compared with the forensic science and DNA testing of the twentieth century.[27] Benjamin goes along with this argument up to a point. He is, in fact, often notoriously optimistic about the utopian possibilities contained in, for instance, technologies of mass reproduction. In the case of the Lisbon earthquake, he thinks that scientific seismology has successfully superseded earlier modes of divination. However, he is careful to point out that seismology does not do away with catastrophe, is even predicated upon it: the apocalypse still looms and science simply makes it easier to anticipate it. If the scientist attempts to predict catastrophe, Benjamin is implicitly arguing, it is because his universe – disenchanted or not – is still one which has a concept of the apocalyptic. In the Paris of the arcades this continuing interaction with fate and destiny takes on different forms. It is there most prominently in the gambler, whose relationship to the roulette wheel is divinatory and includes 'the atavistic sense of clairvoyance'[28] (see '*Jeux/joie/jouissance*' below). It is also active in another form of gambling-cum-forecasting Benjamin examines in the *Arcades Project*: speculation on the stock market. The ways in which modern markets and modern technologies coincide is recorded in 'A Berlin chronicle' where Benjamin calls the telephone 'a truly infernal machine' that introduced him as a child to the mysteries of financial dealings: 'it was only the telephone that intimated to us the occult world of business and traders. My father telephoned a great deal.'[29]

The astral

In Convolute d, Benjamin suggests comparing the last line of a Hugo poem with the last line of Baudelaire's 'Les Aveugles' ('The blind') (d17a, 3). In the latter poem, not reproduced in the *Arcades*, the subjects of the title fix their blank gaze on the heavens, never bowing their heads to the ground:

Leurs yeux, d'où la divine étincelle est partie
Comme s'ils regardaient au loin, restent levés
Au ciel; on ne les voit jamais vers les pavés
Pencher rêveusement leur tête appesantie.

(Their eyes, now devoid of Godly spark
As if gazing in the distance, remain raised
To the sky; never down to the pavement
Do they lower dreamily their heavy brows.)[30]

In the final line, the poet wonders what they are seeking for in the skies: 'But stumbling through the night I wonder what / The blind keep looking for up in the skies?' Unlike the lyric poets who preceded him – Hugo, Lamartine (see D9a, 1 and D9a, 2) – for Baudelaire there are no stars visible in the skies overhead: the promise of transcendence has evaporated. Benjamin takes this as a sign of Baudelaire's modernity: 'That the stars do not appear in Baudelaire is the surest indicator of that tendency of his poetry to dissolve illusory appearances' (J58a, 3). Stars disappear from the skies over the modern city with the advent of artificial lighting. Equally, the stroller in the arcades can be outside, but not fear when the heavens open. The consequences are felt in philosophy as well as poetry, for 'Kant's transcription of the sublime through "the starry heavens above me and the moral law within me" could never have been conceived in these terms by an inhabitant of the big city' (J64, 4). Both modern poetry and modern philosophy, illuminated by gas light, must do without astrological guidance. Benjamin calls this state of affairs in Baudelaire the extinguishing or 'renunciation' of the 'magic of distance' (J47, 6; J47a, 1; J56a, 12).

It seems likely that the 'magic of distance' is equivalent to Benjamin's concept of 'aura', that vexed and awkward term most prominent in the 'Work of art' essay. In Convolute J, Benjamin states that aura, in the form of the 'veil', is 'an old accomplice of distance', and that 'the degree of auratic saturation of human perception has fluctuated widely in the course of history', diminishing particularly in the Baroque and in 'epochs which tend toward allegorical expression' (J77a, 8). By renouncing the possibility of such a distance, whether natural or artificial, does Baudelaire's poetry then continue a process inaugurated by Galileo's telescope in the seventeenth century? And is Benjamin's enthusiasm for the denuding of aura under mechanical reproduction matched by an approval of the extinguishing of the heavens? In so far as Baudelaire does away with 'illusory appearances' yes, but one needs to take into account as well those dialectical companions to Baudelaire, Blanqui and Fourier, who busily reconstruct cosmologies as essential elements of their revolutionary and utopian ideologies. When Fourier 'calculated mathematically the trans-migration of the soul, and went on to prove that the human soul must assume 810 different forms until it completes the circuit of the planets and returns to earth' (W1a), or when Blanqui posited an 'entire universe . . . composed of astral systems . . . . So each heavenly body, whatever it might be, exists in infinite number in time and in space', they were attempting to enlist the stars, not for their ritual or magical value, but for politics[31] (see 'Insurrection', below). Their apposite failure is, of course, what attracts Benjamin to them. He says of Blanqui's *L'Éternité par les astres*, 'This book completes the century's constellation of phantasmago-rias with one last, cosmic phantasmagoria which implicitly comprehends the severest critique of the others.'[32] His insistence on the word 'constella-tion' deliberately betrays his own reluctance to abandon entirely the mythical properties of the stars.

Naming and language

One of the most cryptic features of the *Arcades Project* is the recurring lists of proper names that Benjamin transcribes. Names of arcades (A1, 2), of *magasins de nouveautés* (A3, 11), of Métro stations (C1a, 2), streets (P1a, 3), theatrical plays (G7a, 6), omnibuses (M8a, 6), newspapers (U4a, 6), even drum corps (O7, 3) – Benjamin records them all diligently, but generally without commentary. His interest in names and naming was, of course, long-standing. In 'On language as such and the language of man' (1916), an essay unpublished in his lifetime, which could not be further from the semiology Saussure proposed around the same time, Benjamin distinguishes between divine language and the language of man. He says that the proper name, the human name, is 'the point where human lan-guage participates most intimately in the divine infinity of the pure word', and justifies such recourse to 'mystical linguistic theory' on the grounds that it is preferable to 'bourgeois linguistic theory' in which 'the word has an accidental relation to its object, that it is a sign for things . . . agreed by some convention'.[33] According to Gershom Scholem, this early perspec-tive eventually came into conflict with later, materialist, influences, lead-ing to a 'polarization in Benjamin's view of language':

> that abolition of the magic of language, which conformed to a materialistic view of language, was certainly in unmistakable conflict with all his earlier reflections on language, reflections under theological, mystical inspirations . . . it did surprise me that he could still speak unmetaphorically of 'God's

words', in distinction to human words, as the foundation of linguistic theory.[34]

Benjamin's allegorical approach to the arcades of Paris squares well with the continuing influence of mystical linguistic theory in his thinking, since allegory permits signs to have a destiny or fate, rather than simply an arbitrary meaning. On an occasion when he does gloss one of his lists of names, this allegorical tendency comes through. He calls the Métro 'an underworld of names': 'Combat, Elysée, Georges V, Etienne Marcel, Solférino, Invalides, Vaugirard . . . are transformed into misshapen sewer gods, catacomb fairies' (C1a, 2).

The proper names Benjamin catalogues in the *Arcades Project* are a special sort of name, that is, names generated by the urban environment. In the case of street names, the effect is a linguistic revolution:

> What was otherwise reserved for only a very few words, a privileged class of words, the city has made possible for all words, or at least a great many: to be elevated to the noble status of name. This revolution in language was carried out by what is most general: the street. – Through its street names, the city is a linguistic cosmos. (P3, 5)

Just as the power of thresholds and of stars is diminished in metropolitan modernity, so the magic of names is transformed on the streets of Paris. However, when Benjamin reflects that 'Only the meeting of two different street *names* makes for the magic of the "corner"', he does not seem to be adding names to the catalogue of 'oppressive magic' that makes up the phantasmagoria.[35] In fact, he draws direct connections between naming and historical revolutions. In 'On the concept of history', he reflected on how revolutionaries shoot at clock-towers and institute new calendars, demonstrating an awareness that their actions must be accompanied by a revolution in the measurement of time (Thesis XV). The same principle applies to names in the city, whose durability matches that of the old calendars: 'the unconquerable power in the names of streets, squares, and theaters, a power which persists in the face of all topographic displacement' (P1, 1). In Convolute P ('The streets of Paris'), he records various revolutionary and utopian schemes for the renaming of Paris streets (often along rationalist lines), and in Convolute g ('The stock exchange, economic history'), he notes how the revolutionary bourgeois, after 1789, 'replaced the names of saints in the republican calendar, with the names of metals, plants, and animals' (g2, 2). Unfortunately, the *Arcades Project* does not develop more fully a thesis on naming and utopianism, perhaps because of the impossible tension between Benjamin's vestigial mystical views on language and his conviction that language needed to be purged of its magical elements. However, there are surely affinities here with his claim that historical materialism, in order to succeed, needs to enlist theology in its cause (Thesis I).

If we compare the nineteenth-century magician with his sixteenth-century forebear, the difference in the powers they claim is startling. While the latter manipulates the occult forces of nature, the former has no pretensions beyond being a showman, illusionist, or trickster. Indeed, so little did magicians of the nineteenth century subscribe to the possibility of supernatural forces that they often set out to expose as charlatans those, such as spiritualists and mediums, who did.[36] Much of the analysis of magic in the *Arcades Project* is based on this model of modern magic as mere illusion, even if it is illusion of tremendous ideological force, which transports the inhabitants of the arcades far from the rationalized world that Weber imagines for capitalism. In so far as Benjamin exposes in the *Arcades* these irrational aspects of capitalism, he falls in line with the work of the Frankfurt School and the Institute for Social Research, which critiqued modern mass culture's capacity for deception on a grand scale. And yet (as mentioned in 'Encounters'), Benjamin was also a practising graphologist, who advocated a philosophy that could 'include the possibility of soothsaying from coffee-grounds'.[37] His obvious admiration for Blanqui, who combined mysticism of the wildest kind with insurrectionary activity, has lead Margaret Cohen to suggest that Benjamin, 'Admitting criticism's commerce with irrational forces . . . draws attention to criticism's power both to locate contemporary demons and to press them into . . . service'.[38] Certainly, Benjamin's failure to side entirely with reason earned him a stern reprimand from Adorno, who warned in 1938 that the project 'is located at the crossroads of magic and positivism' and that 'Only theory could break this spell'.[39] While it is true that Benjamin did not share entirely the faith of his contemporaries (including Brecht) that the defeat of capitalism would involve the further extension of reason, neither did he simply want to enlist irrational forces as Cohen suggests. The sort of eccentric and impossible compromise he hoped to reach can be found in the fragment 'On astrology'. The piece is a sort of programme for a future philosophy: he calls it 'the complete prolegomenon of every rational astrology'.[40] A rational astrology would be one 'from which the doctrine of magical "influences," of "radiant energies," and so on has been excluded.' Benjamin wants to discard the irrational aspects of astrology but rescue the 'manifest configurations, mimetic resemblances' which it is able to recognize; in other words, its method of arranging data according to constellations which transform the materials making them up. This is clearly a venture with high risks and serious potential for misunderstanding, but it is difficult to know how to read Benjamin without taking such risks into account.

Notes

1 Max Weber, *General Economic History*, trans. F. H. Knight (New York: Collier Books, 1961), p. 260.
2 Weber, *General Economic History*, p. 265.
3 Fredric Jameson, 'Beyond the cave: demystifying the ideology of modernism', in Francis Mulhern (ed.), *Contemporary Marxist Literary Criticism* (London: Longman, 1992), pp. 168–87 (p. 176).
4 Christopher Hill, *Society and Puritanism in pre-revolutionary England* (London: Secker & Warburg, 1964), p. 486.
5 Buck-Morss, *The Dialectics of Seeing*, p. 81.
6 Rolf Tiedemann, 'Dialectics at a standstill: approaches to the *Passagen-Werk*', in *AP*, pp. 929–45 (pp. 937–40).
7 Jacques Derrida, *Spectres of Marx: The State of the Debt, the Work of Mourning, and the New International*, trans. Peggy Kamuf (London and New York: Routledge, 1994), p. 47.
8 Marx, *Capital*, vol. 1, p. 163.
9 Tiedemann, 'Dialectics at a standstill', p. 938.
10 Margaret Cohen, *Profane Illumination: Walter Benjamin and the Paris of Surrealist Revolution* (Berkeley and London: University of California Press, 1993), p. 11.
11 Christina Britzolakis, 'Phantasmagoria: Walter Benjamin and the poetics of urban modernism', in Peter Buse and Andrew Stott (eds), *Ghosts: Deconstruction, Psychoanalysis, History* (Basingstoke: Macmillan, 1999), pp. 72–91.
12 Louis Aragon, *Paris Peasant*, trans. Simon Watson Taylor (London: Pan, 1980), p. 36.
13 Walter Benjamin, 'Surrealism', p. 209.
14 Walter Benjamin, 'Surrealism', p. 209. In Convolute d ('Literary history, Hugo'), Benjamin asks, 'Why is the nineteenth century the century of spiritualism?' (d18a, 2). The *Arcades* does not give any coherent answer to this question, but Adorno does not hesitate to denounce such pseudo-religions as 'symptom[s] of regression in consciousness', mocking the 'bent little fortune-tellers terrorizing their clients with crystal balls [who] are toy models of the great ones who hold the fate of mankind in their hands'. Theodor Adorno, 'Theses against occultism', *Minima Moralia: Reflections from Damaged Life* [1951], trans. E. F. N. Jephcott (London: Verso, 1981), pp. 238–44 (pp. 238, 240). Benjamin would probably baulk at Adorno's magisterial claim that 'By

its regression to magic under late capitalism, thought is assimilated to late capitalist forms' (p. 239), but in any case he was more interested in the Utopianism of Fourier and the Saint-Simonians and the cosmological speculations of the insurrectionary Blanqui than in the table-turning spectacles of nineteenth-century séances.

15 Letter 168, from Benjamin to Scholem, 30 January 1928, in *Correspondence*, pp. 321–5 (p. 322).

16 Walter Benjamin, 'First sketches', p. 834. See also Q3, 2.

17 Geist, *Arcades*, p. 114.

18 Walter Benjamin, 'The Lisbon earthquake' [1931], in *SW 2*, pp. 536–40. The talk was broadcast by Berliner Rundfunk in October 1931.

19 Benjamin, 'Lisbon earthquake', p. 537.

20 Benjamin, 'Lisbon earthquake', p. 538.

21 Benjamin, 'Lisbon earthquake', p. 538.

22 Benjamin, 'Lisbon earthquake', p. 537.

23 Benjamin, 'Lisbon earthquake', pp. 537–8.

24 Benjamin, 'Lisbon earthquake', p. 539.

25 Benjamin, 'Lisbon earthquake', p. 540.

26 Keith Thomas, *Religion and the Decline of Magic: Studies in Popular Beliefs in Sixteenth and Seventeenth-century England* (Harmondsworth: Penguin, 1973), p. 775.

27 On thief-magic see Thomas, *Decline of Magic*, pp. 252–64.

28 Walter Benjamin, 'Short shadows (II)' [1933], in *SW 2*, pp. 699–702 (p. 700). See also 'Notes on a theory of gambling' [1930], in *SW 2*, pp. 297–8, where Benjamin describes the moment of the wager as a 'marginal case in which presence of mind becomes divination' (p. 298).

29 Benjamin, 'Berlin chronicle', p. 619.

30 Charles Baudelaire, *Complete Poems*, trans. Walter Martin (Manchester: Carcanet, 1997), p. 241.

31 Benjamin, 'Exposé of 1939', p. 25.

32 Benjamin, 'Exposé of 1939', p. 25.

33 Walter Benjamin, 'On language as such and on the language of man' [1916] in *SW 1*, pp. 62–74 (p. 69).

34 Scholem, *Walter Benjamin: The Story of a Friendship*, p. 209.

35 Benjamin, 'First sketches', p. 840.

36 On the nineteenth-century magician see Janet Oppenheim, *The Other World: Spiritualism and Psychical Research in England, 1850–1914* (Cambridge: Cambridge University Press, 1985), pp. 21–7.

37 Scholem, *Walter Benjamin: The Story of a Friendship*, p. 59.

38 Cohen, *Profane Illumination*, p. 257.

39 Letter 110, from Adorno to Benjamin, 10 November 1938, in *Adorno–Benjamin Correspondence*, pp. 280–9 (p. 283).

40 Walter Benjamin, 'On astrology' [1932], in *SW 2*, pp. 684–5 (p. 685).

Empathy/*Einfühlung*

Einfühlung: in Benjamin's nineteenth century, the consumer and the historicist suffer from the same ailment. For the masses at the World Exhibitions as well as the flâneur in the arcades, the commodity-form elicits an 'empathy with exchange-value' (*die Einfühlung in den Tauschwert*) (m4, 7). The historicist establishes an equivalent relation with the past, as illustrated in the following empathetic reverie in a letter from Flaubert to George Sand:

> I see myself at different moments of history, very clearly in various guises and occupations . . . .I was boatman on the Nile, *leno* [procurer] in Rome at the time of the Punic wars, then Greek rhetorician in Suburra, where I was devoured by bedbugs. I died, during the Crusades, from eating too many grapes on the beach in Syria. I was pirate and monk, mountebank and coachman – perhaps Emperor of the East, who knows?[1]

Nothing could be further from the *Arcades Project*'s conception of history than this sensual projection into the past, Flaubert's unmediated identification with imagined historical characters which obliterates all distance and intervening time. Benjamin cites this passage in Convolute M, 'The flâneur', and glosses it with the phrase 'the intoxication of empathy' (*ivresse der Einfühlung*) (M17a, 5). 'Empathy' is the standard translation of *Einfühlung*, which literally means 'in-feeling' or 'feeling into'. The term can be found scattered throughout the *Arcades Project*, and it also appears elsewhere in Benjamin's writings, most notably in 'On the concept of history', where it takes a prominent position in the polemic against historicism in Thesis VII. In spite of its importance in his thought, Benjamin never fully defines the concept, nor does he acknowledge his sources for it, even though he is by no means the first to employ it. There is a wide literature on the subject which predates Benjamin, but his use of the term is far from orthodox. Neither is it consistent, for its relatively straightforward meaning in his critique of historicism is complicated by the metaphysical subtleties which it undergoes when he applies it to commodity fetishism. In the historian it is to be avoided at all costs; in the arcades it is an unavoidable hazard.

The intoxications of historicism

For Benjamin, the slogans of nineteenth-century historiography – Ranke's injunction to see the past *wie es eigentlich war* (as it really was), Michelet's *résurrection intégrale du passé* (complete resurrection of the past) – give no guarantee of a purity of gaze into the past, but are further symptoms of a dreaming century. 'The history that showed things "as they really were"', he writes in Convolute N, 'was the strongest narcotic of the century' (N3, 4). In order to achieve historicism's ambition – reliving an era in all its specificity and difference from the present – the historian must paradoxically enter a state of melancholic forgetfulness. This is because the historicist, according to Benjamin, must 'blot out everything he knows about the later course of history'.[2] The historicist, ever vigilant against anachronism, insists that the past be understood in terms of the past, and not the present, betraying thereby a belief that historical events can be safely consigned to the past *and* at the same time comprehended in their totality. This half-deliberate forgetfulness Benjamin calls empathy, and in 'On the concept of history' – a distillation of Convolute N – it is historical materialism which is to provide the antidote to it. Benjamin's critique of historicism and empathy in Thesis VII has a clear political motivation:

> The nature of this sadness becomes clearer if we ask: With whom does historicism actually sympathize? The answer is inevitable: with the victor. And all rulers are the heirs of prior conquerors. Hence, empathizing with the victor invariably benefits the current rulers.[3]

To project oneself emotionally into the perspective of the dead means to endorse that perspective, and Benjamin appears to leave no room for the perspectives of any but the rulers and their heirs.

Why is empathy inevitably with the victor? Writing well before the 'history from below' which he partly inspired, Benjamin found it difficult to envision any historical remainders uncontaminated by the rulers who, more often than not, hold them up as 'cultural treasures'.[4] For the historicist, the cultural treasure has a totemic value, and in its presence the empathetic relation to the past is summoned up; but the historical materialist views such traces with 'cautious detachment'.[5] And even though Benjamin in the *Arcades Project* prefers the detritus of history – the ruffle on the dress, the mechanical hen which lays praline eggs – to its more familiar treasures, even this detritus he brushes against the grain, resisting the impulse to make of it another 'tradition'. An alternative to empathy is suggested in Convolute N: the concept of 'rescue'. Characteristically, Benjamin has an unconventional understanding of the concept. Phenomena are not rescued, as one might expect, 'from the discredit and neglect into which they have fallen, but from the catastrophe represented very often by a certain strain in their dissemination, their "enshrinement as heritage"' (N9, 4). Benjamin does not set out to save ephemeral phenomena for proper appreciation, but from such appreciation: salvation leads away from heaven, not towards it. Does he then cut off here any possibility of *Einfühlung* for someone other than the victors? This would appear to be the case when, later on in Convolute N, he confirms that 'the basis of the confrontation with conventional historiography and "enshrinement" is the polemic against empathy' (N10, 4). As far as history is concerned, it is not just empathy for the victor but empathy *tout court* which Benjamin rejects.

Antecedents

To understand better the implications of Benjamin's theory of empathy, it is helpful to inquire into some of its possible sources, even though the trail goes cold quite quickly. The only proper names associated with *Einfühlung* in the *Arcades Project* are Flaubert, Baudelaire, Franz Grillparzer (1791–1872) and Fustel de Coulanges (1830–1899). None of them makes direct use of the term, but Benjamin finds in all of their writing features of empathy. He credits the latter two, an Austrian playwright-poet and a French historian, neither of whom makes further appearances in the *Arcades*, with the historicist insistence on examining an historical era without any consideration of what follows it (N7, 5 and N8a, 3). When Benjamin reworks Convolute N as 'On the concept of history', he drops Grillparzer and gives Fustel de Coulanges (pseudonym of Numa Denis) full responsibility for this historicist recommendation.

It may be that Benjamin does not identify his sources for the use of *Einfühlung*, or define it adequately, simply because the term was already in such heavy circulation that its meanings could be taken as given. By the 1920s and 1930s, *Einfühlung* was an accepted, if heavily disputed, term in both aesthetics and psychology, as well as in the dubious hybrids of these two fields. According to H. F. Mallgrave and E. Ikonomou, the minor German aesthetician Robert Vischer coined the term in the early 1870s as a way of 'considering the subjective content that ... the viewer ... bring[s] to aesthetic contemplation'.[6] Vischer was the son of Friedrich Theodor Vischer (1807–1887), the influential Hegelian aesthetician, whose acerbic commentary on fashion in *Mode und Zynismus* (1879) Benjamin cites frequently in the *Arcades*. Robert Vischer introduces his notion of *Einfühlung* in the essay 'On the optical sense of form: a contribution to aesthetics' (1873):

> it seemed to me possible to distinguish between ideal associations and a direct merger of the imagination with objective form .... the body, in responding to certain stimuli in dreams, objectifies itself in spatial forms. Thus it unconsciously projects its own bodily form – and with this also the soul – into the form of the object. From this I derived the notion that I call 'empathy'.[7]

After Vischer, 'empathy' was taken up in the 1890s by Johannes Volkelt and Theodor Lipps, who was most responsible for popularizing the term, concealing some of the mysticism that Vischer gave it by placing it under the aegis of scientific psychology in his *Aesthetics of Space and Geometric-Optical Illusions* (1893–7).[8] Although Lipps was primarily interested in the psychological aspects of aesthetic contemplation, he also used empathy in the sense that is probably more familiar to us now, that is, as a capacity to feel as others feel, and experience what they experience. *Einfühlung* was adopted and modified by, among others, Husserl, and came under attack from a philosophical vantage by the phenomenologist Max Scheler, who suggests in *The Essence and Forms of Sympathy* (1926) that Lipps's empathy does not contain enough in the way of 'intentionality' to be of ethical value and offers the relative *distance* of *Mitgefühl* (sympathy) as a preferable category.[9] Benjamin, then, was by no means alone in his suspicion of empathy.

Whether or not the debates and disagreements about empathy among psychologists and philosophers registered on Benjamin's critical radar, it is little wonder that he made no effort to engage directly with them. Given his antipathy for psychologisms of any variety, and his firm anti-subjectivism (Adorno writes of 'his idiosyncratic distaste for words like "personality"'),[10] neither the philosophical nor the psychological variant of *Einfühlung* was likely to distract him for very long. His polemic against empathy is much more consistent with the one launched by his friend Bertolt Brecht, in the playwright's more general assault on Aristotelian and bourgeois theatre.

Empathy and epic theatre

In the *Versuche* (1930–2) Brecht does not entangle himself in pseudo-scientific proofs of the existence of empathy, nor does he dwell on philosophical speculation about its ethical value or possible substitute terms which might better capture abstractly the interaction between self and other. He simply accepts that empathy takes place and sets out to eliminate it. What Brecht sacrifices by way of nuance is amply compensated for in terms of directness of argument. His case against *Einfühlung*, sometimes translated as identification, is straightforward. The 'Aristotelian' theatre, which is to say most theatre in the Western tradition, and specifically the bourgeois theatre which dominates the stage, is a 'culinary theatre' which serves up generous helpings of illusion, putting its audience in a 'trance'.[11] The theatrical apparatus is well placed to conjure up empathy in its audience: the darkened auditorium and lit stage isolate the spectator, suspenseful plots and sensational action bring her or him to a heightened level of tension, and persuasive, passionate acting encourages identification with the tribulations of a hero. The measure of a play's success has always been its capacity to arouse emotion in its audience, to generate a *correspondence* between the situation on stage and the feelings of those watching. Nothing for Brecht could be more politically disabling than this empathetic power of the theatre, because empathy implies resignation and acceptance of things as they are:

> The dramatic theatre's spectator says: Yes, I have felt like that too – Just like me – It's only natural – It'll never change – The sufferings of this man appal me, because they are inescapable – That's great art; it all seems the most obvious thing in the world – I weep when they weep, I laugh when they laugh.[12]

In contrast, in Brecht's epic theatre, the audience should be astonished at what they see before them, want to stop it, and 'laugh when they weep, weep when they laugh.'

Benjamin's acquaintance and engagement with these arguments dates from his first meetings with Brecht in 1929, and a subsequent radio talk about the playwright broadcast by Frankfurter Rundfunk, as well as a short review of the *Versuche* in the *Frankfurter Zeitung*, both in 1930.[13] His full endorsement and faithful exegesis of Brechtian theory can be found in the short essay 'What is epic theatre?', two versions of which are collected in *Understanding Brecht*. In reference to *Fear and Misery of the Third Reich* (performed in Paris in 1938), Benjamin explains how the resistance to empathy emerges directly from political considerations. For an exiled German actor playing the part of an SS man, 'empathy can scarcely be recommended as a suitable method, for there can be no empathy with the murderers of one's fellow fighters'.[14] But then, nor is empathy necessarily the best method for representing 'one's fellow fighters', because, as Benjamin points out, the objective is a 'relaxed' audience. The essay has the added advantage of explaining what will take the place of empathy in the theatre, if not boredom or empty seats. Instead of empathy, it is the *interest* of the spectator which should be aroused.

A play from the early period of Benjamin's interest in Brecht illustrates this new approach. *The Mother*, first performed in Berlin in 1932, is one of Brecht's didactic plays, a sort of extended tutorial in the class struggle.[15] In a series of loosely connected sketches and songs, it follows the political education of the 'mother', Pelagea Vlasova, in the years leading up to the Russian revolution. The scenes proceed by 'fits and starts' so that the audience concentrates on what is before them and not what is to come next.[16] Each scene poses a problem – the solidarity of workers and soldiers, the role of the intellectual in revolution, nationalism versus internationalism – and asks the spectators to take up a critical attitude towards each of these issues. The loose structure deliberately drains the play of suspense, but even this episodic approach does not forestall an empathetic treatment of the material, because Vlasova, the thread connecting the scenes, begins to take on heroic proportions. The occasion of the execution of her revolutionary son, near the conclusion of the play, is the sort of opportunity the 'dramatic theatre' works hard to bring about, guaranteed as it is to arouse the pity of the audience. In *The Mother*, though, a cool approach is taken: the sympathy an audience might feel is already offered on stage by Vlasova's landlady who tries to console her with wisdom from the Bible, consolation which Vlasova rejects. What follows should deflect the audience's empathy, leading away from Vlasova's grief and into an extended debate about the relative utility of God and political struggle. Rather than feeling strongly about Vlasova, the spectator should ideally feel strongly about one side or other of this debate.

Of the many epic techniques designed to prevent empathy, one is of particular relevance to the *Arcades Project*: the practice of citation. In order to introduce a split between performer and role, Brecht recommends that 'the actor speaks his part not as if he were improvising it himself but like a quotation'.[17] This sort of 'coolness' and distance is accomplished by the Chinese actor, who does not exclude emotion entirely from his performance but generates 'emotions which need not correspond to those of the character portrayed'.[18] In his earliest writings on Brecht, and before he even seized on the term *Einfühlung*, Benjamin concentrates on epic theatre's citational tactics. He draws attention in particular to Brecht's notion of the 'quotable gesture'. This technique isolates a social situation, or even a single action pregnant with contradiction, and, removing it from its original context, re-examines it, repeats it, quotes it, under different circumstances, thereby robbing it of its spontaneity and naturalness and bringing it under renewed scrutiny.

By the time of 'What is epic theatre?' (1939), Benjamin has amplified this one aspect of epic theatre – quotation – and given it a privileged position in Brechtian dramaturgy. He links it to an aesthetics of *interruption*: whereas the dramatic theatre has traditionally relied on continuity, on seamless plotting, epic theatre proceeds by jumps and curves, by a montage of clashing material. Benjamin draws some far-reaching conclusions about interruption and quotation in general:

> We may go even further here and recall that interruption is one of the fundamental methods of all form-giving. It reaches far beyond the domain of art. It is, to mention just one of its aspects, the origin of quotation. Quoting a text implies interrupting its context.[19]

It is hard to resist reading this passage as a commentary on the compositional strategy of the *Arcades Project* itself. There is certainly enough reflection on citation in the *Arcades* to justify this link. For instance, in outlining the historiographical approach taken by the project, Benjamin writes, 'To write history thus means to *cite* history. It belongs to the concept of citation, however, that the historical object in each case is torn from its context' (N11, 3). Context, the pristineness of which is so valued by the historicist, is given short shrift by both epic theatre's quotable gesture and by Benjamin's citational history, which collects quotations like 'rags', and mounts them in a 'literary montage' (N1a, 8).[20] It is no great leap to suggest that Benjamin was trying to achieve for history what Brecht was doing for theatre.

It has been long accepted that the assemblage of quotations which makes up the *Arcades Project* is not just a glorified notebook but contains a principle of construction inspired by avant-garde literary techniques. Thanks in large part to some brief but definitive statements by Adorno, it is usually the surrealists, those exponents of the startling juxtaposition of objects torn from their context, who take credit for influencing the structure of the work. 'The whole . . . can hardly be reconstructed', Adorno says of the *Arcades Project*, 'Benjamin's intention was to eliminate all overt commentary and to have the meanings emerge solely through a shocking montage of the material. His aim was not merely for philosophy to catch up to surrealism, but for it to become surrealistic.'[21] Adorno is not the most likely candidate to acknowledge the importance of epic theatre to Benjamin's citational practice, but the critique of empathy tied up with this practice does imply a radicalization of surrealist montage. It is worth remembering as well that more often than not Brecht's plays were based on historical themes, not because of any tendency towards costume drama (historical *Einfühlung* running riot) but because 'an old story will often be more use to [epic theatre] than a new one' in its efforts to deprive the stage of sensation.[22] In addition, the concept of interruption squares nicely with Benjamin's wider suspicion of the doctrines of progress and historical continuity, doctrines which he claims are part and parcel of the historicist project of empathizing with the past. Whether or not the violent context-shattering powers of the quotation are truly enough to effect the 'tiger's leap into the past' (Thesis XIV) is another matter.

Empathy with exchange-value

Brecht famously kept on his desk a little wooden donkey with the words 'Even I must understand it' written on the sign round its neck. Benjamin, of course, placed no such restrictions on himself, and manages in the *Arcades Project* to reinfuse *Einfühlung* with some of the mystery Brecht stripped it of. For instance, in Convolute m, 'Idleness', this opaque contribution to Benjamin's theory of experience can be found: 'When all lines are broken and no sail appears on the blank horizon, when no wave of immediate experience surges and crests, then there remains to the isolated subject in the grip of *taedium vitae* one last thing – and that is empathy' (m4a, 3). This entry becomes easier to decipher if we know what exactly the 'isolated subject' empathizes with. Running alongside the critique of historical empathy in the *Arcades* is a use of the term in relation to commodity fetishism. This is expressed in fairly conventional fashion in the Exposés of 1935 and 1939 with regard to the display of goods at the World Exhibitions, which

> glorify the exchange value of the commodity. They create a framework in which its use value recedes into the background. They open a phantasmagoria which a person enters in order to be distracted. The entertainment industry makes this easier by elevating the person to the level of the commodity. He surrenders himself to its manipulations while enjoying his alienation from himself and others.[23]

In Convolutes G and m, Benjamin makes this point much more economically with the term *Einfühlung*: 'The world exhibitions were training schools in which the masses, barred from consuming, learned empathy with exchange value. "Look at everything; touch nothing"' (G16, 6 and m4, 7). 'Empathy with exchange value', or 'empathy with the commodity', a phrase which also crops up frequently in the *Arcades Project* – is this all that is left to the modern 'isolated subject' bereft of experience?

'Empathy with the commodity', which Benjamin claims is the same thing as 'empathy with exchange value', poses some startling questions for the very idea of empathy. Empathy, almost paradigmatically, refers to inter-subjective relations. One feels empathy for another person – Flaubert is a boatman on the Nile, the spectator feels the fear and pain of the tragic hero. However, in the reformulation of the *Arcades Project*, empathy can be felt for a thing, the commodity, or even the abstraction animating that strange thing – exchange value. When empathy is no longer subject for subject, but subject for object, the consequences for both subject and object cannot be minor. The subject, by seeing the world from the point of view of the commodity becomes commodity-like, while the object world takes on subjective features (hence Benjamin's interest in advertising and the illustrations of Grandville). Certain figures in Benjamin's Paris of the nineteenth century, such as the prostitute and the sandwich-man, crystallize this pervasive condensation of commodity and subject, which is why 'Love for the prostitute is the apotheosis of empathy with the commodity' (J85, 2 and O11a, 4). By implication, then, the history that recognized the past '*wie es eigentlich war*' was a 'culinary history', written among the luxury goods of the arcades and the world exhibitions, not so much commodified itself, but predicated – in its fantasy of a full reconstruction of the past – on the very fetishistic structure established by a culture of consumption.

In spite of its intimate connection with consumption, however, *Einfühlung* is not primarily experienced by the consumer but by the bystander in the marketplace, and this is the final complication that Benjamin brings to the term. At the world exhibitions, the masses learn empathy with exchange value, but are 'barred from consuming'. When one cannot afford something, exchange value, in the form of the price tag, takes on dimensions that are not otherwise visible. But the true practitioner of empathy for Benjamin is the flâneur:

> Empathy with the commodity is fundamentally empathy with exchange value itself. The flâneur is the virtuoso of this empathy. He takes the concept

of marketability itself for a stroll. Just as his final ambit is the department store, his last incarnation is the sandwich-man. (M17a, 2)

It is a little surprising to discover that one of the heroes of the *Arcades* suffers from the disease of empathy so roundly attacked in the same pages. Is it not the flâneur, that absent, detached, subject of *Les Fleurs du mal*, whose idleness leads Benjamin to the entrance of the arcades, exhibition halls and department stores, those '"despised, everyday" structures' (M21a, 2) which provide the key to the oneiric century? Do not the flâneur's random peregrinations through the city reconfigure its space, rescuing the streets from the fossilization of habitual routes? Yes, but it is also true that Benjamin makes of the flâneur something of a fifth columnist amongst the shoppers: 'The flâneur is the observer of the marketplace. His knowledge is akin to the occult science of industrial fluctuations. He is a spy for the capitalists, on assignment in the realm of consumers' (M5, 6). Just as the flâneur is more than implicated in the capitalist fairyworld he strolls about in, he cannot be extricated from the relations of empathy summoned up by that world. In Convolute J, 'Baudelaire', empathy with the commodity-form goes hand in hand with the allegorist's art:

> Through the disorderly fund which his knowledge places at his disposal, the allegorist rummages here and there for a particular piece, holds it next to some other piece, and tests to see if they fit together – that meaning with this image or this image with that meaning. The result can never be known beforehand, for there is no natural mediation between the two. But this is just how matters stand with commodity and price ... How the price of goods in each case is arrived at can never quite be foreseen, neither in the course of their production nor later when they enter the market. It is exactly the same with the object in its allegorical existence ... The allegorist is in his element with commercial wares. As flâneur, he has empathized with the soul of the commodity; as allegorist, he recognizes in the 'price tag', with which the merchandise comes on the market, the object of his broodings – the meaning. (J80, 2; J80a, 1)

Benjamin suggests that even for the allegorist, who would reconstitute a whole from the shattered shards of modern experience, there is no outside of empathy. Not for the *Arcades Project*, then, the outright elimination of empathy in the manner of Brecht. The flâneur and allegorist recognize the 'inferno' which 'rages in the soul of the commodity, for all the seeming tranquility lent it by the price' (J80, 2; J80a, 1), but they can do so only from within empathy, for there is no question of any magical escape from commodity culture, even less of a return to uncontaminated use-value. For the collector, on the other hand, who wrenches the object or quotation from its context and places it within a new system of meaning, both exchange-value and use-value fall by the wayside. What results is actualization, a special kind of 'nearness' antithetical to *Einfühlung*: 'The true method of making things present is to represent them in our space (not to represent ourselves in their space [i.e., empathy]). (The collector does just this, and so does the anecdote.)' (H2, 3).[24]

Notes

1 *The Letters of Gustave Flaubert, 1857–1880,* trans. Francis Steegmuller (Cambridge, Mass.: Harvard University Press, 1982), p. 89.
2 Benjamin, 'On the concept of history', p. 391 (Thesis VII).
3 Benjamin, 'On the concept of history', p. 391 (Thesis VII).
4 Benjamin, 'On the concept of history', p. 391 (Thesis VII).
5 Benjamin, 'On the concept of history', pp. 391–2 (Thesis VII).
6 Harry Francis Mallgrave and Eleftherios Ikonomou, 'Introduction', in Mallgrave and Ikonomou (eds), *Empathy, Form, and Space: Problems in German Aesthetics 1873–1893* (Chicago: University of Chicago Press, 1994), p. 21.
7 Robert Vischer, 'On the optical sense of form: a contribution to aesthetics' (1873), in *Empathy, Form, and Space,* p. 92.
8 Mallgrave and Ikonomou, 'Introduction', p. 29.
9 See Brian Poole, 'From phenomenology to dialogue: Max Scheler's phenomenological tradition and Mikhail Bakhtin's development from "Toward a philosophy of the act" to his study of Dostoevsky', in Ken Hirschkop and David Shepherd (eds), *Bakhtin and Cultural Theory,* 2nd edn, (Manchester: Manchester University Press, 2001), pp. 109–35.
10 Adorno, 'Portrait of Benjamin', p. 235. Adorno goes on, 'His target is not an allegedly over-inflated subjectivism but rather the notion of a subjective dimension itself. Between myth and reconciliation, the poles of his philosophy, the subject evaporates' (p. 235). He adds, 'one will search his writings in vain for a concept like autonomy' (p. 236).
11 See Bertolt Brecht, 'The modern theatre is the epic theatre', in *Brecht on Theatre: The Development of an Aesthetic,* 2nd edn, trans. and ed. John Willett (London: Methuen, 1974), pp. 33–42.
12 Brecht, 'Theatre for pleasure or theatre for instruction', in *Brecht on Theatre,* pp. 69–77 (p. 71).
13 Walter Benjamin, 'Bert Brecht' and 'From the Brecht commentary', in *SW 2,* pp. 365–71 and 374–7.
14 Walter Benjamin, 'What is epic theatre?', in *Understanding Brecht,* trans. Anna Bostock (London: NLB, 1973), pp. 15–22 (p. 22).
15 Brecht, *The Mother,* in *Plays: One* (London: Methuen, 1987), pp. 143–206.
16 Benjamin, 'What is epic theatre?', p. 21.

17 Brecht, 'Short description of a new technique of acting which produces an alienation effect', in *Brecht on Theatre*, pp. 136–47 (p. 138).

18 Brecht, 'Alienation effects in Chinese acting', in *Brecht on Theatre*, pp. 91–9 (p. 94).

19 Benjamin, 'What is epic theatre?', p. 19.

20 For further discussion of the function of quotation in Benjamin see Sigrid Weigel, *Body- and Image-space: Rereading Walter Benjamin*, trans. G. Paul (London and New York: Routledge, 1996), pp. 13, 38, and Irving Wohlfarth, 'On the messianic structure of Walter Benjamin's last reflections', *Glyph* , 3 (1978), pp. 148–212 (p. 181).

21 Adorno, 'Portrait of Benjamin', p. 239.

22 Benjamin, 'What is epic theatre?', p. 16.

23 Benjamin, 'Exposé of 1935', p. 7.

24 For more on the collector see 'Encounters' and 'Method'.

~

Insurrection

Walter Benjamin began his reflection on the arcades at the conclusion of an age of insurrections. In the wake of 1917 he had had the opportunity of experiencing first-hand, with some translation difficulties, the morne anonymity of socialist Russia and its immense potential for the transformation of human nature, the failure of the Spartacist revolution in 1919–20, the insurrectional movements agitating Fascist Europe, the 1934 attempted coup in France, the riotous new dawn of 1936, the rumours of the Spanish civil war.[1] All of this was merely in the political field while the artistic movement he most closely associated with, the surrealist movement, presented itself in terms of manifestos, war declarations to the established literature of their age and revolutionary aspirations. The simple fact that the notion of 'movement' was central in the literary phraseology expresses in itself the turmoil and immense portentousness of the 1930s. To a visitor and later exile, Paris itself could be read in revolutionary terms.[2] The streets bore the names of the great revolutionaries of the past: Raspail, Blanqui, Barbès . . . to take the Underground in Paris is to take a crash course in revolutionary nomenclature. The history of nineteenth-century Paris, which forms the backdrop to the *Arcades Project*, is replete with insurrections and revolutionary movements which followed each other at regular intervals throughout and, apart from the great successful insurrections of 1830 and 1848, smaller ones and abject failures represented as many missed opportunities: 1832, 1839, 1848, 1849, 1851, 1870, 1871 . . .

With a career covering all of these periods of insurgency, and standing high among the revolutionary figures of the nineteenth century, none achieved the controversial centrality of Auguste Blanqui. The young bourgeois, who declared himself a proletarian at the time even when the word was acquiring definite meanings, grew into one of the most contested leaders of the French revolutionary left.[3] His work and life haunt the *Arcades Project* for more than one reason.

First of all Blanqui represents the mixture of high intellectualism and action that Benjamin admired. To Walter Benjamin, Blanqui became the embodiment of the revolutionary spirit and, at least implicitly, a herald of potentially revolutionary alternatives to the models developed between 1905 and 1936.

Blanqui was a small man who lacked physical courage in the heat of the insurrection, unlike Barbès, and whose enduring virtue was to survive stoically long stays in prison earning in the process the titles of 'l'enfermé' and that of 'le vieux'. Always arrested while attempting to escape or in hiding, Blanqui never intended to lead the way on the barricades. His aims were strategic and his method was organizational. Blanqui had begun his political career when the *charbonnerie*, a secret society inspired by the Italian Carbonari, was still alive. He kept alive this system, relying on an elite of highly trained and committed men who could, at the given time, show the path of the insurrection to the masses, who would then overwhelm the conservative forces. In practice, the groups of Blanquists were always too few, too ill-equipped to lead the path and they never acted in isolation. The myth of the sleek machine working through the crowd which Benjamin notes in Convolute V9, 1 was in itself a product of Blanqui's own considerable self-promoting propaganda. This secrecy which accompanied all his acts and which is found even in the organized chaos of his private papers had other side effects and Blanqui was denounced as an informer and traitor.[4] The 'affaire Taschereau', which exploded on 31 March 1848, accused Blanqui of betraying the insurrection of 12 May 1839 that had cost fifty lives and 190 wounded. In 1839 Blanqui and Barbès functioned in the same revolutionary family, but, while Barbès was arrested in the action, Blanqui fled only to be arrested five months later. The evidence against Blanqui included some rather strange judicial U-turns whereby Blanqui's death penalty was repealed and his prison sentence turned into a stay in a sanatorium. Blanqui was then freed in 1848.[5]

Even now the controversies are far from solved, and Blanqui's latest and most comprehensive archivist is of the opinion that Blanqui had indeed betrayed and that this betrayal led him to further his extreme views in the hope of recovering the political high ground among the partisans of the extreme left.[6] This attack on Blanqui's character stuck to him and his leadership of the left was thus considerably diminished until the 1860s when his renewed acquaintance with the prison made him a cause célèbre. In 1879 his election to the assembly as the deputy for Bordeaux was jeopardized by the use that republicans made of the *affaire*. Blanqui certainly was not the pure leader of the left that Benjamin tends to imagine. The conflict between Barbès and Blanqui became open in 1849 and the scission of the two factions has even been compared to the bitter divisions between Marxists and Bakuninists.[7]

When Walter Benjamin was writing, the scholarship on Blanqui was still limited[8] and many of the important studies, such as Dommanget's, had only just begun, but there is evidence that Benjamin had the opportunity to read them.[9] Benjamin relied predominantly on the hagiographic texts published in the late nineteenth century.[10] With these documents in hand, the old insurrectionists offered very solid credentials for revolutionary action, including the grudging respect of Karl Marx. Under some pressure from his friends and fellow philosophers to articulate more firmly the political content of the *Arcades Project*, Benjamin used Blanqui's writings and a few more conventional documents pertaining to the Commune of Paris of March to May 1871. Blanqui's thoughts were indeed worthy of Marxist interpretation and, while their political economic content seems a little insubstantial compared with the *magnum opus* of Marx, they could have formed the basis of a straightforward revolutionary interpretation, with the obvious caveat that Blanqui offered a dictatorship for the proletariat rather than the dictatorship of the proletariat as the best mode of revolutionary government.[11] Unfortunately Blanqui also dismissed any form of economic determinism: 'the so-called necessity of economic laws regulating society is pure nonsense. Nothing more arbitrary and more irregular than the advancement of human acts which vary according to billions of whimsies. Nothing is less akin to the immutable and fatal order of the natural world.'[12] But it is Blanqui's lesser-known mystical prose that enthused Benjamin. Blanqui was tied in some ways to some of the more idealistic dimensions of Utopian socialism, and his cosmic vagaries resembled Fourier's (seeW2a, 6). More than any of his social and critical documents, than his manifestos and social analyses, what interested Benjamin was the revolutionary's ability to combine messianic mysticism and action. Blanqui alone had been recognized with the gift of animating large crowds from within, as in the largely peaceful but potentially revolutionary demonstration in the honour of Victor Noir in 1870 (V9, 1).[13] Of all revolutionaries his reliance on conspiracies, secret societies, subterranean politics, plots and *mots d'ordre* made him emblematic of hidden forces working throughout nineteenth-century society and its social and urban architecture.

As a theoretician, Blanqui also recognized revolutionary action as an aim in itself and for itself. The insurrection as an act was central to

Blanquism: 'As to socialism in practice it is but the revolution itself – without any sectarian engagements or churches, it is eclectic and borrows from all the systems the means of accomplishing its mission: throw down [social order] to rebuild on the basis of equality.'[14] Led by an elite and taking the form of a dictatorship of men of action, the revolution was no new dawn but a revolt, a rebellion, a mark of extreme and pure freedom inscribed in the instant in which it took place and which alone could interrupt the inevitable march of time. For Blanqui the insurrection was not a step toward a future, it was an absolute moment of decisiveness interrupting human history and, in Benjamin's terms, the catastrophic march of history.

> It is just as worthy of humane ends to rise up out of indignation at prevailing injustice as to seek through revolution to better the existence of future generations. It is just as worthy of the human being; it is also more like the human being. Hand in hand with such indignation goes the firm resolve to snatch humanity at the last moment from the catastrophe looming at every turn. That was the case with Blanqui. He always refused to develop plans for what comes later. (J61a, 3)

Blanqui always and constantly denied himself the liberty of shaping the future. 'Isn't it madness to imagine that, by a simple rolling over (*culbute*), society will fall back on its feet, rebuild from new? No! Things do not happen this way, neither in human society nor in nature.'[15] He could not foresee a future without revolution and his revolution was perhaps only the harbinger of other revolutions building on as yet unformed social forces. The revolutionaries would not live to see the post-revolutionary era and this formulation was almost an oxymoron in itself. Unlike Marx, Blanqui refused to adopt an understanding of history that could take Hegelian portentousness. History according to Blanqui was summed up by a then and now, leading to the insurrectionary act and the revolution. Paradoxically considering these self-limitations to socialist and Utopian reveries, Blanqui was also the author of a short and deeply puzzling meditation on eternity and history: *L'Éternité par les astres*. This short text was written in 1871 while he was the single prisoner in the austere Fort du Taureau on the coast near Roscoff and Morlaix,[16] and sent to the publishers in February–March 1872.[17] Blanqui, like many socialists of his age, was not the pure product of reason-led philosophy. His readings betray not only a deep interest in materialistic and factual information but a curiosity on the limits of knowledge, the boundaries of human comprehension bordering on the occult (as we have discussed in 'Magic'). Indeed, while in prison in 1865 his non-fiction library kept in his cell was composed half of recent books devoted to occultism and half scientific accounts and descriptions of the cosmos.[18] This could be read as a desire to dabble in occult mumbo jumbo, symptomatic of the fact that 'occultism is a theory of progress which cannot confess what it is seeking [and] Socialism is a form of occult which does not want to reflect on its origins'[19] – or as a desire to understand more fully the spiritual and even mystical dimensions of radical materialism. This is not in itself very shocking. The modern imaginary and modern ideas of science remained open to magic, occult and esoteric manifestations to an extent unimaginable in the twenty-first century.[20] The apparent confusion of genres hides some of the common ground between science, positivist speculation and attempts to comprehend manifestations beyond human understanding. Blanqui, when he undertook his cosmological reinterpretation of human history, was developing his messianic theories and astral reveries from a positivist and materialistic standpoint without any apparent contradictions. The internal coherence of his logic was enough to distinguish his musing from the clerical attempts to reconcile reason and faith. Blanqui's messianism, like his reasoned extrapolations, remained materialistic and they ran through his work over a long period. *L'Éternité* was not an isolated incident or the depressed rambling of a prisoner for life facing the ocean, it was the culmination of a long reflection fed by years of reading and its themes recur in a diversity of Blanqui's texts. Benjamin was thus right to identify its cosmology as central to the revolutionary's ideology.[21]

To sum up the argument, Blanqui, taking as his premises the infinity of space and time and the finite number of elements composing the universe, postulated that human flesh and history were neither unique nor endowed with any special quality, being material and hence replicable ad infinitum. Humanity might be acting over and over again the same play, shaping itself along the same iniquities and producing the same (therefore not unique) individuals, by sheer chance, to live the same or only slightly dissimilar lives. History 'was to complete the existence of the planet until its last day has been followed billions of times. It will only be a copy printed beforehand for centuries.'[22] To Walter Benjamin this speculation that history is but reiteration and variation of materially determined human existence resembled Nietzsche's theory of eternal return and, starting from entirely different premises, created an intellectual bind between the French revolutionary and the German philosopher. In other terms history in its reiteration resembled the mass production of commodities. According to Blanqui these parallel histories would then differ not because of preordained forces but through the will of the individuals to revolt. In the absence of a grander philosophy of history than one based on the gathering of atoms, one could shape the future only through action, finding solace perhaps in the fact that, somewhere, somehow, another humanity had won that particular revolt, but the notion of progress, contingent on a particular planetary setting, had its limits: 'what we call progress is locked on each earth and disappears with it . . . The universe repeats itself endlessly and remains at a standstill. The universe plays undisturbed the same representations in the infinity.'[23]

Blanqui wrote these speculative notes in his last prison, a few months after the crushing of the single most successful Blanquist revolution: the Commune of Paris. A parallel could indeed be made between the reveries of a man of action constantly imprisoned and those of Walter Benjamin whose apocalyptical dreams of social retribution only matched in their open-endedness those of Blanqui.

But the melancholy figure of Blanqui is a haunting representation of Benjamin's disenchantment with progress and with socialism. Benjamin's materialism is beyond progress (N2, 5) and his socialism is disenchanted:

> It may be considered one of the methodological objectives of this work to demonstrate a historical materialism which has annihilated within itself the idea of progress. Just here, historical materialism has every reason to distinguish itself sharply from bourgeois habits of thought. Its founding concept is not progress but actualisation. (N2, 2)

In some respects revolution and fashion share the same value-free recurrence (B4) and in the long term provoke the same indifference.

The meditation of *L'Éternité par les astres* could seem superficially to match that of Baudelaire's correspondences which mapped, in romantic and spiritualistic terms, the bridges between material and spiritual world and between past and mournful present. The great difference of course is the absence of spirituality of Blanqui's reverie and, in Baudelaire, the absence of purpose in revolutionary action. Baudelaire's attitude towards the poor and revolutionary movements was at the very least ambiguous, fluctuating between short-lived periods of enthusiasm in 1848 and withdrawing from political activities during the Second Empire.[24] As he put it, 'in the historical action which the proletariat brings against the bourgeois class, Baudelaire is a witness; but Blanqui is an expert witness' (J76a, 1). Some of his poems were rich in social meanings and in *Les Fleurs du mal* the poem entitled 'The ragpickers' wine' ('*Le vin des chiffoniers*') had a central role. Benjamin read into these fragments selectively; appropriations of Baudelaire by the left provided the material for this reading. Félix

Pyat, an extremist leader of the Commune of Paris, referred back to the poem in his own melodrama *Le Chiffonnier de Paris* (J88; 88a, 1). The fact that Pyat belonged to an eccentric leftist tradition was not picked up by Benjamin.[25] This poem mattered above all else because it contained intrinsically a philosophical strength, which, if we are following some of Tiedemann's views on the sociological content of Benjamin's idiosyn-cratic mixture of theory and subtle empiricism, approached Benjamin's most ambitious theoretical aims.

Still, Benjamin was as ever sensitive to the contradictions and nuances of artists' politics and he noted how the proletarian insurrection of Lyon in 1832 had had little impact on Baudelaire.[26] The insurrection that mat-tered, and the one to which Blanqui was closest, was the ever-renewed Parisian insurrection inscribed in the densely inhabited space of Paris between 1815 and 1871. This dense space is precisely that of the arcades themselves. The *passages couverts* of Paris cut through the central arrondissements of the *rive droite* and were not simply linking together fashionable neighbourhoods but linking together densely populated dis-tricts. Indeed by cutting through the concentric rings of boulevards the arcades lead to the step of Montmartre, the sacred mountain of the Catholic church and the dens of iniquity of the people, the hill where the unplanned insurrection of March 1871 was to originate.[27]

The Commune of Paris represents an obligatory stage in Walter Benjamin's reflection on modernity. It may be that it was at the sugges-tion of Adorno that Benjamin felt that he had to add a section on the Commune of Paris, but it seems difficult to imagine that he could have missed the opportunity to relate his reflection on social and cultural phantasmagoria to the greatest moment of revolutionary reverie of the nineteenth century. When Benjamin was writing, the dominant left-wing interpretation was that of Lenin and of the Soviet historiography which saw in the Commune of Paris an unadulterated model of proletarian, class-led insurrection which took on the mantle of the Terrorist phase of the French revolution (1793–4) (k1, 3).[28] Lenin himself rests under a red flag of the Commune of Paris. The weight of received wisdom and dogma could have been constraining, but Benjamin was particularly inspired by his readings of Jean Cassou and Engels himself to undermine a naive reading of the Commune which insisted on the fact that Marx 'had upgraded the unconscious tendencies of the Commune into more or less conscious projects' (k3a, 1). The Commune offered confused messages and its spontaneity itself proved a riddle to all non-dogmatic historians.[29] For Benjamin it offered the opportunity to reflect on proletarian censorship, on the revolutionary engagement of Rimbaud, Courbet and Vallès.[30] Rimbaud was then in the process of reinventing French poetics; Vallès's extraordinary style composed of disjointed and broken phrases, using slang and challenging 'good taste', prefigured a new prose while Courbet's challenge to academicism had also opened up avenues for art.[31] While politically the Commune of Paris was marked by a surge of power, an irruption of hitherto voiceless figures on the centre stage, it also offered creators the possibility to dream the future, even though the Commune itself, dominated by Blanquists, refused to do so in a coherent manner. Indeed, its own rejection of the future was associated with its fear of militaristic drifts. In turn, this antimilitarism led to an increased reliance on insurrectionary strategies to defend Paris when the Versailles forces of French Parliament advanced.

In very subtle ways the fragments of the Commune convolute are revisionist of the then current historiography. Benjamin stressed the Sorelian dimensions of this violent moment and its aesthetic qualities, and its reliance on symbolic acts to compensate for its limited historical consciousness of class struggles. Benjamin also explored the struggles of the Commune and their investment in the subterranean remains of ancient Paris (Convolute C). Communards were obsessed with the defence of the underground passages of Paris. Already in October 1870 conservative forces had crowded in the Town Hall taken over by Blanqui using an underground passage and had forced on the insurrectionists a negotiated settlement.[32] The catacombs and subterranean passages of the Commune of Paris belonged to the social and political fantasy of Eugène Sue's *Mystères de Paris* or to Victor Hugo's Gothic reconstructions (Convolute d, more particularly d4a, 2). With the Commune they became strategic priorities in their own right, mingling thus fact and fiction, dream and war.

This is only one example showing how, by looking at the act of insurrection for itself and by abstracting it from any progress dominated vision of history, Walter Benjamin highlighted its aesthetic qualities and how it produced unconscious meanings and new urban forms. Allied to aesthetics, politics could then become a threat indeed and Benjamin's well-known axiom that Fascism represented the intrusion of aesthetics in politics illustrates the potential dangers latent in insurrectional politics when they become aesthetic statements. This axiom used in relation to the sources used in the *Arcades Project* reveals interesting parallels. Benjamin thus identifies the resonantly Romantic politician and poet as a proto-fascistic leader: 'Lamartine's politico-poetic program, model for fascist programmes of today' (d18, 5). Meanwhile he fails to note the better known drifting to the right of the Blanquists who, individually for political expediency, courted the charismatic leadership of General Boulanger.[33] The 'nationalist' epithet attached to Blanqui by Marxists dates from this period and reveals a later scission.

Also interestingly absent from the *Arcades Project* are the anarchist forces working through the Commune of Paris and earlier. Bakunin and Kropotkin are thus absent even though their ideas and militantism agitated the French left and represented an important social and revolutionary force in late nineteenth-century France.[34] The association of anarchists and artists was obvious in the many sources used by Benjamin, and one must wonder why Benjamin chose to ignore them. Several explanations come to mind. A possible one would be that to discuss in the same breath Marx and Bakunin was almost impossible by the mid-1930s and the war raging in Spain among the left showed the breadth of that chasm. The second possible explanation would be that by 1870 anarcho-syndicalism was strongest in the provinces and that the insurrectional theme followed by Benjamin was deemed to be almost exclusively Parisian. A third explanation could be that the theme of 'Paris, capital of the nineteenth century' covered merely the lifetime of Baudelaire and Blanqui, excluding thus the revolutionary aesthetics of propaganda by deed developed in the 1880s and 1890s. Ultimately it could also be the case that these political forces seemed too steeped in progressive and dialectic teleology to serve the *Arcades Project*.

Tiedemann noted in his classic 1965 study of the theoretical system of Benjamin that his work tended towards a 'dialectic at a standstill'.[35] This apparently self-contradictory concept argues that the old thesis-antithesis-synthesis explanatory scheme could be disconnected from its teleological historicism and that conflicts did not necessarily lead to a resolution adopting and merging forces present in the earlier phases in order to produce progress. Even though progress was undoubtedly the overarching ideology of the nineteenth century, historical pessimism was its mirror ideology and insurrections could take place in the name of the one or the other. Indeed in Blanqui's materialism progress had a limited part to play and historical awareness remained more an incantation of the names of Baboeuf and of leading revolutionaries of the past than a projection in the future. Insurrections were fed by social decay and fermentation, despair and the absence of progress rather than the awareness of rising social forces or the power of new systems: 'All the powers of thought, all the efforts of intelligence will never anticipate this creative phenomenon [of the revolution] which will only explode at a given moment. One can prepare the cradle but not bring to life the being we wait for [*l'être attendu*].'[36]

Notes

1 See Benjamin, 'Moscow'.
2 See Ferguson, *Paris as Revolution*.
3 Maurice Paz, *Un Révolutionnaire professionnel: Auguste Blanqui* (Paris: Fayard, 1984).
4 Blanqui's papers are collated somewhat messily in the manuscript department of the Bibliothèque Nationale. They were deposited in 1899 but Paz's authoritative catalogue appeared only in his 1974 thesis. Bibliothèque Nationale NAF 9583 fol. 388.
5 Paz, *Un Révolutionnaire*, pp. 91–103.
6 Paz, *Un Révolutionnaire*, p. 12. This went in opposition to Maurice Dommanget, who attempted to put an end to speculations in 1948 with *Un Drame politique en 1848: Blanqui et le document Taschereau* (Paris: Les Deux Sirènes, 1948). This is the line taken by Philippe Vignier's contributors in *Blanqui et les Blanquistes* (Paris: SEDES, 1986). Some of this debate probably has to be recast in the post-1968 context and linked to the parallels made with the terrorist drift of the French extreme left making mendacious parallels with Blanqui possible.
7 Paz, *Un Révolutionnaire*, pp. 121–6.
8 There were, however, key texts by Alexandre Zévaès, *Auguste Blanqui, patriote et socialiste français* (Paris: Marcel Rivière, 1920) and 'Une Révolution manquée', *Nouvelle Revue Critique*, 17 (1933), 89–95.
9 Maurice Dommanget, *Auguste Blanqui à Belle Ile* (Paris: Librarie du Travail, 1935) and *Auguste Blanqui au début de la Troisième République, 1871–1880, dernière prison et ultimes combats* (Paris, La Haye: Mouton, 1971).
10 Gustave Geffroy, *L'Enfermé* (Paris: Charpentier, 1897). On the other hand, Benjamin ignored Suzanne Wassermann, *Les Clubs de Barbès et de Blanqui en 1848* (Paris, É. Cornély, 1913).
11 For instance M. J. Villponteix and D. Le Noy, 'Révolution et dictature', in Vignier, *Blanqui et les Blanquistes*, pp. 105–20.
12 Papiers Blanqui, Bibliothèque Nationale NAF 9590 274 66.
13 Victor Noir had been sent by Rochefort to Pierre Bonaparte, a relative of Napoleon III, to invite the latter to a duel. Bonaparte had murdered Noir. The demonstration has traditionally been presented as a missed opportunity for an insurrection.
14 Papiers Blanqui, BN NAF 9584[2] 155–6 (text of 1848).
15 Auguste Blanqui, *Textes choisis*, Les Classiques du Peuple (Moscow: Éditions Sociales, 1955), p. 152.

16 Yves Le Manach, 'Auguste Blanqui et L'Éternité', *Banc Public*, 91 (2000); www.bancpublic.be/PAGES/622000an.htm [accessed 2 December 2004].

17 Papiers Blanqui, BN NAF 9587, 486, letter of 28 March 1872.

18 Papiers Blanqui, BN NAF 9587, 311, 329. These included A. Debay, *Histoire des sciences occultes* (Paris: E. Dentu, 1860); Louis Figuier's materialistic *Histoire du merveilleux* (Paris: Hachette, 1860) and Alfred Maury, *La Magie et l'astrologie* (Paris: n.p., 1860).

19 Philippe Muray, *Le Dix-neuvième siècle à travers les âges*, 2nd edn (Paris: Gallimard, 1999), p. 11. The theme is recurrent throughout for instance on *L'Éternité*, pp. 224, 244–5.

20 For a recent synthesis of French practices see Bernadette Bensaude-Vincent and Christine Blondel (eds), *Des Savants face à l'occulte, 1870–1940* (Paris: La Découverte, 2002).

21 A clear example can be found in Auguste Blanqui, *Science et foi* (Conflans-Sainte-Honorine: Edition de la Revue L'Idée Libre, 1925), pp. 9–11; originally written in *Candide*, 13, 14, 15, 16 (1865) in answer to the French academician and mystical R. P. Gratry, *La Crise de la foi* (Paris: C. Douniol, 1863).

22 Louis-Auguste Blanqui, *L'Éternité par les astres* [1872], ed. Lisa Block de Behar (Geneva: Fleuron, 1996), p. 109.

23 Blanqui, *L'Éternité par les astres*, pp. 151–2.

24 Richard Burton, *Baudelaire and the Second Republic: Writing and Revolution* (Oxford: Clarendon Press, 1991).

25 Pyat was a spiritualist and Utopian socialist at heart who used out of context Revolutionary language.

26 Fernand Rude, *L'Insurrection Lyonnaise de novembre 1832: Le Mouvement ouvrier à Lyon de 1827–1832* (Paris: Anthropos, 1969).

27 See Chevalier, *Montmartre du plaisir et du crime*.

28 For an introduction to this literature see Eugene Schulkind, *The Paris Commune of 1871: The View from the Left* (New York: Grove Press, 1974), and Eugene Kamenka, *Paradigm for Revolution? The Paris Commune, 1871–1971* (Canberra: Australian National University Press, 1972).

29 See Robert Tombs, 'Prudent rebels: the Second Arrondissement during the Paris Commune of 1871', *French History*, 5: 4 (1991), 393–413, and '"Les Communeux dans la ville": des analyses récentes à l'étranger', *Le Mouvement Social*, 179 (1997), 93–104.

30 Jules Vallès, *Oeuvres complètes: Souvenirs d'un étudiant pauvre, le candidat des pauvres, lettre à Jules Mirès* (Paris: Éditeurs Français Réunis, 1972).

31 Rachael Langford, *Jules Vallès and the Narration of History: Contesting the French Third Republic in the Jacques Vingtras Trilogy* (Bern: Peter Lang, 1999).

32 Bertrand Taithe, *Citizenship and Wars: France in Turmoil, 1870–1* (London: Routledge, 2001), p. 33.

33 Patrick H. Hutton, *The Cult of the Revolutionary Tradition: The Blanquists in French Politics, 1864–1893* (Berkeley: University of California Press, 1981);

James R. Lehning, *To Be a Citizen: The Political Culture of the Early French Third Republic* (Ithaca: Cornell University Press, 2001), pp. 155–81.

34 See Petr Kropotkine, *Anarchistes en exil: correspondance inédite de Pierre Kropotkine* (Paris: Institut d'Études Slaves, 1995); Marie Fleming, *The Anarchist Way to Socialism: Elisée Reclus and Nineteenth-century Europe* (London: Croom Helm, 1979).

35 Rolf Tiedemann, *Études sur la philosophie de Walter Benjamin*, rev. edn of 1973 (Arles: Actes Sud, 1987). See also Tiedemann, 'Dialectics at a standstill', p. 943.

36 Papiers Blanqui, BN NAF 9584[2] 57, 161.

The Angel of History

The Angel of History doesn't appear in the *Arcades Project*. In fact, it appears only once in all of Benjamin's work, in Thesis IX of the eighteen theses he wrote in February 1940, to which he gave the title 'On the concept of history' (they are sometimes called 'Theses on the philosophy of history'). In this, his final extant written work, Benjamin engages in a metaphysical reverie on the occasion of Paul Klee's inkwash drawing, *Angelus Novus*, which he had bought in 1920:

> My wing is ready for flight
> I would like to turn back
> If I stayed everliving time
> I'd still have little luck
> – Gerhard Scholem, 'Greetings from the Angelus'

> There is a picture by Klee called *Angelus Novus*. It shows an angel who seems about to move away from something he stares at. His eyes are wide, his mouth is open, his wings are spread. This is how the angel of history must look. His face is turned towards the past. Where a chain of events appears before *us*, *he* sees one single catastrophe, which keeps piling wreckage upon wreckage and hurls it at his feet. The angel would like to stay, awaken the dead, and make whole what has been smashed. But a storm is blowing from Paradise and has got caught in his wings; it is so strong that the angel can no longer close them. This storm drives him irresistibly into the future, to which his back is turned, while the pile of debris before him grows toward the sky. What we call progress is *this* storm.[1]

At the time Benjamin was trying to convert sections of the *Arcades Project* into a book-length study of Baudelaire. 'On the concept of history' articulated the methodological framework for this study (and for the *Arcades Project* in general), but Benjamin himself downplayed its significance. Confiding in Gretel Karplus (a close friend, married to Theodor Adorno), he confessed that his comments had 'such an experimental character that they will not serve alone as the methodical preparation for the sequel to the Baudelaire essay', a hedging of bets that seems odd in the face of the prophetic verve of the theses themselves.[2]

As we observed earlier, 'On the concept of history' frequently draws on the material brought together in the 'methodological' Convolute N, 'On the theory of knowledge, theory of progress'. The concept of the dialectical image which flashes up at a moment of danger, the acknowledgement of theology as a source, the vision of history as catastrophe, the critique of the historiographical idea of progress: these motifs circulate, often in the same form of words and with the same citations, through both texts. But two characters and one concept from Benjamin's late theses are missing from the *Arcades*: the Messiah, the aforementioned angel, and the idea of redemption. 'The past', Benjamin says in Thesis II, 'carries with it a secret index by which it is referred to redemption'.[3] In the *Arcades Project* the past is incomplete, carrying a 'secret index' that points beyond it, but it points not to a redemptive end of history but to the moment of awakening ('The imminent awakening is poised, like the wooden horse of the Greeks, in the Troy of dreams' (K2, 4)). The utopian energies laid up in the past are figured as dreams in need of realization, rather than as pointers towards the Day of Judgement. The one mention of messianic powers is safely tucked away at the end of Convolute N, after a series of lengthy quotations from Karl Korsch. But what follows is a curious equation – 'The now of recognizability is the moment of awakening' (N 18, 4) – as if Benjamin was saying goodbye to the language of dream and awakening and welcoming a new vocabulary in its place.

But though the angel isn't there in person, it sends a delegate. Otto Karl Werckmeister has shown that the Angel of History has many precursors in Benjamin's writing, some of them angelic in name and form, others not.[4] He draws our attention to what might otherwise seem a fairly innocuous cross-reference in N9, 7, where Benjamin speaks not of the 'redemption' of the past but of the 'rescue' of 'what in the next moment is already irretrievably lost'. In this regard Benjamin advises us to look to 'my introduction to Jochmann, concerning the prophetic gaze that catches fire from the summits of the past'. The text referred to is Benjamin's introduction to 'The regression of poetry' by Carl Gustav Jochmann, published in the Frankfurt School's journal, the *Zeitschrift für Soizalforschung*, in 1940.[5] Jochmann figures a few times in the *Arcades*, occasionally as the editor of a cited text, at other points as a critic of the progressivist view of human history. But in this excerpt he figures as the bearer of 'a prophetic gaze' that will be taken over and transformed into the horrified glance of the angel of history.[6]

Benjamin's introduction to Jochmann lauds him for his indifference to his contemporaries and his future reputation: 'He turns his back on the future (which he speaks of in prophetic terms), while his seer's gaze is kindled by the vanishing peaks of earlier heroic generations and their poetry, as they sink further and further into the past.'[7] In the draft materials for 'On the concept of history' Benjamin admits that the stance he attributes to Jochmann is itself a refunctioning of Friedrich Schlegel's claim that the historian is a prophet facing backwards.[8] In Benjamin's vision of Jochmann's gaze, the latter is purposefully fixed on a past that recedes and threatens to vanish irretrievably unless the historian does something about it. But whereas Jochmann's gaze 'catches fire' from past achievement, the Angel's is fixed in horror by the sheer accumulation of human catastrophe: the torch Jochmann passes from Schlegel to the Angel has gone very cold.

Why? The standard answer, which is probably also the right one, advises us to look at the dates: the introduction to Jochmann is composed in the first half of 1939, 'On the concept of history' roughly a year later. Between these two fall the Molotov–Ribbentrop Pact, the German invasion of Poland and the Soviet attack on Finland. But the difference between these two scenes involves more than what the backward gaze reveals. For the Angel of History has grander aspirations than Jochmann, or at least so it would seem from Benjamin's descriptions, and whereas in the introduction to Jochmann the past recedes from view, in 'On the concept of history' it is the Angel that recedes, forced backwards by the storm called 'progress'.

The critique of progress is notionally central to the *Arcades*. It is, Benjamin claims, 'one of the methodological objectives of this work to demonstrate a historical materialism which has annihilated within itself the idea of progress', which is accused of being a 'bourgeois habit of thought' (N2, 2). It is a bourgeois habit of thought which had coloured much of the historical materialism around at the time, in the form of Second Internationalist confidence that (as Benjamin put it in 'On the concept of history') the working class 'was moving with the current'.[9] The substance of the *Arcades Project*, however, is about decline rather than progress; its task is to elaborate on the discovery of the surrealists, the 'first to perceive the revolutionary energies that appear in the "outmoded"'.[10] For sure, the panoramas, arcades, mirrors and lithographs that are the focus of Benjamin's historical exertions are products of nineteenth-century technological advance, and their dream content depends on this to a great extent. But Benjamin's interest depends upon fashion as much as progress in the *Arcades*, and he is only truly interested in technological achievements once they have become dated. The polemic with progress is therefore announced, but not developed and when it is developed, it is in the form of strings of quotations from Turgot and Hermann Lotze added to Convolute N in the period between 1937 and 1940.[11]

The Angel of History has the merit of bringing together, in a single image, the redemption of what threatens to disappear from historical view and the 'progress' it must struggle against, thereby integrating motifs that remained disjunct in the *Project* itself. It articulates not just desirable and lamentable approaches to the writing of history, but the struggle between them as itself an historical event and problem of the first order. Peter Osborne sees in this argument Benjamin's 'determination to derive a new form of historical experience immanently, from the experience of the crisis of the old one – to redeem this crisis *as* historical experience'.[12] And the stakes could not be higher. '*Even the dead* will not be safe from the enemy if he is victorious', remarks Benjamin: losing this struggle means ensuring that the sleep of the nineteenth century is permanent.[13]

The Angel is losing the struggle: but what would it like to do? Strictly speaking, of course, angels are not supposed to do anything. They are divine messengers, creatures of God's will, who sing the latter's praises and announce its actions to the creatures of the earth (of course, occasionally they go bad, setting off civil war in the heavens). Gershom Scholem, who was the source of most of Benjamin's knowledge of angels (and was the intended heir to *Angelus Novus* when Benjamin planned a suicide in 1932), speculates that Benjamin has purposefully split the role of the redeeming Messiah into the angel who fails in the task and the actual Messiah who can accomplish it.[14] He describes the Angel's mission in terms of 'the kabbalistic concept of *tikkun*, the messianic restoration and repair which mends and restores the original being of things, and of history as well, after they have been smashed and corrupted by the "breaking of the vessels"'.[15] Benjamin does not, however, speak of the redemption of a world which is corrupt because it is creaturely, but of a world which has been, for the majority of its inhabitants over the entirety of its history, a catastrophe. In this context 'progress' means more than a Whiggish view of the national past: it means the subjection of historical evolution to a crude cost-benefit calculus, in which the suffering of the past is somehow indemnified by the benefits of the future.

To the extent that the Angel summarizes history as a single catastrophe and sees it from above, it appears 'irredeemably' (if one can pardon the expression) theological. 'In this respect,' Osborne comments, '"theology" stands for that moment of totalising transcendence of the given which is intrinsic to the concept of history itself.'[16] But the progressivist view of history is also a totalization of history, albeit a 'bad' totalization, which disavows itself as totalizing. To see a history transcending generations as 'progress' is to take a God's eye view of it, in so far as it involves trading off the miseries of past historical actors against a future they cannot experience. The champions of progress don't renounce a view of the whole – they set up a Messiah false in form and false in content. Benjamin draws heavily on Scholem's interpretation of the Jewish messianic tradition, which emphasizes the apocalyptic nature of the Messiah's coming. In the Jewish tradition of the Bible and the apocalyptic writers, Scholem argues, there is 'no progress in history leading to the redemption [. . .] It is rather transcendence breaking in upon history, an intrusion in which history itself perishes, transformed in its ruin because it is struck by a beam of light shining into it from an outside source.'[17] The Social Democrats of the Second International, and the Stalinists who design 'Socialism in One Country', rationalize messianism, retaining the utopian goal, but turning it into the 'infinite task' of history itself.

Benjamin was scathing about this rationalization:

> Once the classless society had been defined as an infinite task, the empty and homogenous time was transformed into an anteroom, so to speak, in which one could wait for the emergence of the revolutionary situation with more or less equanimity [. . .] (Classless society is not the final goal of historical progress but its frequently miscarried, ultimately achieved interruption).[18]

It was not just that 'progress' was a recipe for political quietism; it rationalized and thereby justified the past course of history, which would then appear as the necessary prelude to the utopia of its end, a hard road that had to be taken. But if that history was a history of defeated struggle, then the past was an accumulation of unfinished business, which it was the task of the revolutionary class to address. 'Like every generation that preceded us, we have been endowed with a *weak* messianic power, a power on which the past has a claim'.[19]

The most radical, and in a certain sense theological, aspect of Benjamin's philosophy of history is this central claim that past history is 'incomplete'. If 'Historical "understanding"' is to be grasped, in principle, as an afterlife of that which is understood' (N 2, 3), this is possible only because every historical object is in some sense not yet dead (which is why the dead, though dead, may still not be safe). The dialectical image rescues that which threatens to be lost, by fixing on that within it which refuses to be sealed off in its specific time and place. As we have discussed above in 'Judaism', this essentially theological motif of recovery and restoration did not go uncontested by colleagues such as Horkheimer. But it is essential to Benjamin's conception. His rhetoric of awakening continually reminds us that waking does not seize on the dream, but is, in some sense, its culmination or realization. The historian willing to exercise a weak messianic power therefore sees the present as a moment when past energies may be brought into play, by means of the dialectical image.

'Doesn't a breath of the air that pervaded earlier days caress us as well? In the voices we hear, isn't there an echo of now silent ones?'[20] The key to the messianic 'intrusion' (to use Scholem's word) is that it not only creates, or recreates, a utopia on earth, but that it repairs the damage done in human history. Benjamin focuses on the necessary corollary of this: that each moment of history is reparable, containing the seed of its possible redemption. The *Arcades Project* focuses attention on a 'dream kitsch' that seems particular to the nineteenth century; but the method Benjamin works out in the course of his studies assumes that every historical object or event has dream content that might, in the right political circumstances, find its awakening. This will appear absurd to any kind of history that aims at establishing factual content, but the point of the argument is to facilitate a new kind of historical experience, in the sense of a new relation between the present and 'what has been'.

In any case, what it displaces is not the detached establishment of facts but a relation to the past scarred and distorted by all the worst features of modernity. Benjamin's critique of progress fixes not on any particular prejudices at work in the minds of modern historians (and the practitioners of cultural history in particular) but on the *form* of the historical experience they create. This experience is modelled on the commodity. In the *Arcades* notes that were pulled together in 1938–9 as 'Central Park' Benjamin argues that commodity production is responsible for a form of time that that finds itself reflected in the innermost and outermost elements of our experience. The continual production of what is new and yet always the same forces us to experience time as Nietzschean 'eternal recurrence', which in turn alters our experience of historical succession and our psyche. 'The idea of eternal recurrence transforms the historical event itself into a mass-produced article' (J62a, 2), and the chains of events parading through history are like so many commodities following one another on the market (while, on the other hand, the mass-produced article appears in our psyche as 'the obsessional idea, [. . .] manufactured in countless copies').[21] The sealed-up quality of the historical event reflects not the irrevocability of historical life itself but the transformation of our past into 'empty, homogenous time', in which the distance between what has been and the present becomes abstract and calculable. By contrast, 'it is the inherent tendency of dialectical experience to dissipate the semblance of eternal sameness, and even of repetition, in history' (N9, 5).

The Angel of History does not therefore offer us metaphysics in place of sober science. It offers a metaphysics of remembrance in place of the 'bad' metaphysics of commodified historiography. The catastrophe depicted in Benjamin's thesis is not just an accumulation of suffering but the very fact that we are not the Angel, because we lack the capacity for the kind of historical experience that would reveal the continuity of history as catastrophe. This returns us to the question of the Angel's identity. While several commentators have assumed that the Angel embodies the perspective of the materialist historian, the distinction drawn between how *we* see the past and how the Angel sees it indicates a more complex situation. The Angel is arguably a place-holder, a signifier for the position from which we *ought* to see the past, a signifier the theological character of which reminds us that this is a position we cannot yet occupy. Not least because, if we take the full weight of Benjamin's argument, only a political revolution can redeem the past, because only politics can address the unfinished business it has left for us. If that revolution would be the secular equivalent of the coming of the Messiah, it may be that the Angel represents a historical consciousness in the service of it.

That historical consciousness consists of dialectical images 'that emerge suddenly, in a flash' (N9, 7). Their suddenness and evanescence point to the inevitably circular element in Benjamin's argument. On the one hand, our secular experience of modernity is dominated by the commodity form and not yet genuinely historical; on the other hand, the Angel's perspective is theological and not possible 'within history' itself. To get from one to the other requires a break which is itself the ultimate form of historical experience, in which 'the truly new makes itself felt for the first time' (N9a, 7). The only genuine historical experience possible would seem to be the experience of 'crossing over' to the sphere of genuine historical experience.

The *Arcades* speaks of bringing 'the entire past [. . .] into the present in a historical apocatastasis' (N 1a, 3), meaning the 'setting aright of all that through Adam had fallen into sin, death, hell and eternal damnation'.[22] But as Irving Wohlfarth has shrewdly observed, the theory of history proposed in the *Arcades* implies that every history written *before* the Judgement Day will be pre-messianic: not a completed work, but fragmented piecework structured around a still history in ruins.[23] Werckmeister has taken an even more sober view. In the continuing metamorphoses of Benjamin's angels he sees a defeated militancy and the gradual 'transfiguration of the revolutionary into the historian'. Despite the talk of the 'blasting of historical continuity' and the 'destructive' element of materialist historiography (N10a, 1), Benjamin's Angel has renounced open political activity and 'reduced the notion of "saving" to a recovery of what dominant historiography has forgotten, passed over in silence, or suppressed'.[24]

This would seem to open the door to using Benjamin as philosophical ballast for the practice of 'history from below' or scholarship aiming at the illumination of a 'tradition of the oppressed'.[25] That is certainly an irreducible element of the materialist historiography Benjamin evokes. But as we have argued in 'Empathy', his own practice in the *Arcades Project* tells a slightly different story: 'What are phenomena rescued from?' he asks: 'Not only, and not in the main, from the discredit and neglect into which they have fallen, but from the catastrophe represented very often by a certain strain in their dissemination, their "enshrinement as heritage"' (N 9, 4). While the everyday life of the oppressed is documented in fits and spurts throughout the *Arcades*, most of the objects rescued are drawn from the world of the Parisian middle and upper classes. Benjamin is at pains to avoid a 'revisionist' history that simply re-allocates the rights and wrongs of the past, because such a history does not address the essential structures of modernity, seeking only a more just allocation of resources within their confines. Habermas has argued that Benjamin's project demands that we imagine the possibility of a world that is just and prosperous but miserable, denuded of the semantic resources we need for a meaningful historical existence.[26] To avoid this fate Benjamin insists that we confront the phantasmagoria of the commodity world and nineteenth-century urban existence.

The *Arcades Project* therefore 'deals with awakening from the nineteenth century' (N4, 3) in the belief that until we have awoken from the dreams of the city, fashion and the commodity, we will be unable to make any real progress. The Social Democratic belief that a more just distribution of the goods lay around the corner was, for Benjamin, evidence enough that the left would make no headway whatsoever until it acknowledged the distance between the commodity world and the promise of redemption. In large part, this reflects the mindset of what has been called 'romantic anti-capitalism' by Michel Löwy, as exemplified by the work of Georg Lukács, whose *History and Class Consciousness* was to some extent Benjamin's guide to the Marxist tradition. For Benjamin and others of his generation, commodification and reification, not exploitation, were the central issues of the capitalist economy, and it is these dragons he sets out to slay before all others. Benjamin believed that by their very nature they demanded a historiography composed of dialectical images, not persuasive stories. In this lies his strength as well as his weakness as a theorist of history.

Notes

1 Benjamin, 'On the concept of history', p. 392.
2 Letter from Benjamin to Gretel Adorno, April 1940, as cited in Lutz Niethammer, 'The blown-away angel: on the posthistory of a historical epistemology of danger', in *Posthistoire: Has History Come to an End?*, trans. Patrick Camiller (London: Verso, 1992), pp. 101–34 (p. 103). 'Confiding' is the right word here because, as far as one can tell, Benjamin chose not to tell Adorno, then his principal correspondent, about the text, nor Scholem.
3 Benjamin, 'On the concept of history', p. 390.
4 O. K. Werckmeister, 'Walter Benjamin's angel of history, or the transfiguration of the revolutionary into the historian', *Critical Inquiry*, 22:2 (Winter 1996), pp. 239–67. Lutz Niethammer has objected to the interpretation of the angel by reference to draft materials 'as if they has not been discarded'. In a perhaps unconscious slip, he complains of the 'distorting effect of such montages'. Given Benjamin's technique, and his stated aim to use montage, this seems a very odd objection. See Niethammer, 'The blown-away angel', p. 130 n38.
5 Walter Benjamin, 'Carl Gustav Jochmann's "Die Rückschritte der Poesie"', *Zeitschrift für Sozialforschung*, 1–2 (1939–40).
6 Benjamin himself makes clear the centrality of this gaze in the draft materials for 'On the concept of history' that have been translated into English as 'Paralipomena to "On the concept of history"' [1940], in which he remarks that 'The passage on Jochmann's visionary gaze should be worked into the basic structure of the Arcades'; in *SW 4*, pp. 401–11 (p. 407).
7 Walter Benjamin, '"The regression of poetry" by C. G. Jochmann' [1940], in *SW 4*, pp. 356–80 (p. 360).
8 Benjamin, 'Paralipomena', p. 407. The original sentence is found in fragment 80 of Friedrich Schlegel, *Athenaeum Fragment* (1798).
9 Benjamin, 'On the concept of history', p. 393 (Thesis XI).

10 Benjamin, 'Surrealism', p. 210.

11 See sections N11a–N14a. According to the editorial apparatus of the *Gesammelte Schriften*, entries N8 – N20 were made between December 1937 and May 1940.

12 Peter Osborne, *The Politics of Time: Modernity and Avant-Garde* (London: Verso, 1995), p. 141.

13 Benjamin, 'On the concept of history', p. 391 (Thesis VI).

14 Gershom Scholem, 'Walter Benjamin and his angel', in *On Jews and Judaism in Crisis* (New York: Schocken Books, 1976), pp. 198–236 (p. 235).

15 Scholem, 'Benjamin and his angel', p. 233.

16 Osborne, *Politics of Time*, p. 141.

17 Gershom Scholem, 'Toward an understanding of the messianic idea in Judaism', in *The Messianic Idea in Judaism* (London: Allen & Unwin, 1971), pp. 1–36 (p. 10).

18 Benjamin, 'Paralipomena', p. 402 (Thesis XVIIa)

19 Benjamin, 'On the concept of history', p. 390 (Thesis II).

20 Benjamin, 'On the concept of history', p. 390 (Thesis II).

21 Walter Benjamin, 'Central park' [1939], in *SW 4*, pp. 161–99 (p. 166). Peter Osborne argues persuasively that the commodity form establishes a rhythm Benjamin finds everywhere in modernity: in warfare, mechanized labour, the jostling of the crowd, gambling, and fashion. See *The Politics of Time*, 134–8.

22 This definition of apocatastasis is drawn from Christian pietistic treatises cited in H. D. Kittsteiner, 'Walter Benjamin's historicism', *New German Critique*, 39 (1986), 179–215 (p. 186).

23 Irving Wohlfarth, 'Re-fusing theology: some first responses to Walter Benjamin's Arcades Project', *New German Critique*, 39 (1986), 3–24 (pp. 5–6).

24 Werckmeister, 'Benjamin's angel of history', p. 261.

25 Niethammer is clearly of this opinion, pointing to E. P. Thompson's work as an example of historical scholarship that aids the tiger's leap into the past (Niethammer, pp. 119–20).

26 Jürgen Habermas, 'Consciousness-raising or rescuing critique', in *Philisophico-Political Profiles*, trans. Frederick G. Lawrence (Cambridge: Polity Press, 1983).

Awakening

How many readers of Benjamin have waited patiently for the lightning flash of understanding, the moment when one of his tricky analogies suddenly reveals itself (and how many have felt that mere wakefulness while reading the *Arcades* would be achievement enough)? The *Arcades Project* was written 'rung by rung, according as chance would offer a narrow foothold' (N2, 4) and reading it is just as arduous and precipitous a climb. We can adapt an analogy of Benjamin's to explain the problem:

> All historical knowledge can be represented in the image of balanced scales, one tray of which is weighed with what has been and the other with knowledge of what is present. Whereas on the first the facts assembled can never be too humble or too numerous, on the second there can only be a few, heavy massive weights. (N6, 5)

The *Project* does not stint on the first tray, although it fills it with texts and sources, quotations and aphorisms, rather than facts. But knowledge arrives only when the scales balance just so, and the reader may find herself or himself throwing any number of concepts on to the other tray in the vain hope that one of them will do the trick. 'Knowledge of the present' in this context means some understanding of Benjamin's method and argument, but these are nowhere laid out in traditional form. Instead, the *Project* holds out the rather misty possibility that its truth can be suddenly grasped in a moment of sharp but unmistakeable insight, when that which seems wholly esoteric and impenetrable – one of Benjamin's treasured dialectical images – becomes lucid and full of meaning.

Knowing that he was trying to establish a new model for the comprehension of the historical past, Benjamin devotes large chunks of the *Arcades* to the exposition of his method. Unfortunately, understanding what Benjamin means by 'understanding' depends in its turn on a grasping of analogies, similes and metaphors every bit as enigmatic as those used to describe Paris. There is no evading the need for sudden insight, no traditional back door that will allow us to get Benjamin's point without submitting to the peculiar epistemology of his beloved dialectical images. All of which means that to understand Benjamin's method we must clarify his claim that his own historical work is 'an experiment in the technique of awakening' (K1, 1). The metaphor of awakening first pokes its sleepy head out of the covers in Convolute I, and raises itself, bleary-eyed, to face the break of day in Convolutes K and N. But it doesn't make its way out of bed by the end of the *Project*: we have to grasp it by the hair and do that for it. Benjamin's strictness and consistency mean it will take something of an awakening to understand the metaphor of awakening itself.

At first glance, it looks an easy one to crack. After the 'dream-filled sleep [that] came over Europe' (K1a, 8) enrobed capitalism in swathes of illusion, our task is surely to rub the dust from our eyes, look at the world in the cold light of day and see European capitalism for what it is, abetted by the piles of quotations Benjamin erects around the text. If the early convolutes present the frayed image of a capitalist consumer paradise that has lost its dazzle, later ones push the point about capitalism home by detailing the social movements and sheer poverty of those forced to produce the goods that lure the keen, but slightly bored, consumer.[1] In classic Marxist form, we are reminded that commodities are the phantasmatic form in which labour presents itself. That Benjamin chose to preface Convolute N with Marx's famous claim to Arnold Ruge ('The reform of consciousness consists *solely* in . . . the awakening of the world from its dream about itself') should more or less settle the argument.[2]

But Benjamin has something quite different in mind, in three decisive respects. First because, as we shall see, the point is not to be awake but to be waking up. The wakeful eyes of the present do not dispel the dreamy illusions of the past, for the moment at which one attains the truth is the moment of awakening itself. 'The new dialectical method of doing history presents itself as the art of experiencing the present as waking world, a world to which that dream we name the past refers in truth' (K1, 3). Secondly, the moment of truth is the *moment* of awakening: an instant when we are poised on the threshold between dream and total wakefulness, when the dream is present but in transfigured, not-yet-forgotten form. The truth that emerges in the 'flash of awakened consciousness' (K1, 2) is not a permanent possession but something fitful and passing. Once we are fully awake, ready to meet the world on its own terms, the moment of possible understanding has passed. Finally, Benjamin insists on awakening as a stage in the realization of the dream itself, which 'waits secretly' for it (K1a, 2). The present does not focus on a past which is a 'fixed point': 'There is a not-yet-conscious knowledge of what has been: its advancement has the structure of awakening' (K1, 2).

Waking up

The dialectical moment of awakening is not the same as wakened consciousness but is a threshold moment got between sleep and wake. In awakening, the dream has not faded but is already being wrenched from the dreamworld into the present. Benjamin's focus on this transitional moment alerts us to the fact that Freud, the traditional first port of call for a theory of dreams, isn't the point of reference here (his query to Adorno on the existence of 'a psychoanalytic study of waking' by Freud and his school seems to have drawn a blank).[3] Instead, Benjamin turns to Paris's own poets of half-sleep:

> Is awakening perhaps the synthesis of dream consciousness (as thesis) and waking consciousness (as antithesis)? Then the moment of awakening would be identical with the 'now of recognizability,' in which things put on their true – surrealist – face. Thus, in Proust, the importance of staking an entire life on life's supremely dialectical point of rupture: awakening. Proust begins with an evocation of the space of someone waking up. (N3a, 3).

While Proust famously begins not with waking up but with going to bed ('For a long time I used to go to bed early'), the opening pages of *In Search of Lost Time* are preoccupied with the process of awakening and falling back to sleep and the strange half-states of dream and consciousness that permit remembrance. That search for lost time makes Proust stand out in an age of forgetting: he 'could emerge as an unprecedented phenomenon only in a generation that had lost all bodily and natural aids to remembrance and that, poorer than before, was left to itself to take possession of the worlds of childhood in merely an isolated, scattered, pathological way' (K1, 1). Proustian remembrance offers the possibility of reconstructing the past in the present, just as his protagonist reconstructs the room in which he is lying.

If Proust provides the rationale for awakening, it is surrealism that justifies the vision of Paris as a dream city. 'The Surrealists . . . are less on the trail of the psyche than on the track of things': they define dreaming not as a mental state but as a property of objects, in particular objects which have become in the most literal sense possible, outmoded.[4] Just as significant, however, is the distance Benjamin strives to keep between his historical project and the profane illumination of the surrealists. '[W]hereas Aragon persists within the realm of dream, here the concern is to find the constellation of awakening' (N1, 9). The 'constellation of awakening' although it appears esoteric in this context, is in fact an exact choice of words. For Benjamin intends the metaphor of constellation to be understood in the deepest possible sense. Just as the constellation which appears to us as an image in the night sky is in fact a juxtaposition of stars which are more and less distant from us, so the constellation that triggers awakening appears when the present and the past are set together in a single, albeit dialectical image. (In fact, if we bear in mind that the light that makes up a constellation is a composite of light from different times, depending on the distance it has had to travel to reach us, the metaphor is even more apposite.)[5]

'What Proust intends with the experimental arrangement of furniture in matinal half-slumber, what Bloch recognises as the darkness of the lived moment, is nothing other here than what is to be secured on the level of the historical, and collectively' (K1, 2). The point of awakening is crucial, because only there does the dream content become, in Benjamin's sense of the term, historical. To regard the worn-out arcades, the outrageous forms of *Jugendstil*, the wax museums and panoramas, as so much trivia or false consciousness is to ignore their Utopian charge; for this reason, 'In order to understand the arcades from the ground up, we sink them into the deepest stratum of the dream' (H1a, 5). At the same time, that dream content itself remains stuck in the phantasmagoria of the nineteenth century, working in unconscious form, until it is appropriated in the moment of awakening.

As if to secure the need for half-sleep, Benjamin insists it is illumination, not darkness, that characterises the dreams of the nineteenth century. Theories of ideology have traditionally taken their cue from the Enlightenment, contrasting the clear-sightedness of science with the foggy mysteries of religion and the dark clouds seeded by despots. The ideology of capitalist society, however, develops after and on the basis of the Enlightenment, and in the arcades the illuminated object is the ideological phenomenon *par excellence*. That is why so much of the *Arcades Project* is devoted to the 'art of the dazzling illusion' (R1, 1) produced by street-lighting, mirrors (which merit their own convolute!), panoramas, shop displays and so on. The dream-state of the nineteenth century is characterized not by fuzziness or irrationality but by an abundantly clear naturalistic presentation of objects in museums, shop windows, exhibitions and, of course, arcades. And if this is the kind of dream one must 'wake up' from, then clearly no amount of light will do the trick. In the *Arcades Project* the dreams are already well-lit, and waking up is hard to do.

The panorama which provides the jumping-off point for Convolute Q is one such well-lit dream, and its cousin the diorama is not only well lit, but lit so as to produce a naturalistic mimicry of the day's changing lighting. One cannot fault the panorama for vagueness or for lack of world-historical ambition, and, while Benjamin subtly mocks its aspirations to a 'perfect imitation of nature', it's also clear from the company it keeps that it is not ideological because it *fails* to imitate. Convolute Q discusses the panoramas and their kin, but also the wax museum, photography and the works of Dickens and Balzac, and here, as throughout the *Arcades Project*, the juxtaposition of a series of apparently analogous phenomena goads us into searching for the principle underlying the series (also see 'Advertising'). What's striking in Convolute Q is the inclusion of such darlings of Marxist literary criticism as Dickens and, more particularly, Balzac, both of whom were lauded by Marx and Engels, and virtually deified by Lukács for providing educative, realistic pictures of the emerging capitalist order. Benjamin doesn't dispute their status as the greatest of nineteenth-century realists. But when he points to the coincidence that 'in the same year in which Daguerre invented photography, his diorama burned down' (Q2, 5), he seems to be telling us that fidelity to nature is itself the distinguishing feature of the ideological.

Balzac is therefore strikingly realistic, and this is the problem. His dedication to a contemporary description of the social world, which goes so far as lifting five hundred of his characters directly from Parisian life, puts him on a par not with great social thinkers, but with Madam Tussaud and her kind. For both wax museum and Balzac novel make a vast and accurate display of the historic world their 'panoramic' principle. And their aggregation of precisely rendered persons and objects – in the wax museum, taken from the past; in Balzac, from the present – is exactly what is dreamlike about them. In the realist novel and the wax museum, history appears as aggregate and succession, a collection of objects and events that fill up time without, so to speak, altering its shape. 'The dreaming collective knows no history. Events pass before it as always identical and always new' (S2, 1), and the more exactly the event or personage is rendered, the more its effect is like the shock of the commodity or being jostled in the street.

In Balzac, dreams and fantasies are the illusions young men have before the hard facts of Parisian life teach them a lesson. For Benjamin, on the contrary, these hard facts are themselves the dreamworld from which the modern critic and historian must awaken. This can make sense only if we assume that the collective dreams are not merely individual dreams writ large but something quite different from ideas and images floating through the mind. Collective dreams are embodied in structures external to the individual yet internal to the collective: 'architecture, fashion – yes, even the weather – are, in the interior of the collective, what the sensorial of organs, the feeling of sickness and health, are inside the individual' (K1, 5). An exact rendering of these phenomena lulls us back to sleep.

Awaking with a start

And yet we can be forgiven for noticing that the experience of awakening resembles, in its suddenness and transitoriness, the shocks of modern life. The 'flash of awakened consciousness' is just as fleeting, in its structure if not in its effects, as the appearance of the commodity, the difference lying in the dialectical tension that supposedly marks this moment. In this sense, Benjamin's theory of awakening seeks not to escape from modernity but to mobilize its structures in the service of a new kind of historical experience which reflects the significance of 'the moment of truth' in twentieth-century tragic writing as Franco Moretti has demonstrated.[6] Whereas the novel – the very genre whose death Benjamin recounts as the death of storytelling – depends on compromise and the normalized structures of everyday life, tragedy assumes as its narrative crux a moment when 'life' falls away to reveal 'truth'. As Moretti notes, 'the interdependence of truth and crisis anticipates the classical rhetoric of *revolutionary* politics', and the two arguably greatest classics of this genre are George Sorel's *Reflections on Violence* and Carl Schmitt's *Political Theology*, both of which Benjamin read and took to heart.[7]

As we have discussed in 'Insurrection', it was the revolution as dramatic, aesthetic gesture that drew Benjamin to Blanqui. But one can see the tragic world-view reflected in his epistemology as well, which supposes that truth is not something arrived at by careful steps but grasped suddenly, albeit not intuitively. Benjamin is hardly alone in this. The rejection of the traditional models of judgement in favour of sudden grasping mark the conceptions of truth articulated by philosophers as different as Husserl and Wittgenstein. When Benjamin objects to Gottfried Keller's dictum that 'the truth will not escape us' (N3a, 1), he insists on a revolutionary epistemology that turns modern shock on its head. Like awakening, the moment at which it is possible to grasp the utopian substance of the past without sinking into it is fleeting. For that reason he will present catastrophe and progress as a matter of opportunities missed and taken, in the belief that political opportunities knock only once. For that reason also, he will make 'presence of mind', alertness to these opportunities, the key feature of the mature revolutionary consciousness.

Awakening as the dream's 'realization'

Presence of mind is required, because the opportunities for awakening are not dictated subjectively. 'The facts become something that just now first happens to us, first struck us' (K1, 2), not because we were not paying attention earlier but because the present situation enables the object to become something we experience as both utopian and embedded in its history. The surrealist interest in the outmoded and the worn-out was not accidental, for it is only when commodities and their structures lose their lustre that their dream content can appear in sober form. In an early study of surrealism, 'Dream kitsch', Benjamin asks: 'And which side does an object turn toward dreams? [. . .] It is the side worn through by habit and patched with cheap maxims, the side which things turn toward the dream is kitsch.'[8] In kitsch the dream content misfires, making its awakening possible. It is therefore the most explosive form of all, for it reflects a misplaced grandeur of aspiration.

Can there be no intimation that an object or structure will some day 'awaken'? In a different text, Benjamin suggests this is possible. In 'A Berlin chronicle' of 1932, Benjamin argues that we have misunderstood the commonplace phenomenon of *déjà vu*. When we experience *déjà vu* we feel as if we have been somewhere before. 'But', he asks,

> has the counterpart of this entranced removal ever been investigated – the shock with which we come across a gesture or word the way we suddenly find in our house a forgotten glove or reticule? And just as they cause us to surmise that a stranger has been there, there are words or gestures from which we infer this invisible stranger, the future, who left them in our keeping.[9]

As we discuss in '*Jeux/joie/jouissance*', Benjamin's vision of the revolutionary consciousness emphasizes a quality of readiness or presence of mind that divines signs of the future in the present, the 'splinters of messianic time' that stand out from the apparent continuity of historical 'development'.[10] Benjamin's musings are followed by a story in which, hearing news of a relative's death from his father, he 'infers this invisible stranger, the future' and memorizes the moment, knowing it will be significant. When years later he discovers the man has in fact died of syphilis, it's a sign that what Benjamin infers is the fact of a crisis, in this case the crisis of sexuality (crossed with death). The past is full of such moments, but they will not 'awaken' of themselves, that is, as part of a 'natural' historical development. Their awakening demands someone with an interest in their awakening, in, as it were, bringing the crisis to expression.

'Just as Proust begins the story of his life with awakening, so must every presentation of history begin with awakening' (N4, 3). Throughout the *Arcades Project* 'awakening' is the privileged metaphor for genuinely historical experience. The surrealists made the necessary equation between the realization of dreams and political revolution; Proust provided a model for the kind of awareness this entailed. But this metaphorical web was not the only one Benjamin would employ in his search for a way to grasp lost times. As the Second World War began to reveal its horrors, Benjamin found other words for the promise of happiness and the knowledge that enables us to realize it. Instead of dreams, Benjamin spoke of the promise of redemption; instead of half-sleep, the moment of danger; instead of awakening, our weak messianic power. 'On the concept of history', composed in 1940, retains the structure of the earlier epistemology; but it puts the metaphor of awakening to bed.

Notes

1 T. J. Clark has suggested there is a contradiction in the *Arcades* between Benjamin's descriptions of the dreaming collectives – organized around the consumerism of the arcades – and his growing recognition of the dull, cruel, impossible-to-glamorize exploitation that lay at the heart of capitalist social relations. See his 'Reservations of the marvellous', pp. 7–9.

2 Letter from Marx to Arnold Ruge, September 1843, p. 209.

3 Letter 35, from Benjamin to Adorno, 10 June 1935, in *Adorno–Benjamin Correspondence*, pp. 98–101 (p. 99).

4 Walter Benjamin, 'Dream kitsch: gloss on Surrealism' [1927], in *SW 2*, pp. 3–5 (p. 5). It is worth noting that this line reappears in the *Arcades Project*, but with the amendment that 'we' are 'less on the trail of the psyche' (I1, 3)

5 Note Scholem's comment: 'The origin of the constellations as configurations on the sky surface was, so he asserted, the beginning of reading and writing', in *Walter Benjamin: The Story of a Friendship*, p. 61.

6 Franco Moretti, 'The moment of truth', in *Signs Taken for Wonders*, 2nd edn (London: Verso, 1988), pp. 249–61.

7 Moretti, 'Moment of truth', p. 258.

8 Benjamin, 'Dream kitsch', p. 3.

9 Benjamin, 'A Berlin chronicle', pp. 634–5.

10 Benjamin, 'On the concept of history', p. 397 (Thesis A)

~

Advertising

A calligram in the sand

Benjamin cites many advertisements in the *Arcades Project*, but he analyses only one in detail. It is in fact only a fragment, a memory of an advertisement, a poster for Bullrich Salt he saw many years previously on a Berlin streetcar and recollected only much later. He introduces the forgotten advertisement by way of a lengthy drama of involuntary memory. This imitation of Proust is marked in the following citation by an ellipsis:

> Many years ago, on the streetcar, I saw a poster that, if things had their due in this world, would have found its admirers, historians, exegetes, and copyists just as surely as any great poem or painting. And, in fact, it was both at the same time. As is sometimes the case with very deep, unexpected impressions, however, the shock was too violent: the impression, if I may say so, struck with such force that it broke through the bottom of my consciousness and for years lay unrecoverable somewhere in the darkness. I knew only that it had to do with 'Bullrich Salt' [. . .] I had it once more. Here is what it looked like. In the foreground, a horse-drawn wagon was advancing across the desert. It was loaded with sacks bearing the words 'Bullrich Salt.' One of these sacks had a hole, from which salt had already trickled a good distance on the ground. In the background of the desert landscape, two posts held a large sign with the words 'Is the Best.' But what about the trace of salt down the desert trail? It formed letters, and these letters formed a word, the word 'Bullrich Salt.' Was not the preestablished harmony of a Leibniz mere child's play compared to this tightly orchestrated predestination in the desert? And didn't that poster furnish an image for things that no one in this mortal life has yet experienced? An image of the everyday in Utopia? (G1a, 4)

There is good reason to think that this poster is for Benjamin paradigmatic of advertisements. Like surrealism, which borrows from them, advertisements tear objects from their 'normal' setting and juxtapose them with others. The subsequent clash, in surrealism at least, establishes shocking connections and thereby illuminates the thing which might otherwise remain invisible, quotidian. In the case of Bullrich Salt, torn from the bathroom cabinet and thrust into the desert, the surrealist isolation of the object is no less than a step into something not 'yet experienced'.

If the salt is 'everyday', though, what is Utopian in this picture? One reading might be that Utopia is glimpsed in the miraculous appearance in the desert of the banal commercial name. With Benjamin's Angel of History in 'On the concept of history', the opening towards Utopia is undecidable in its outcome: it could head in the direction of redemption and the promised land, or could just as easily move towards destruction. The same crossroads of possibility applies here: *Bullrich-Salz*, after all, claims to relieve constipation, and is still widely sold in German pharmacies. There is another way of reading that final sentence in the dizzying accretion of rhetorical questions which concludes the passage. Might not utopia here be the impossible convergence of word and thing, the closing of the gap opened up by language? By virtue of 'predestination in the desert', 'Bullrich Salt' needs nothing more than its own materiality to convey its meaning. This sort of figure, where the letters of a word are made up of the very substance that the word signifies, is a calligram. In only the second entry in the *Arcades Project*, Benjamin shows an interest in calligrams. He cites Eduard Kroloff, who describes two calligramatic shop signs, at least one of them in an arcade:

> The name of the jeweler stands over the shop door in large *inlaid letters* – inlaid with fine imitation gems . . . In the Galerie Véro-Dodat, there is a grocery store; above its door, one reads the inscription: 'Gastronomie Cosmopolite.' The individual characters of the sign are formed, in comic fashion, from snipes, pheasants, hares, antlers, lobsters, fish, bird kidneys, and so forth. (A1, 2)

As Judith Williamson points out, calligrams are common in advertising, and she sees them as the culmination of the ruse of advertising: 'actual objects are turned into words, appropriated by a language that claims to *be* "reality" in being "made" of objects'. She concludes that in the calligram, 'the advertisement reaches a final point in its imaginary joining of sign and referent'.[1] Why is Benjamin blinded by this simple ploy of advertising, and so clearly mesmerized by the Bullrich Salt poster, not to mention ordinary shop signs? One might equally ask why so many contemporary analysts of advertising fail to notice the utopian impulse which accompanies its commercial priorities: the promise of plenitude glimpsed within an exhortation to acquisitiveness.

Benjamin's perspective on advertising diverges from many more recent thinkers on the subject because he does not share their theory of language. Broadly speaking, the semiotic approach to advertising takes as its first premise that advertising, like any code, is an arbitrary system of differences. That is to say, there is no 'natural' connection between the signifier of advertising (the consumer product) and its signified (wealth, happiness, sexual desirability, sophistication, and so on). Nevertheless, advertisements constantly attempt to disguise the arbitrary nature of the bond they establish between product and 'lifestyle'. In advertising's war of attrition against Saussurean linguistics, the calligram is regarded as particularly treacherous by the semiotician, because in its doubling as word and thing, sign and object signified, it suggests that the relation between signifier and signified is not arbitrary, but that there can indeed be a one-to-one correspondence between the two.

Benjamin, of course, never subscribed to this fundamental principle of modern linguistics. In 'On language as such and on the language of man' (1916), he deliberately rejects the view that 'the word has an accidental relation to its object, that it is a sign for things (or knowledge of them) agreed by some convention'.[2] He strikingly calls this 'bourgeois linguistic theory' and instead argues that '*It is . . . the linguistic being of man to name things.*'[3] Although the mysticism of this early essay was gradually displaced by a materialist outlook, some of it still remained in his 'micrological' approach to the everyday world of objects. His interest in calligrams is based less on a nostalgic wish to make good the gap of language, for the word to mystically become 'the essence of the thing',[4] than on a desire to redeem all matter, to rip the object from the arbitrariness of commodification. Redemption is certainly the future that Benjamin foresees for this forgotten poster, a mere piece of urban residue which, 'if things had their due in this world [*wenn es auf der Welt mit rechten Dinge zuginge*]' would receive the same attention 'as any great poem or painting'.[5] One of the techniques of redemption for Benjamin was of course allegory. His allegorical approach to the arcades of Paris squares well with the continuing influence of mystical linguistic theory in his thinking, since in allegory signs are not arbitrary but are fated in their destination, rather than simply an arbitrary meaning. It is worth noting that the last sentence of his commentary on the Bullrich poster, which has been translated as 'An image of the everyday in Utopia' reads in German *Ein Gleichnis für den Alltag der Utopie* where *Gleichnis* can mean allegory or parable, as well as image.[6]

The porous borders of advertising and 'the great poem of display'

In some respects, Benjamin's perspective on advertising resembles recent attempts to challenge the consensus view on advertising's unparalleled capacity to dupe and its unequivocal complicity with capitalist economy. For instance, Mica Nava has powerfully argued that advertising should no longer be considered a universal scapegoat in analyses of commodity culture. Nava surveys a wide range of approaches to advertising – semiotic, historical, journalistic, Marxist – and finds that the majority of cultural critics distrust or even condemn it flatly, treating it as '*the* iconographic signifier of multinational capitalism, and therefore in some ethical sense, beyond redemption'.[7] Even though they start from widely different premises, Vance Packard in *The Hidden Persuaders* (1957), Judith Williamson in *Decoding Advertisements* (1978) and Thomas Richards in *Commodity Culture of Victorian England* (1991) all share the 'conviction that advertising, of all instances of visual communication in contemporary consumer culture, is somehow uniquely powerful and culpable in the perpetration of desire and the production of commodity signs'.[8] While not trying to rescue advertising from its involvement in consumption, Nava is keen to show that market research is far from being the sinisterly exact science that Packard made it out to be, that more often than not advertisements fail to interpellate their subjects in the manner Williamson claims and that in Richards's book 'the consumer who is gullible and easily duped by the machinations of the advertisers is usually explicitly female'.[9] Nava has been instrumental in underlining and undermining some basic assumptions about advertising culture and has brought about an important reorientation of current debates. It is a reorientation which had already been anticipated in the *Arcades Project*, except that Benjamin's method is dialectics, while Nava's is positivism. Certainly, Benjamin, unlike many Marxists, could not be accused of the 'iconophobia' which, according to Nava, handicaps so many cultural critics.[10] This is not to say that he did not at times regard advertising with the suspicion typical of his colleagues at the Institute of Social Research, Adorno and Horkheimer, who are near the top of Nava's list of culprits. For instance, he writes, in true Frankfurt School style, that 'Advertising is the ruse by which the dream forces itself on industry' (G1, 1). But he also emphasizes the radical implications that advertising has for language, for objects, for politics and for the street. It was Benjamin, after all, who proclaimed – sounding like Baudrillard before his time – that 'The "unclouded", "innocent" eye has become a lie . . . Today the most real, mercantile gaze into the heart of things is the advertisement. It tears down the stage upon which contemplation moved, and all but hits us between the eyes with things as a car, growing to gigantic proportions, careens at us out of a film screen.'[11]

For Nava, one of the main problems with much criticism of advertising is its tendency to isolate its object of study, to grant it a formal specificity. She contests the presupposition that 'as a consequence of the unique relationship between advertising and commodities, advertising imagery can easily be distinguished at a formal level from all other cultural representations'.[12] The borders of advertising, she implies, are by no means discrete. It is not just the ubiquity of product placement which guarantees a bleeding of boundaries between media. Leaf through any fashion or decoration magazine and it is difficult to establish any major differences between the pictorial conventions of the features and the advertisements. Television advertisements borrow their style and techniques from cinema and music videos, and advertisements in their turn pioneer techniques such as digitalization. Given such high levels of cross-fertilization, it is hardly justifiable to separate advertising from the rest of visual culture, which consequently needs to be examined as a whole. It could be said that Nava uses this point to get advertising off the hook, but her case could equally be used to argue how thoroughly the logic of advertising has in fact infiltrated the entire visual field.

The *Arcades Project* dedicates a convolute (G) to advertising, but it does not enjoy it in splendid isolation. Instead, Benjamin, whose surprising groupings include Saint-Simon and railroads (Convolute U) and anthropological materialism and history of sects (Convolute p), places advertising with exhibitions and Grandville, the caricaturist and illustrator of the mid nineteenth century. What are the correspondences between these seemingly disparate topics? It is Benjamin's thesis that they participate equally in a visual regime that puts the object on display, and by doing so renders it evanescent, otherworldly. So, Grandville's cosmic-comic engravings, in which 'the Milky Way appears as an 'avenue' illuminated at night by gas lamps' (G16, 3), correspond to the advertisements for Fanta Beer – 'it refreshes like ambrosia!' (G2a, 9) – or Essence D'Amazilly – compared to 'the waters of the Fountain of Youth' (G3a, 1) – which invest products with mythic qualities. Even though Grandville's pictures pre-date the explosion of visual advertising in the late nineteenth century, they prophesy this development: 'Grandville's works are the sibylline books of *publicité*. Everything that, with him, has its preliminary form as joke, or satire, attains its true unfolding as advertisement' (G1, 3).

Forming a bridge between Grandville and the advertising boom of the end of the century are the Great Exhibitions, beginning with the Crystal Palace in 1851 and the Paris *Exposition Universelle* of 1855. Exhibitions prepare the ground for advertising by establishing the basic rule, 'look but don't touch'. Benjamin's hypothesis of a continuum of advertising is confirmed by the historian of exhibitions Paul Greenhalgh, who claims that the Great Exhibitions were in fact the culmination of a century of development of 'the principle of display'.[13]

Like many historians of advertising who have followed him, Benjamin locates the beginnings of modern advertising in the rise of the mass circulation press.[14] Just as industrially produced goods required means of promotion in an increasingly anonymous market, so the burgeoning newspapers depended on advertising revenue to ensure their survival.[15] Here again Benjamin emphasizes the slippage between advertising and other kinds of text. He regularly detects, for instance, the presence or influence of advertising in literary activity, whether it be Balzac's pioneering use of the *annonce déguisé* (disguised advertisement) (A9, 2), the way Baudelaire's 'famous mythomania was a publicity stunt' (J59, 6), or Fourier's deployment of 'the tactics of commercial advertising' to 'launch his system' (A11a, 1). This thesis is taken even further in 'Literary history, Hugo' (Convolute d), where Benjamin suggests a thorough interpenetration of novelistic, advertising and journalistic discourse. He cites Alfred Nettement's argument in *Histoire de la littérature française* (1859) that the serial novel acted as 'bait' in journals which needed subscribers in order to satisfy their advertisers who in turn kept the journals afloat (d9a, 1). Not only do advertising's imperatives bring about the serial novel but the novel in turn takes on the stylistic features of its new host, which leads Benjamin to note: 'The journalistic strain in the novels of Dumas: the first chapter of *Les Mohicans de Paris* already provides information about what impost must be paid, in the event one is arrested, for the privilege of an individual cell; where the Paris executioner lives; and what the best-known apache pubs of Paris are' (d14, 6). The convergence between journalism and *publicité* is summarized by the one term *publiciste*, which was used for three separate but interrelated meanings: political writer, journalist, and advertiser. The fact of advertising, and its ubiquity, are intimately related, then, to wider questions of the commodification of art and writing in general.

For Benjamin, there is no point in treating advertising as a distinct phenomenon, although it is certainly a privileged element in Balzac's 'great poem of display [*étalage*]' that 'chants its stanzas of color from the

Church of the Madeleine to the Porte Saint-Denis' (A1, 4). The continuum of display ranges well beyond Grandville and the great Exhibitions. It takes in the sandwich-man, the window display and display cabinet, the decorative movement *Jugendstil*, the advertising pillar and tower, the shop sign, and the lettering and posters on walls and the sides of buildings. More recently, historians of advertising have confirmed the value of Benjamin's concentration on a more generalized culture of display rather than the specificity of advertising. Often this has simply meant expanding the definition of what constitutes advertising. For instance, Uwe Spiekermann, in his analysis of commerce in nineteenth-century Berlin, notes that shop windows began to be used for display in the period 1835–70, well in advance of formal advertising. He concludes that window-displays are a form of proto-advertising and that consumer society developed in the mid-nineteenth century rather than the 1890s as many historians claim.[16] Stefan Haas explains how near the end of the century architectural form acceded to commercial content:

> With the new glass architecture of the International Style, the city changed into a single enormous display window of the urban dynamic. The need for a display window now increasingly determined the architecture, whereas before the architecture had determined the presentation of the merchandise. Architecture became subordinate to advertising.[17]

Greenhalgh, meanwhile, notes that the major department stores, Le Printemps, Le Louvre and Le Bon Marché, all contributed pavilions to the Expos in Paris, and concludes that the 'exposition was in a very real sense a massive display unit, a shop window arranged and constructed in the way the stores themselves were'.[18] Proto-exhibitions, premature department stores, the arcades clearly mark an earlier instance of urban space being designed with display in mind.

(Arts and) Technologies of advertising

In the pages of *One-Way Street*, where the indulgence in aphorism reaches new levels, Benjamin makes some bold claims about the implications of advertising for the city and for textuality in general:

> Script – having found, in the book, a refuge in which it can lead an autonomous existence – is pitilessly dragged into the street by advertisements and subjected to the brutal heteronomies of economic chaos. This is the hard schooling of its new form. If centuries ago it began gradually to lie down, passing from the upright inscription to the manuscript resting on sloping desks before finally taking itself to bed in the printed book, it now begins just

as slowly to rise again from the ground. The newspaper is read more in the vertical than in the horizontal plane, while film and advertisement force the printed word entirely into the dictatorial perpendicular. And before a contemporary finds his way clear to opening a book, his eyes have been exposed to such a blizzard of changing, colourful, conflicting letters that the chances of his penetrating the archaic stillness of the book are slight.[19]

Already here can be seen the stirrings of the sort of logic which animates 'The work of art in the age of its technological reproducibility' a decade later. Just as the work of art ceases to exist in its privileged form once submitted to new means of (re)production, the printed word is torn from its private repose and thrust into a very public verticality by visual technologies as diverse as newsprint, advertising and silent film. The argument is homologous to that of the later essay: for the lost 'archaic stillness of the book', which Benjamin pseudo-nostalgically invokes, simply substitute the 'unique existence' of the artwork which 'mass existence' supposedly abolishes.[20] In a somewhat tortuous fashion Benjamin suggests that the printed book emerges (or 'takes itself to bed') simultaneously with the establishment of a bourgeois private sphere. In other words, printing is subject to changes in the socio-economic formation, its horizontality auguring the rise of a new dominant class. However, other than invoking 'economic chaos', Benjamin is evasive when it comes to accounting for the underlying conditions which stimulate the renewed verticality of printed letters. He does not answer this question: he is evidently more reluctant to draw conclusions about the state of the economic base than he is to reflect on a relatively autonomous superstructure. What he envisions is no less than a revolution in reading, with advertising putting language itself – now 'a blizzard of changing, colourful, conflicting letters' – on display, producing an *étalage de mots*.[21]

With advertising, then, the printed word takes to the streets. In the Berlin of Benjamin's childhood and the Paris of the 1920s and 1930s, enormous outsized letters towered over passers-by on the exposed walls of buildings, and an increasingly elaborate range of shop signs competed with each other for attention. The fronts of the same shops, which might have been bare at the beginning of the nineteenth century, were bound by the end of it to be plastered with a heterogeneous assemblage of *annonces* and *affiches*, mingling different typefaces, colours and sizes. So pervasive now are the signs and advertisements that fill urban environments that we can hardly perceive them any longer as anything but integral elements of the streets, divorced from the strangeness which marked their first apparition. As Stefan Haas argues, advertising 'transformed the city into

a text'.[22] In fact, advertising was both by-product and engine of urbanization: not only were large cities the main site for new developments in
advertising but advertisements were instrumental in the illumination so
characteristic of the modern city.[23] And if the city is routinely treated as
'legible' by urban theorists and historians, it is in large part thanks to
advertising, which established the printed word in the street and provides
the paradigm for the city as text.

In the 'Work of art' essay, Benjamin belatedly recognizes the double-
edged nature of such technological developments. While he is keen to
stress that mass reproduction makes art's 'cult value recede into the
background [...] because it encourages an evaluating attitude in the
audience', he admits that the same technologies may be 'pressed into
serving the production of ritual values' by fascism.[24] His way out of this
difficulty is not entirely satisfactory: he proposes that, once authenticity
is no longer a criterion of artistic production, *politics* becomes the practice in which it is based.[25] Advertising is subject to a similar dichotomy,
and is equally up for grabs in the *Arcades Project*. Although Benjamin
concentrates on the display of commodities in Convolute G, he also notes
the various workers' committees dispatched to the Great Exhibitions and
remarks on the proliferation of political posters around 1848 (G7, 1). The
extent to which posters in particular were a site of contestation in the
city's graphic field is recorded by Aaron Segal, who also provides some
startling statistics:

> By the eve of the Great War, Lyons alone earned close to 60,000 francs per
> year and Paris over half a million for walls, urinals and columns maintained
> by contractors . . . From the 1880s, departments and municipalities distin-
> guished public and private wall spaces. Nantes and Lyons began to restrict
> posters to designated locations.[26]

The convergence of advertising and politics found its most potent expression in the political poster, which became a basic staple of European
politics in the first half of the twentieth century.[27] Advertising, then, was
a key component in the 'massification' of the political field.

Clearly then, it is not just the printed word but art in general which is
submitted by advertising to the 'brutal heteronomies of economic chaos'.
One of the refrains of the *Arcades Project* is the gradual displacement
during the nineteenth century of the architect by the engineer, of the
École des Beaux Arts by the École Polytechnique. This displacement is
realized in the very construction of the arcades, where iron (and with it
glass) is introduced as a building material for pragmatic commercial
reasons rather than for architectural ones. The strength of iron in

comparison with earlier materials means that less of it needs to be used, leaving more space for glass, and therefore for the display of goods. Posters, meanwhile, which are routinely hailed as the 'public art' of the 1870s onwards, are dependent on an early technique of mass printing, lithography. Lithography had been invented in 1798, but it was not until Jules Chéret produced the first colour lithograph design, *Orphée aux Enfers*, in 1858 that the potential of the technique was realized.[28] And for those many historians of 'poster art' who wish to claim Chéret as an artist rather than an advertiser,[29] it is enough to cite Benjamin on those who would elevate the photographer to artist: 'they undertook nothing less than to legitimize the photographer before the very tribunal he was in the process of overturning'.[30] Photography eventually replaced or even became poster art, and today the vast majority of commercially produced photographs are destined for advertisements.[31]

Although advertising has fairly comprehensively unseated art in the domain of visual representation, there is one sense in which it could be argued that it carries on art's function. To make this connection we can turn to one of Benjamin's Parisian contemporaries and wartime guardian of the *Arcades Project*, Georges Bataille, who considered art and fiction a kind of 'nonproductive expenditure' along with 'luxury, mourning, war, cults . . . games, spectacles . . . perverse sexual activity'.[32] Given that British companies alone spend approximately £43 billion a year on advertising,[33] and that there is much evidence to suggest that advertising does not always, or even usually, make positive returns on its investments,[34] it could be argued that it attests not to an economy based on utility but to one closer to potlatch. That is to say, advertising could be considered a form of useless expenditure, one of the ways in which capitalist economies shed their surplus, their excess, disposing of it as waste, but disguising it as 'value-added'. This argument could, at any rate, be fruitfully applied to the almost viral proliferation of Great Exhibitions, *Expositions Universelles* and World's Fairs in the period from 1851 up until the outbreak of the Second World War, when the world's nations found other means of non-productive expenditure. Paul Greenhalgh can barely conceal his disapproval when he describes the dizzying excesses carried out in order to display national products and imperial spoils: 'The highest, biggest, newest and costliest of artefacts and structures become the commonplaces of all events, often in vulgar exercises tantamount to criminal waste.'[35] Thanks to government subsidy, the exhibitions usually made small profits, although the Paris Expo of 1878 made heavy losses and the international exhibition in Vienna in 1873 nearly bankrupted the city.[36] There were various attempts to extol the utility of the exhibitions (their contribution to peace, education, progress),[37] but they were really fuelled by *rivalry*, an altogether different economic principle and also a key motive force in the practice of potlatch. That Benjamin did not take up this nationalistic aspect of the Exhibitions is consistent with the rest of the *Arcades Project*, which is oddly silent on this issue.

Notes

1 Judith Williamson, *Decoding Advertisements: Ideology and Meaning in Advertising* (London: Marion Boyars, 1978), pp. 92, 95.
2 Benjamin, 'On language as such', p. 69.
3 Benjamin, 'On language as such', p. 64.
4 Benjamin, 'On language as such', p. 69.
5 Benjamin, *Das Passagen-Werk*, vol. 1, p. 235.
6 Benjamin, *Das Passagen-Werk*, vol. 1, p. 236.
7 Mica Nava, 'Framing advertising: cultural analysis and the incrimination of visual texts', in Mica Nava, Andrew Blake, Iain MacRury and Barry Richards (eds), *Buy this Book: Studies in Advertising and Consumption* (London: Routledge, 1997), pp. 34–50 (p. 34).
8 Nava, 'Framing advertising', p. 39.
9 Nava, 'Framing advertising', p. 37.
10 Nava, 'Framing advertising', p. 47.
11 Benjamin, 'One-way street,' p. 476.
12 Nava, 'Framing advertising', p. 43.
13 Paul Greenhalgh, *Ephemeral Vistas: The* Expositions Universelles, *Great Exhibitions and World's Fairs, 1851–1939* (Manchester: Manchester University Press, 1988), p. 3.
14 See, for instance, E. S. Turner, *The Shocking History of Advertising!* (Harmondsworth: Penguin, 1965) or Gillian Dyer, *Advertising as Communication* (London: Methuen, 1982)
15 See Clemens Wischermann, 'Placing advertising in the modern cultural history of the city', in Clemens Wischermann and Elliot Shore (eds), *Advertising and the Modern European City: Historical Perspectives* (Aldershot: Ashgate, 2000), pp. 1–31 (pp. 1–10).
16 Uwe Spiekermann, 'Display windows and window displays in German cities of the nineteenth century: towards the history of a commercial breakthrough', in Wischermann and Shore, *Advertising and the Modern European City*, pp. 139–71 (pp. 142, 165).
17 Stefan Haas, 'Visual discourse and the metropolis: mental models of cities and the emergence of commercial advertising', in Wischermann and Shore, *Advertising and the Modern European City*, pp. 54–78 (pp. 65–6).
18 Greenhalgh, *Ephemeral Vistas*, p. 190.
19 Benjamin, 'One-way street', p. 456.
20 Walter Benjamin, 'The work of art in the age of its technological repro-

ducibility (third Version)' [1939], in *SW* 4, pp. 251–83 (p. 254).

21 Benjamin, 'One-way street', p. 456.

22 Haas, 'Visual discourse and the metropolis', p. 61.

23 Wischermann, 'Placing advertising', p. 10, and Haas, 'Visual discourse and the metropolis', p. 67.

24 Benjamin, 'Work of art (third version)', p. 269.

25 Benjamin, 'Work of art (third version)', p. 257.

26 Aaron J. Segal, 'Commerical immanence: the poster and urban territory in nineteenth-century France', in Wischermann and Shore, *Advertising and the Modern European City*, pp. 113–38 (p. 132).

27 For accounts of the political role of posters, see, for example, John Tisa (ed.), *The Palette and the Flame: Posters of the Spanish Civil War* (Wellingborough: Collett's, 1980); Stephen White, *The Bolshevik Poster* (New Haven: Yale University Press, 1988); and Victoria E. Bonnell, *Iconography of Power: Soviet Political Posters under Lenin and Stalin* (Berkeley: California University Press, 1997).

28 John Barnicoat, *Posters: A Concise History* (New York: Thames and Hudson, 1972), p. 7.

29 See Barnicoat, p. 12; Bevis Hillier, *Posters* (London: Spring Books, 1974), pp. 36–9; and Jane Abdy, *The French Poster: Chéret to Cappiello* (London: Studio Vista, 1969), pp. 9–10.

30 Walter Benjamin, 'Little history of photography' [1931], in *SW* 2, pp. 507–30 (p. 508).

31 Dyer, *Advertising*, p. 2.

32 Georges Bataille, 'The notion of expenditure' (1933), in *Visions of Excess: Selected Writings, 1927–1939*, trans. and ed. Allan Stoekl (Minneapolis: University of Minnesota Press, 1985), pp. 116–29 (p. 118). Benjamin attended meetings of Bataille's Collège de Sociologie during the late 1930s, but even though Bataille apparently 'held him in the highest esteem', Benjamin 'worried that the College was toying with explosive ideas without realistically weighing up the consequences'; Michel Surya, *Georges Bataille: An Intellectual Biography* (1992), trans. Krzysztof Fijalkowski and Michael Richardson (London and New York: Verso, 2002), pp. 266, 268. Benjamin clearly found Bataille unpredictable. He asked Horkheimer that criticism of Bataille should be excluded from a letter of his to be published by the Institute journal because 'he is hardly the kind of person to react serenely to its contents' (Letter from Benjamin to Max Horkheimer, 3 August 1938, quoted in part in a note to his letter to the Adornos of 28 August 1938, in *Adorno–Benjamin Correspondence*, pp. 275–6 n6). On Benjamin's relationship to the College see Michael Weingrad, 'The College of Sociology and the Institute of Social Research', *New German Critique*, 84 (2001), pp. 130–61.

33 *The Guardian*, 3 December 2002, Media section, p. 4.

34 See Nava, 'Framing advertising', pp. 40–3.

35 Greenhalgh, *Ephemeral Vistas*, p. 12.

36 Greenhalgh, *Ephemeral Vistas*, pp. 34, 41.

37 See Greenhalgh, *Ephemeral Vistas*, pp. 17–23.

Nations

The story of Benjamin's key work is one of border-crossings; of capital cities echoing and reflecting each other beyond borders and time. From his 'Berlin childhood', to the dawn of a new age in Moscow or the rebirth of modernity in Paris, Benjamin seemed to make a point of not mentioning nationalities in his published work and of scrupulously editing out the usual rhetorical tropes of national characters and types which fed the majority of tourist narratives. Benjamin the German Jew, writing about French literature and Paris, thinking afresh internationalist ideology, seems to escape the conventions of national attachments. Even if, in his 1923 letter to Florens Christian Rang, Benjamin argued his complex intellectual identity was deepened through his attempt to redeem the writings of the past, there is little dialectical engagement between nationalism and modernity in the *Arcades Project*.[1] Almost inconceivably his *magnum opus* on modernity seems to ignore what most historians of either France or Germany have considered to be the political linchpin of European modernity: the national phenomenon which, from the 1770s (years of the early arcades) until the 1910s (years of the last few bloated arcades of Europe), was deemed to be the spirit of history in both the Hegelian and Herderian sense.[2] National *identity* has been deemed by philosophers and sociologists to constitute one of the central manifestations of a collective super ego, disciplining the violence of the unconscious which sociologists such as LeBon saw as malleable by demagoguery and authoritarian leaders.[3] A few years after the great war of nationalism, in the midst of political conflicts which focused equally on ideology and nationalism, Benjamin chose to ignore the latter dimension. At least that is what it seems. In fact one could read the entire *Arcades Project* as a critique, albeit by default, of nationalism while Benjamin's life seems a denial of the national identikit one is encouraged to resemble from childhood. The fact that Benjamin had to live through the complexities of renegotiated national identities further complicates the issue.

Against nations

This silence on nations could be explained in different ways. Perhaps the association of the national phenomenon with right-wing politics from the late nineteenth century onwards, in the French case since the Dreyfus affair, stained it with false consciousness. Furthermore, its abstract qualities could not be explained in the concrete and material terms that define the *Arcades Project*. Yet much of the literature used by Benjamin was about nation-making, be it in the writings of commentators on Paris as modern Babylon, travel writers defining their otherness in Paris or French intellectuals codifying the social themes of their national consciousness. The *physiologies* and other forms of cultural portraits and stereotyping aimed at producing a recognizable image of Paris which could then be exported and sold as a place to tour and consume as Frenchness, sweet and corrupt.[4] Much of the German literature on Paris, which forms some of the most important quarries of information collated in the *Arcades Project*, is in fact devoted to the establishment of 'national character',[5] the definition of alterity[6] and the constitution of moral alienation *against* Paris or the French. The nationalism latent in so many of these works is not commented upon or criticized, just as Benjamin feigns to ignore the right-wing politics of so many of his sources. When quoting the writing of historians, he tends to follow the obscure method that consists of turning around the prose of his objective intellectual enemies in order to uncover whatever insights they might unwittingly reveal. Symptomatic in this sense is his use of Léon Daudet, famous anti-Semite and royalist, who since the Dreyfus affair and until his death denounced all forms of Jewish and 'anti-national' interference while ridiculing the 'stupid nineteenth century'.[7] The Nietzschean dimensions of Daudet's proto-Fascism thus recur in the quotes selected in the *Arcades Project*. Similarly the hyper-nationalist and racist author of *La France Juive*,[8] Édouard Drumont, is summoned to provide critical judgement on nineteenth-century authors such as Toussenel (G12a, 5).[9] In many other instances the political leaning of the sources is decidedly to the right. There is a morbid fascination with the literary insights of men, some of them contemporaries of Benjamin, obsessed with national identity which is reflected also in the systematic use of authors specializing in the depiction of their own national character through a description of

Paris. The Babylonian nature of Parisian vices and mores formed the lurid appeal of many nineteenth-century depictions used by Benjamin. Far from recoiling or contextualizing the lurid appeal of these texts to their original readership, Benjamin engages with them as if they were a quarry of evidence.

While nationalism and the value system attached to this ideology coloured the entirety of these texts, Benjamin nevertheless seems to quote them for their judgements and authoritative statements. One is thus faced with a puzzling riddle supplementary to the many riddles of the *Arcades Project*. On what would such authority be grounded for Benjamin? If a wholesale rejection would have been childish and censorious, Benjamin nevertheless seems to sail close to an inimical wind. Whether this reflected a genuine fascination with anti-liberal authors or a desire to reclaim utopian fragments in otherwise politically objectionable texts is up for discussion. As a result, the nation and nationalism are embossed in the palimpsest of the *Arcades* and simultaneously omnipresent and glaringly absent. When Benjamin does refer explicitly to sources that deal with nations and nation building, it is in an 'international' context: those moments when nations parade alongside each other in the great displays of consumerism and production of the international exhibitions. He also refers to Victor Hugo's *Manifesto to the Peoples of Europe* which paradoxically mimicked some of the dreams of Hugo's arch-enemy Napoleon III in calling for a 'concert' of European nations, a united order if not a united states of Europe.

It is thus significant that a rare mention of the French revolution should appear only fleetingly in the discussion of 'economic history' and only in parallel with the celebration of the centenary of ironwork constructions (Convolute g) side by side with a series of quotes exposing the latent protectionism of the French. Of course the Third Republic in 1889 celebrated the centenary of the French revolution with the modernist statement of the Eiffel Tower (which is mentioned only in the precursor to the *Arcades Project*, the 1928–9 text 'The ring of Saturn, or some remarks on iron construction') and a largely boycotted universal exhibition, and it invited this parallel, but Benjamin seems particularly dogged in his neglect of metanarratives of nation building.[10] Thus the discussion of the aptly titled *xeonomania impugned* caricature of 1818 which invites the French to celebrate simultaneously their victorious and glorious past and their commercial and manufactured goods is juxtaposed with Michelet's denunciation of Napoleon III's 'second coup' of the Cobden–Chevalier free trade treaty of 1860.[11]

This single reference to the nationalism of Michelet is extraordinary considering the number of quotations from – and the general reverence in which Benjamin holds – Michelet. Most references from Michelet thus refer not to his resurrectionist practices, as an 'eater of dust', a consumer of the archives, but to his social and literary criticism, particularly his essay on *Le Peuple*.[12] Michelet in *Le Peuple* remained specific, he was writing about the French people rather than the idea of 'the people' as opposed to class for instance.[13] It is the 'people' which was the main actor of Michelet's account of the French revolution in so far as it incarnated the 'spirit of France'. In his quotations, Benjamin prefers to narrow him down to a literary critique of petty bourgeois aspirations or to highlight his populist idealism. Other references to Michelet reflect more particularly his ambivalent position towards Lamartine (p. 798) and his forms of aestheticized demagoguery. Michelet's nationalism, while repressed in Benjamin's careful excision of quotes, re-emerges as a strand of populism. Either pared down to its materialistic underpinnings or revealed as the troubled exaltation of the masses, nationalism is implicitly denounced as one of the dreams of the bourgeois century.

On the other side of the political spectrum Benjamin conveniently chooses to ignore the exalted idealism of the idea of nation.[14] He does not, for example, pay attention to the Mazzinians, or the Garibaldians who all developed important movements in Europe and whose messianic dimensions played an important rôle in the shaping of a radical nationalist tradition.[15] Blanqui himself, one of Benjamin's few crucial human figures, was usually dismissed by the Marxist internationalists as an example of a 'nationalist socialist' who opposed the spirit and even the action of the first Workers' Internationale.[16] When discussing the Commune and many other radical Utopian socialist movements in the *Arcades Project*, Benjamin excludes any reference to their cosmopolitan dimensions.[17] German, Hungarian and Polish men joined in the Commune of Paris in the same way that multitudes of Italians, Greeks, Spanish, Irish volunteers had come to the rescue of the French republic in the armies raised by Garibaldi in 1870. There were parallels with the International Brigades of Spain in the 1930s, all of which Benjamin chose to ignore even in his later writings of the late 1930s. He withdrew the *Arcades Project* from its most important contextual setting: the shaping of modern France and of nationalities throughout Europe. Even the late *passages couverts* that burgeoned throughout Europe in the late nineteenth century did so because these buildings were in themselves objects of pride and an opportunity to outdo national industrial competitors with a demonstration of ever higher and more complicated metallic structure. Yet Benjamin said nothing about that aspect of the imperial dynamic of the later arcades.

In spite of all this the *Arcades Project* sets itself as a counter-narrative of nation making. The historicist tradition Benjamin so relentlessly attacks is explicitly present in the arcades under the shape of the wax gallery of Musée Grévin (Q2, 2), the mirror of nothingness which, like the mirrors of the arcade, reflects not a concrete object but a dream. The historical portraits of the wax museum had for him the spectacular but obsolete realism and fixity of the historicist narratives of the ruling elites of the past.

Yet to scorn the rigidity of historicism was to ignore much of the historiography Benjamin could have engaged with. The *Arcades Project* was undoubtedly designed to be a history of sorts, yet it never fully engaged with the constraints of historical method or with any of the narrative conventions of what the French and German historians were increasingly redesigning as the central social science. The absence of nations or nationalism in the narrative of modernity in the imperial capital of France and its empire might then be a more crucial omission and a source of unease with Benjamin's limited engagement with historical questions or concerns.[18] Even though the revolution, economic determinism and occasionally orthodox accounts of the class struggle figure prominently in the drafts and organizational principles of the *Arcades Project*, Benjamin seems to have alternative definitions of all these central analytical devices. The correspondence with Adorno clearly reflects the latter's puzzlement at Benjamin's uses of Marxist terms and methods. As Arno Münster has argued, Benjamin might have been more Blanquist than Marxist and perhaps had found in Sorel the fusion that enabled him to extol messianic aspirations for his historical project.[19] The idea of the nation fell through the cracks, perhaps because it never played such a central role in Marxist historical analysis, except as the archetype of false consciousness. Not even at the level of the 'collective unconscious' which figures in the exposé of 1935 did the nation appear.[20] In his musings on the forms that history might take after the revolutionary awakening, the idea of nation could only figure as a pale reverie of the nineteenth-century bourgeoisie, yet a less significant one than its dreams of abundance or of stolid material success.

Yet, in his daily life, Benjamin could not ignore how the national idea conditioned the terms of his existence and gradually narrowed his options. Even if we put to one side the details of his biography, we have to contend with the fact that Benjamin lived through the most charged era of nationalism: the Great War, and the period following the armistice of 1918. More than any other nineteenth-century dream, the idea of the nation haunted the interwar period. The ideologies of the Soviet and Fascist blocs might have outwardly promoted internationalist ideals, but they remained rooted in ultra-nationalism. Even the great democratic regimes oscillated between a narrow definition of themselves and their imperial mission, always framed in national terms. In this context, Benjamin's neglect of the nation seems more like denial than transcendence.

Cosmopolitan Benjamin?

Even before the difficult circumstances of the late 1930s one could have asked some simple yet complex questions of Benjamin's identity. The first one arises from a reading of Tiedemann's 1964 thesis on the philosophy of Walter Benjamin, which received the imprimatur of Adorno and which was published in 1965 in *Frankfurter Beiträge zur Soziologie*.[21] To put it crudely, the matter is whether Benjamin was *really* German. This question might seem absurd considering the language used in most of the texts or indeed the passport used by Walter Benjamin until July 1939, when he lost the right to use his official nationality without acquiring a new one. Yet in his philosophy and in the *Arcades Project* there is an element of doubt. Autobiographical texts by Benjamin refer to his Berliner identity but always in a dialectical relation to his Parisian identity rather than to his German identity.[22] Though his literary and philosophical heritage was undoubtedly German, his 'heirs' and posthumous patrons have insisted a little too heavily and a doubt creeps in. Adorno and Tiedemann sought to anchor Benjamin among the German philosophers of the past rather too vigorously. It is because Benjamin did not really belong among the Frankfurt School that he had to be recovered as an original but integral strand of it. It is because he was no longer very German that Benjamin had to become German again, albeit posthumously in the reconstruction of the Federal University system. Benjamin was an intellectual martyr, and his errant and hesitant career, his lack of 'rootedness' to use Simone Weil's concept, has meant that his real sense of belonging to a particular national tradition could be and was contested.[23] An equally puzzling question is whether Benjamin was French. As Christopher Forth has shown, such a question about Nietzsche had, for a short period between 1900 and 1914, been answered positively.[24] For Benjamin the case is if anything stronger. In his curriculum vitae of 1929, Benjamin referred to his dual belonging to French and German literary worlds and of his difficulties as a translator.[25] Benjamin spoke and wrote in French as well and the *Arcades Project* was truly a bilingual collage of German and French texts.[26] Increasingly in the 1930s, he used French in his epistolary exchanges with his friends. The 1939 draft of the *Arcades Project* was written in French and, in spite of some of his writing being rejected by the *Nouvelle Revue Française*, the book might well have been written in either German or French. The model of Joseph Conrad was available to all exiles.[27] In fact the final product, the compilation of notes and quotes reflects this genuine bilingual and bicultural engagement.

Benjamin felt an uncommon affinity for Marcel Proust, and his journalistic writings show his desire to disseminate French ideas as well as his desire to meet the great French writers of his time.[28] His enthusing for Paris as the capital of the nineteenth century reflected not the fleeting infatuation of a tourist but a real intellectual homecoming, seeking a role for himself in the ruins of the nineteenth century. Obviously, exile from Germany had made the Parisian stay a necessity, but it is also clear that Benjamin resisted to the last minute calls to move to New York or Jerusalem. Benjamin was not really one of Remarque's exiled drifters.[29] He might have been learning some Hebrew and might have been tempted to rejoin his intellectual comrades abroad; he remained in France and died there by his own hand. Stalling at the border was indeed Benjamin's fate in many ways. Ultimately, it may be that the national phenomenon was opposed, even as an abstract concept, to the urban and intellectual condition of Benjamin. In a sense he was consciously unwilling to engage with nation making and nationalism even when he was quoting nationalists or describing objects or people who contributed as *lieux de mémoire* or actors to the shaping of nations. And this unwillingness was, for nationalist detractors, the main characteristic of 'cosmopolitanism' or the ideology of the '*apatrides*', the men without homeland.[30] Reflecting recently on similar issues, commentators have conceptualized this distance as either an ironic standpoint or a superior attachment to Kantian cosmo-politics.[31] In the era of *apatrides*, men and women denied political rights of any kind, repelled by the nation in which they were born and unwelcome in the territory where they lived, experienced this distance in a tragic mode.[32]

Was Benjamin in this sense cosmopolitan? The term *cosmopolitan* has attracted a fashionable literature, devoted to the tracing down and microdefinition of identity, positing cosmopolitanism as a sign of openness and cross-fertilisation,[33] opposed to what Ulrich Beck named the 'monologic imagination which excludes the otherness of the other'.[34] In the French context inherited from the late nineteenth century, the term had mostly very negative connotations.[35] The cosmopolitans were the dangerous men of the Commune, the Polish agitators, the Italian terrorists, the tumultuous mass of intellectuals expelled from their own countries who sought to plant the seeds of revolutionary turmoil in foreign soil. Their otherness was opposed to both the 'blood and soil' nationalism of the right inspired by Maurras and Barrès[36] and to the Revolutionary universalism of the left, which could not conceive of the legitimacy of difference and divergence.[37] From the right, conservatives such as Maxime Du Camp in 1877 theorized afresh the revolution as another incarnation of this cosmopolitan contagion.[38] The Paris police prefecture then attempted to keep its information constantly actuated on these dangerous foreign elements, and the whole notion of cosmopolitanism was one of dangerousness.

The 1930s witnessed a revival of this anxiety. In 1932 a Russian refugee murdered the French president Paul Doumer; in 1934 a Croatian refugee assassinated Alexander I of Yugoslavia and the French foreign minister Louis Barthou in Marseille. Last but not least, the 1934 major financial scandal, which ended with the murder of the Russian Jew Stavisky, revived anti-Semitic and xenophobic tropes.[39] By 1939 France had received so many refugees from Spain and Germany that they represented nearly 10 per cent of its population. Over three hundred thousand Germans resided in France by 1939. The mass arrival of professionals led to their gradual exclusion on grounds of nationality by the mid-1930s, and even French Jewry resented the '*boche*' attitude and cultural imperialism of the newcomers.[40] Vociferous nationalist professional unions, fearing a glut of expertise and the competition of foreigners especially, had targeted doctors, university lecturers and lawyers, petitioning relentlessly for restrictive regulations.[41] Naturalization became increasingly difficult in the late 1930s and professional openings narrowed down in a country increasingly involved in the worldwide economic downturn. The mass arrival of republican Spaniards had led to the creation of internment camps which later served as concentration camps under Vichy. According to his biographer, Benjamin attempted in 1938 to obtain French citizenship, but in vain; he was not alone in being scorned, as Picasso himself suffered the same humiliation.[42] By February 1939 his German citizenship expired according to the laws of the Reich, yet Benjamin did not acquire a new nationality, having to be content with a *carte de séjour* renewable annually and which required police and health registration. Ironically it is as an enemy alien that Benjamin was interned in September 1939, only to be released very swiftly at the insistence of his intellectual friends.

His subsequent flight from Paris is well documented, yet it is at the Bibliothèque Nationale – note the name – that Benjamin hid his writings while the Gestapo deemed him sufficiently important to raid his flat in Paris. Dying at the border of France does not seem such an accident after all.

Notes

1 Letter 122, from Benjamin to Florens Christian Rang, 18 November 1923, in *Correspondence*, pp. 214–17 (pp. 214–15).
2 For instance, see Stuart Woolf (ed.), *Nationalism in Europe, 1815 to the Present: A Reader* (London: Routledge, 1996), and R. Brubaker, *Citizenship and Nationhood in France and Germany* (Cambridge, Mass.: Harvard University Press, 1992).
3 Susanna Barrows, *Distorting Mirrors: Visions of the Crowd in Late Nineteenth-Century France* (New Haven: Yale University Press, 1981); Robert Nye, *The Origins of Crowd Psychology: Gustave Le Bon and the Crisis of Mass Democracy in the Third Republic* (London: Sage, 1975).
4 See Ferguson, *Paris as Revolution*, pp. 81–5.
5 G. Varouxakis, *Mill on Nationality* (London: Routledge, 2002).
6 On which see Michel de Certeau, *Heterologies: Discourses on the Other* (Manchester: Manchester University Press, 1986).
7 Léon Daudet, *Le Stupide XIXe Siècle: exposé des insanités meutrières qui se sont abattues sur la France depuis 130 ans, 1789–1919* (Paris: Nouvelle Librairie Nationale, 1922).
8 Édouard Drumont, *La France juive: essai d'histoire contemporaine* (Paris: C. Marpon & E. Flammarion, 1886).
9 Alphonse Toussenel (1806–1885), allegorist and author of books on animals and Jews.
10 Walter Benjamin, 'The ring of Saturn or some remarks on iron construction' [c. 1928–9], in *AP*, pp. 885–7 (pp. 886, 887).
11 A. A. Iliasu, 'The Cobden–Chevalier commercial treaty of 1860', *The Historical Journal*, 14: 1 (1971), 67–98.
12 See Steedman, *Dust*, pp. 38–40.
13 The idea of the 'people' as mode of political configuration has been well explored for Britain in Patrick Joyce, *Visions of the People* (Cambridge: Cambridge University Press, 1991).
14 See for instance Maurizio Viroli, *For Love of Country: An Essay on Patriotism and Nationalism* (Oxford: Oxford University Press, 1995).
15 H. Bellman, *Architects of the New Age: Bright, Kossuth, Lincoln, Mazzini and Tolstoy; with an Introductory Essay* (London: S. Low, Marston, 1929); D. Mack Smith, *Mazzini* (New Haven: Yale University Press, 1994).
16 Jean Maitron, *Le Mouvement anarchiste en France*, vol. 1 (Paris: Gallimard,

1975); Un bourgeois républicain, *Histoire de l'internationale, (1862–1872)*, London, Paris and Brussels (n.p.: Combe et Vande Weghe, 1873).

17 In the proper sense of the word, the Commune of Paris fostered, among many diverging political messages, calls for universal rights. A. Bellina, *Les Polonais et la Commune de Paris* (n.p.: n.pub.., 1871).

18 Similar unease arises when reading philosophical discussions on Benjamin's contribution to historical thinking. The opposition offered by Jeanne-Marie Gagnebin between the 'homogenous and empty concept of time of historical causality' and Benjamin's 'fuller concept of "time of now" *Jeztzeit*' makes sense only if one accepts the straw man she offers. Even by the 1930s, historians of the early *Annales* school were revisiting in depth the concepts of historical time and of causality. J. M. Gagnebin, *Histoire et narration chez Walter Benjamin* (Paris: L'Harmattan, 1994), p. 147; see also Marie-Cécile Dufour-El Maleh, *La Nuit sauvée: Walter Benjamin et la pensée de l'histoire* (Brussels: Ousia, 1993).

19 Arno Münster, *Progrès et catastrophe, Walter Benjamin et l'histoire: Réflexion sur l'itinéraire philosophique d'un Marxisme mélancolique* (Paris: Kiné, 1996), pp. 53–6, 64.

20 Walter Benjamin, 'Exposé of 1935', p. 11; see also Rainer Rochlitz, *Le Désenchantement de l'art: la philosophie de Walter Benjamin* (Paris: Gallimard, 1992), p. 277.

21 Tiedemann, *Études* (the translation of the revised (1973) edition into French).

22 Benjamin, 'A Berlin chronicle', p. 597.

23 Simone Weil, *L'Enracinement* (Paris: Gallimard NRF, [1943] 1949).

24 Christopher Forth, *Zarathustra in Paris: The Nietzsche Vogue in France, 1891–1918* (DeKalb: Northern Illinois University Press, 2001).

25 Benjamin, 'Curriculum vitae III', p. 78.

26 Jean-Maurice Monnoyer (ed.), *Walter Benjamin*, avec les témoignages d'Adrienne Monnier, de Gisèle Freund et de Jean Seltz (Paris: Gallimard, 1991).

27 Béatrice Caceres and Yannick Le Boulicaut, *Les Écrivains de l'Exil: Cosmopolitisme ou ethnicité* (Paris: L'Harmattan, 2002), pp. 47–70.

28 Robert Kahn, *Images, passages: Marcel Proust et Walter Benjamin* (Paris: Kiné, 1998). See, for example, Benjamin's enthusiastic account of an interview with André Gide (Letter 168, from Benjamin to Scholem, 30 January 1928, in *Correspondence*, pp. 321–5 (p. 324)). The published account of the interview is 'Conversation with André Gide' [1928], in *SW 2*, pp. 91–7.

29 E. M. Remarque, *Liebe Deinen Nächsten* (Munich: Desch, 1953).

30 Patrick Weil, *The Transformation of Immigration Policies: Immigration Control and Nationality Laws in Europe: A Comparative Approach*, Series, EUI working paper EUF; no. 98/5 (San Domenico: European University Institute, European Forum, c. 1998); Bernard Lejuif, 'Les Apatrides' (Thèse de doctorat, Université de Caen, 1939).

31 See David Ingram, 'Between political liberalism and postnational cosmopolitanism: toward an alternative theory of human rights', *Political Theory*, 31: 3 (2003), 359–91; Bryan S. Turner, 'Cosmopolitan virtue, globalization and patriotism', *Theory, Culture and Society*, 19: 1–2 (2002), 45–63 (pp. 55–6); G. Raulet, 'Citizenship, otherness and cosmopolitism in Kant', *Social Science Information — Sur Les Sciences Sociales*, 35: 3 (September 1996), 437–46. See also the American-inflected version of this debate: Richard Rorty, *Achieveing Our Country: Leftist Thought in Twentieth-century America* (Cambridge, Mass.: Harvard University Press, 1998), and Martha Nussbaum et al., *For Love of Country: Debating the Limits of Patriotism* (Boston: Beacon Press, 1996).

32 I. P. Lipovano, *L'Apatridie* (Paris: Les Éditions Internationales, 1935), p. 22.

33 Ulf Hannerz, 'Cosmopolitans and locals in world culture', *Theory, Culture and Society*, 7: 2 (1990), 237–51.

34 Ulrich Beck, 'The cosmopolitan society and its enemies', *Theory, Culture and Society*, 19: 1–2 (2002), 17–44 (p. 18).

35 Pascal Bruckner, *Le Vertige de Babel* (Paris: Arléa, 2000).

36 Maurice Barrès, *La Terre et les morts, sur quelles réalités fonder la conscience française* (Paris: Bureau de la Patrie Française, 1900).

37 Sophie Wahnich, *L'Impossible Citoyen, l'étranger dans le discours de la Révolution française* (Paris: Albin Michel, 1997).

38 Maxime du Camp, *Les Ancêtres de la Commune, l'attentat Fieschi* (Paris: Charpentier, 1877).

39 Paul Jankowski, *Stavisky: A Confidence Man in the Republic of Virtue* (Ithaca and London: Cornell University Press, 2002); Vicki Caron, *Uneasy Asylum: France and the Jewish Refugee Crisis 1933–1942* (Palo Alto: Stanford University Press, 1999).

40 Ralph Schor, *L'Opinion française et les Étrangers 1919–1939* (Paris: Publication de la Sorbonne, 1985), pp. 613, 618.

41 Apatrides had thus lost the right to manage a newspaper or publication, to belong to a union, to act as lawyer or doctor. By 1939 there were voices asking to prevent them from using their university diploma in any capacity whatever (Lejuif, 'Les Apatrides', pp. 88–94).

42 Bernd Witte, *Walter Benjamin: An Intellectual Biography*, trans. James Rolleston (Detriot: Wayne State University Press, 1991), p. 189.

Jeux/joie/jouissance

Desire is both too narrow and too broad a concept to encompass the central idea of Convolute O, 'Prostitution, gambling'. Roland Barthes's concept of *le plaisir* is perhaps closest to the range of experiences to which Benjamin refers. Benjamin is interested in regulation, but does not, on the face of it, adhere to a Foucauldian theory of desire as itself a product of regulation. His concept of 'naked lust' seems closer to a Freudian 'drive' and he turns to psychoanalytic articles by Edmund Bergler to find a connection between gambling and sexuality. However, three factors complicate the idea of naked lust as essential human drive: first, Benjamin's focus on the temporality of pleasure; second, the structure of the convolute itself, which is typical of the *Project* in the sense that it takes a theoretical idea and then follows its material manifestations in the context of nineteenth-century Paris; and third, the mystical connection between pleasure and the divine.

Woodrow Wyatt, the right-wing Labour peer, used to claim that, where moralists saw gambling as the ruin of the working class, betting might instead be seen as a force for good. Placing a bet, he argued, was one of the few times that the working man was called upon to make a critical judgement, and this use of his intellectual faculties in judging a horse's form, the terrain and the other variables was a good preparation for making political judgements in a democracy. It is unlikely that Benjamin would have agreed with this rather instrumentalist justification of gambling – an industry in which Lord Wyatt took more than a philosophical interest – still less that he would have applauded it as a bulwark of liberal democracy. Rather, Benjamin sees gambling on political uncertainty as symptomatic of capitalism's short-sightedness: 'It is not by accident that people bet on the results of elections, on the outbreak of war, and so on.' The proletariat, by contrast, is less taken in by the ebbs and flows of what is essentially the same system: 'He is better positioned to recognize constants in the political process' (O13, 5).

But where Benjamin comes some way to meeting Wyatt is in the idea that the predictive or divinatory element of gambling fosters a form of thinking premonitory of the temporal thinking that might break out of the dull constraints of the everyday. As limited as the form of gambling is, it offers the prospect of something else, something better. The time of desire, Benjamin suggests, contains 'an extract of the future', or traces of what he describes elsewhere, as messianic time.[1] To illustrate the gambler's conception of time, he suggests Baudelaire's 'L'Horloge':[2]

> *Souviens-toi* que le Temps est un joueur avide
> Qui gagne sans tricher, à tout coup! c'est la loi
> La jour décroit; la nuit augmente; *souviens toi!*
> Le gouffre a toujours soif; la clepsydre se vide
>
> (Remember Time is a greedy gambler
> Who wins without cheating! it's the law
> The day runs down; the night comes on; *remember!*
> The water clock empties itself; the abyss is always thirsty)[3]

As desperate a condition as this depicts, it suggests to Benjamin the possibility of something beyond that state. The mystery of the lucky name or number lies in the prospect that it will reveal the future. Reducing that future to a monetary 'win' is, literally, a cheapening of a form, thinking that might allow us to break free of historicism and a devaluing of what becomes a key concept in Convolute O: *Geistesgegenwart* or 'presence of mind'.[4]

> The proscription of gambling could have its deepest roots in the fact that a natural gift of humanity, one which, directed toward the highest objects, elevates the human being beyond herself, only drags her down when applied to one of the meanest objects: money. The gift in question is presence of mind [*Geistesgegenwart*]. Its highest manifestation is the reading that in each case is divinatory. (O13, 3)

The best definition of 'presence of mind' comes in 'The path to success, in thirteen theses', published in 1928:

> The questions is not whether the mind is present, or what form it takes, but only *where* it is. That it happens to be present here, at this very moment, is possible only if it enters into a person's intonation, his smile, his conversational pauses, his gaze, or his gestures. For only the body can generate presence of mind.[5]

As an embodied state, *Geistesgegenwart* involves a commitment of body and mind towards the future. It informs all divinatory activities. Thus in 'One-way street':

He who asks fortune-tellers the future unwittingly forfeits an inner intimation of coming events that is a thousand times more exact than anything
they might say. He is impelled by inertia, rather than by curiosity, and nothing is more unlike the submissive apathy with which he hears his fate
revealed than the alert dexterity with which the man of courage lays hands
on the future. For presence of mind is an extract of the future, and precise
awareness of the present moment is more decisive than foreknowledge of
the most distant events.[6]

In gambling, like fortune-telling, a future orientated activity, presence of
mind is achieved before, but not through the placing of the bet: 'gambling
generates by way of experiment the lightning-quick process of stimulation at the moment of danger, the marginal case in which presence of
mind becomes divination – that is to say, one of the highest, rarest
moments in life'.[7] If for Baudelaire time is a gambler, to gamble is also to
control time, to concentrate pleasure into a short period and thus to
achieve presence of mind. In Convolute O, Anatole France is cited:

what is gambling . . . but the art of producing in a second the changes that
Destiny ordinarily effects only in the course of many hours or even many
years, the art of collecting into a single instant the emotions dispersed
throughout the slow-moving existence of ordinary men, the secret of living
a whole lifetime in a few minutes. (O4a)[8]

France goes further to suggest that not only can the bet encompass a
whole life, but all material possessions:

The stake is money – in other words infinite possibilities . . . Perhaps the
next card turned, the ball now rolling, will give the player parks and gardens,
field and forests, castles and manors lifting heavenward their pointed turrets
and fretted roofs. Yes, that little bouncing ball holds within it acres of good
land . . . it contains treasures of art, marvels of taste, jewels of price, the most
exquisite bodies in all the world, nay! even souls – souls no one ever
dreamed were venal, all the decorations, all the distinctions, all the elegance,
and all the puissance of the world. (O4a)

But Benjamin feels that the full possibilities inherent within the time of
gambling have been missed by most commentators. Anatole France
focuses on the time of winning, rather than the anticipatory, speculative
time before the bet is placed. The anticipation of betting compresses time,
provoking the gambler's 'intoxication', but this intoxication is productive
of new constellations, which the gambler projects into the future:[9]

Such intoxication depends on the peculiar capacity of the game to provoke
presence of mind through the fact that, in rapid succession, it brings to the

fore constellations which work – each one wholly independent of the others – to summon up in every instance a thoroughly new, original reaction from the gambler. This fact is mirrored in the tendency of gamblers to place their bets, whenever possible, at the very last moment – the moment, moreover, when only enough room remains for a purely reflexive move. (O12a, 2)

Although Benjamin remarks that 'the gambler's reaction to chance' (that is the bet itself) 'is more like that of the knee to the hammer in the patellar reflex', this should be seen as more of a mechanical than a natural response, as gambling is a 'drastic expression' of the 'lack of consequences that defines the character of the isolated experience <*Erlebnis*>' (O12a, 1) (which we have discussed in 'Modernity/Modernism'): 'The ideal of the shock-engendered experience <*Erlebnis*> is the castastrophe. This becomes very clear in gambling: by constantly raising the stakes, in hopes of getting back what is lost, the gambler steers towards absolute ruin' (O14, 4). In his small way the gambler repeats the movement of the Angel of History. Thus, as with the shock experience that is *Erlebnis*, the intoxication induced by gambling is both disenabling – 'Only the future which has not entered as such into his consciousness is parried by the gambler' (O13, 2) – and productive – in creating the presence of mind that might, if it could see beyond the limited structure imposed by money and the commodity form, be able to think of genuinely new futures: 'What if one were to store up all the energy and passion ... which every year is squandered at the gaming tables of Europe?' (O13a,5).[10] As Miriam Hansen suggests, the 'rare gift of proper gambling pursued – and misused – by individuals in a hermetically isolated manner and for private gain, becomes a model of mimetic innervation for a collective that seems to have all but lost, literally, its senses; which lacks that bodily presence of mind that could yet turn the threatening future into a fulfilled "now"'.[11]

Convolute O pursues gambling and prostitution as dialectical images (on which see 'Method'). Like the other convolutes that link more than one characteristic of Paris in the nineteenth century the relationship between those characteristics – in the case of O, the desires or pleasures that connect them – cannot be reduced to one thing. Rather, each concept is represented as a constellation. Thus, gambling is represented in relation to its historical emergence as a bourgeois pursuit in the aftermath of the Napoleonic wars, its prohibition and then regulation at the same time as the *Bourse* institutionalized betting on the stock market. Prostitution is represented in relation to its specific forms in nineteenth-century Paris and the state's attempts to regulate public sexuality. Benjamin's invocation of the divine, however, suggests that those manifestations are not historically inevitable. The commodity form imposes its temporality on pleasure/desire. For example, although the essence of gambling is uncertainty, it organizes uncertainty into knowable, albeit limited, structures: 'Isn't there a certain structure of money that can be recognized only by fate, and a certain structure of fate that can be recognised only by money?' (O3, 6). But these structures of desire, as mysteries, contain the possibility of other forms of pleasure, and perhaps other forms of pleasure than those known by nineteenth-century capitalism. Pleasure begets pleasure. One kind of intoxication can lead to another. Engels is cited on French wine: 'with a few bottles you can pass through . . . all intermediate stages from the Musard quadrille to the Marseillaise, from the mad gaiety of the cancan to the wild ardor of revolutionary fever' (O9a, 5).

The historical and geographical reasons for linking gambling and prostitution are that both were associated with the arcades. But the Convolute's opening paragraph makes the connection poetically in the form of a brief piece of fiction, in which the gambler takes the part of the protagonist. That the prostitute is not the protagonist, except by her association with the gambler, raises the issue of gender in the *Arcades Project*: how, or perhaps whether, its structure, its particular form, is gendered. All Benjamin's city figures, the idler, the gambler, the brooder, the student, the collector and the flâneur are masculine. The prostitute is the one exception. Only two sections in Convolute O give a voice to prostitutes, and one of those is the ventriloquized voice of pornography (O8, 2), found *merkwürdig*, 'noteworthy', because this example brings together the theological and the obscene. In the rest of the convolute, the allegorical figure of the prostitute has an ambivalent position that never realizes itself as subject, while the allegorical figure of the gambler takes the stage as an agent of transformation:

> Hasn't his eternal vagabondage everywhere accustomed him to reinterpreting the image of the city? And doesn't he transform the arcade into a casino, into a gambling den, where now and again he stakes the red, blue, yellow *jetons* of feeling on women, on a face that suddenly surfaces (will it return his look?), on a mute mouth (will it speak?). (O1, 1)

Consciously or unconsciously, Benjamin's 'fiction' sets up a series of correspondences with the great works of modernist prose. The most significant work here for Benjamin was Marcel Proust's *In Search of Lost Time*. But this is just one instance of texts which themselves respond to the city through a series of linguistic constellations, projecting form on to chaotic and unknowable cityscapes. Chance and the arbitrary nature of the city encounter are responded to with internally coherent forms that are themselves arbitrary. In these worlds, as in what was for Benjamin the original modernist creation, Baudelaire's *Fleurs du mal*, encounters with prostitutes are both arbitrary and systematic. Modern prostitution is produced by the economic forces that create the capitalist city in the first place. But the actual encounter between the two participants is down to chance. Their significance is complex, with elements of fantasy, desire, pleasure, anxiety, guilt, shame, indifference, regulation and exploitation. In Benjamin's emblematic encounter, however, it is the gaze the gambler directs at the woman he finds to be 'his type' that constitutes his subjectivity.

> What, on the baize cloth, looks out at the gambler from every number –
> luck, that is – here, from the bodies of all the women, winks at him as the
> chimera of sexuality: as his type. This is nothing other than the number,
> the cipher, in which just at that moment luck will be called by name, in order
> to jump immediately to another number. His type – that's the number that
> pays off thirty-six fold, the one on which, without even trying, the eye of the
> voluptuary falls, as the ivory ball falls into the red or black compartment.
> (O1, 1)

That gaze opens up a whole other set of fictional correspondences in modernist literature from Baudelaire's 'A une passante' onwards where the gaze, met or unmet, constitutes a (usually masculine) subjectivity. But for Benjamin, the network of desiring gazes constitutes the arcades as spectacle as much as the gazes are themselves a product of the city's spectacular spaces. According to one of Benjamin's key sources, F. F. A. Béraud, prostitution produces a 'sort of phantasmagoria' in 'the comings and goings of these women along a routine circuit, which has the effect of multiplying them to infinity' (O6a, 2). In the context of prostitution's regulation at the end of the 1830s, the selling of commodities and of sex as commodity are both done through visual signals:

> *filles publiques* are installed as milliners, seamstresses, sellers of perfume,
> and the like. Women who work in these stores and shops will station them-
> selves at open doors or windows in order to send signals to passersby . . .
> There are others more ingenious who close their doors and windows but
> send signals through glass panes unprovided with curtains; or the curtains
> are left open just enough to permit easy communication between outside
> and interior . . . All these shops are found in the arcades.[12] (O5a, 1)

Gambling and prostitution meet in their investment in the speculative gaze. In Benjamin's fiction the gambler and the prostitute actually meet:

He leaves the Palais-Royal with bulging pockets, calls to a whore, and once more celebrates in her arms the communion with number, in which money and riches, absolved from every earthen weight, have come to him from the fates like a joyous embrace returned to the full. For in gambling hall and bordello, it is the same supremely sinful delight: to challenge fate in pleasure (O1, 1).

Their encounter, which takes the gambler from *les jeux* (gaming) to *la joie* (the joy of winning) to potential *jouissance* gives to sexual pleasure the place reserved for revolution elsewhere: a messianic moment that breaks free from history's predestined path of liberal progress. In what is a familiar part of Benjamin's methodology in the *Arcades Project*, the everyday is the outward sheath of the marvellous and the extraordinary, the possibility of something other than what is. But the next three sentences develop the enigma that the convolute offers to elucidate, offering it first as a religious mystery:

> Let unsuspecting idealists imagine that sensual pleasure, of whatever stripe, could ever determine the theological concept of sin. The origin of true lechery is nothing else but this stealing of pleasure from out of the course of life with God, whose convenant with such life resides in the name. The name itself is the cry of naked lust [*nacktes Lust*]. This sober thing, fateless in itself – the name – knows no other adversary than the fate that takes its place in whoring and that forges its arsenal in superstition. (O1, 1)

It is 'the name' here that offers the mystery. It appears to refer to the manifestation of 'luck' referred to earlier in the passage in 'the number, the cipher, in which at just that moment luck will be called by name'. But the idea of naming also relates to Benjamin's earlier theory of language in which the names of things have a divine mystical relationship with the things themselves (discussed in 'Magic' above). Here the name is both arbitrary – the lucky number – and connected to a concept of the eternal, pleasure 'stolen from out of the course of life with God'. But this is the theology of damnation rather than redemption. Baudelaire, in 'Le Jeu', a poem referred to but not cited in the *Arcades* (O13a, 5), describes those who 'soûl de son sang, préférait en somme / La douleur à la mort et l'enfer au néant!' 'drunk on blood, prefer, in sum / Suffering to death and Hell to nothingness!'.[13] The gambler's superstitious belief in fate and in the prostitute as 'his type' acts as a way of controlling the unregulated pleasures that are available in nineteenth-century Paris.

However, the analogy of the temporality of gambling with prostitution is not necessarily a good one. As in Benjamin's revealing fiction of the gambler and the prostitute, the equivalent state of mind to *Geistesgegen-*

wart is the anticipatory moment experienced by the punter before the encounter, the choosing of the object of desire for perfect pleasure, where ideal sex corresponds to the ideal win. In Benjamin's opening fiction the win buys the sex. But in a failure to appreciate the different positions of the punter and the prostitute, Benjamin appears to include the prostitute herself in this temporality. The fiction concludes: 'Thus in gambler and prostitute that superstition which arranges the figures of fate and fills all wanton behaviour with fateful forwardness, fateful concupiscence, bringing even pleasure to kneel before its throne' (O1, 1). It might be countered that the prostitute, like the idler, the gambler, the student, the collector, the brooder and the flâneur, is an allegorical figure. However, these other characters in Benjamin's urban panorama are all allegories of subjectivity. Each embodies and acts out one of the *Project's* complex concepts, existing only in relation to the constellation of citations that forms the individual convolute and the *Project* as a whole. The prostitute by contrast is an allegory not of a subjectivity but of an object and a practice. Even if we reread 'the gambler' and 'the prostitute' as figurative, representations of a future orientated consciousness, they are not equivalent. The prostitute here takes up the position of the bet in relation to the gambler's subjectivity. When Benjamin writes in the key paragraph on thresholds (see 'Modernity/Modernism') that 'Prostitutes . . . love the thresholds of . . . dream gates' (O2a, 1), the word 'love' seems to refer to the exploited women who emerge gradually in the latter passages of Convolute O, whereas it should more properly be applied to a masculine imagination that loves to position the figure of the prostitute at the gateway to fantasy.[14]

As a consequence, the discussion of sexuality in the convolute becomes one which is highly gendered, and the use of prostitution as a figure for sexual relations in nineteenth-century capitalism almost entirely elides women's agency: 'Love for the prostitute is the apotheosis of empathy for the commodity' (O11a, 4). There is no equivalent moment of anticipatory consciousness to that gifted to the gambler. That said, the metaphor works in a way that involves Benjamin's usual complex handling and provides at least a starting point for an alternative approach to the history of sexuality. Convolute O traces the particular forms in which sex is commodified. Benjamin picks out the example of prostitutes advertising cures for sexually transmitted diseases to illustrate interlinking of sexual and medical discourses (O1, 5). He explores the relationship between bourgeois morality and payment for sex, so that shame after the event extracts more money from the punter than the price of the service itself

(O1a, 4). The role of masquerade in public sexuality (O2, 1–2) has a dia-
logic relationship with the discussion of fashion in Convolute B. Hence,
the unexpected reappearance of the history of decorative shawls in
Parisian society (see O8a, 2 – O9a, 3). The spur of sex as commodity to
new technologies of contraception is noted as a parallel to industrial
innovation. To this extent, the spread of prostitution 'less as the opposite
than as the decline of love' has a 'revolutionary aspect' in its ability to
shatter earlier social bonds. Benjamin writes that 'this decline fuses, as
though of its own accord, with the very same aspect in the decline of the
arcades' (O2, 3). In the dream of prostitution it is possible to precipitate
an awakening – a potential new era of social relations.[15]

The situation in the nineteenth century is seen as a systematization of
prostitution as the norm of public sexuality. Béraud's extensive discussion in *Les Filles publiques de Paris et la police qui les régit* illustrates the
involvement of the state in even the most minute details of the sex trade.
The most radical element of the discussion is the recognition of prostitution as labour so that the familiar citations about the fickleness of
womankind (e.g. O1a, 1) are followed by the recognition, subsequently
supported by feminist histories of prostitution, that there was no clear
division between 'unrespectable' prostitutes and 'respectable' working-
class women. Prostitution existed on a spectrum, with gifts from lovers at
one end, extra money for treats and holidays in the middle to a full-time
occupation at the other (O6, 2). The economic necessity that institution-
alizes prostitution and the superexploitation it involves is made clear by
its description by nineteenth-century factory workers as the 'Xth working
hour' (O10, 1)[16] or the 'fifth quarter of their day' (O10, 6).[17] If the stock
exchange brings the logic of the casino to the economy (O4, 1),[18] prostitution brings the labour relations of the factory to sexual intercourse.

Gambling and sexual pleasure are brought together in two excerpts
from an essay by Edmund Bergler, 'On the psychology of the gambler' in
Imago.[19] In its juxtaposition with the other excerpt in the convolute, these
citations offer a psychoanalytical account of gambling as 'the only occasion when the pleasure principle, and the omnipotence of its thoughts
and desires, need not be renounced, and on which the reality principle
offers no advantages over it' (O11, 2).[20] Bergler sees gambling as ultimately a masochistic, self-destructive impulse, but the quotation he uses
from Ernst Simmel's essay on the psychology of the gambler suggests that
a kind of polymorphous sexuality is briefly achieved:

> Thus, in the last analysis, the passion for gambling satisfies the claim of the
> bisexual ideal, which the narcissist discovers in himself; at stake is the for-

mation of a compromise between masculine and feminine, active and passive, sadistic and masochistic; and in the end it is the unresolved decision between genital and anal libido that confronts the gambler in the well known symbolic colours of red and black. The passion for gambling thus serves an autoerotic satisfaction, wherein betting is foreplay, winning is orgasm, and losing is ejaculation, defecation, and castration. (O11a, 1)[21]

The meaning of this for Benjamin would seem to be, given the citation that follows, that capitalism makes 'erotic freedom' possible and renders '"conjugal slavery"... unendurable' (O11a, 2), but the possibility of new formations of pleasure is visible only in such degraded forms offered by prostitution and gambling. [22] Ernst Simmel's account might lead us to reinterpret the original encounter between gambler and prostitute, with which Convolute O begins. The prostitute as seen by the gambler is no more than another opportunity for autoerotic satisfaction. 'His type' is his own desires made manifest. Thus, the search for satisfaction in the dream world of the nineteenth century is doomed to failure. But this is not to say even within the closed circle of masculine desire, 'drunk on blood, prefer, in sum / Suffering to death and Hell to nothingness!', there is not a world of erotic freedom which might be awakened. The women in which he sees himself are given just one satirical paragraph. The *Pétition des filles publiques de Paris à MM. Le Préfet de police* alludes not just to the hypocrisy that constructs the institution but to its function as a mirror for the male ego:

> The business in itself is unfortunately quite ill-paid, but with the competition of other women and of elegant ladies, who pay no taxes, it has become wholly unprofitable. Or are we all the more blameworthy because we take cash while they take cashmere shawls? The city charter guarantees personal freedom to everyone; if our petition to Monsieur le Préfet proves unavailing, then we shall apply to the Chambers. Otherwise, it would be better to live in the kingdom of Golconda,[23] where girls of our sort formed one of the forty-four divisions of the populace and, as their sole responsibility, had only to dance before the king – which service we are prepared to render His Honor the prefect, should he ever wish it. (O10, 5)[24]

Notes

1 Walter Benjamin, the section 'Madame Ariane: second courtyard on the left', in 'One-way street', p. 482.
2 A discussion of Baudelaire and gambling is offered in 'On some motifs in Baudelaire', pp. 329–32. For a full discussion of Benjamin's understanding of *Spiel*, including *Hasardspiel*, see Miriam Hansen, 'Room-for-play: Benjamin's

gamble with cinema', *October*, 109 (2004), 3–45.

3 Baudelaire, 'L'Horloge', in *The Flowers of Evil: A New Translation with Parallel French Text*, trans. James McGowan (Oxford: Oxford University Press, 1998), pp. 160–2. Translation modified.

4 On this concept see Hansen, 'Room-for-play', p. 10.

5 Walter Benjamin, 'The path to success, in thirteen theses' [1928], in *SW 2*, pp. 144–7 (p. 147).

6 Benjamin, the section 'Madame Ariane: Second Courtyard on the Left', in 'One-way street', pp. 482–3.

7 Walter Benjamin, 'Notes on a theory of gambling' [1930], in *SW 2*, pp. 297–8 (p. 298).

8 Anatole France, *Le Jardin d'épicure* (Paris: n.pub., 1895).

9 This is reminiscent of that which Benjamin saw as the surrealists' 'most particular task', to 'win the energies of intoxication for the revolution', 'Surrealism', p. 216.

10 Cited from Ludwig Börne, 'Das Gastmahl der Spieler', in *Gesammelte Schriften* (Hamburg and Frankfurt am Main: n.pub., 1862), vol. 3, pp. 38–9. The citation also appears (albeit in a slightly different translation) in 'On some motifs in Baudelaire', p. 330.

11 Hansen, 'Room-for-play', p. 10. The citation from Benjamin comes from the 'Madame Ariane' section of 'One-way street', p. 483.

12 Cited from F. F. A. Béraud, *Les Filles publiques de Paris et la police qui les régit*, vol. 2 (Paris and Lepizig: n.pub., 1839), pp. 152–3.

13 See also Benjamin's comment that 'Gambling is the infernal counterpart to the music of the heavenly hosts' (O10a, 6). 'Le Jeu' is also briefly discussed in 'On some motifs in Baudelaire', p. 330.

14 One might compare the use of the prostitute as a figure for the threshold between bourgeois home and public sphere in 'A Berlin chronicle'.

15 As in the 'Exposé of 1935': 'Every epoch, in fact, not only dreams the one to follow it but, in dreaming, precipitates its awakening' (p. 13).

16 Cited from Karl Marx, *Der historische Materialismus*, ed. Landshut and Mayer (Leipzig: n.pub., 1932), p. 318.

17 Cited from Jean Journet, *Poésies et chants harmoniens* (Paris: La Librairie Universelle de Joubert, 1857), p. lxxxi (Editor's Preface)

18 Cited from Paul Lafargue, 'Die Ursachen des Gottesglaubens', *Die Neue Zeit*, 1 (1906), 512.

19 Edmund Bergler, 'Zur Psychologie des Hasardspielers', *Imago*, 22: 4 (1936).

20 Cited from Bergler, 'Zur Psychologie', p. 440.

21 The original of this quotation is drawn from Ernst Simmel, 'Zur Psychoanalyse des Spielers', *Internationale Zeitschrift für Psychoanalyse*, 6 (1920), 397. Benjamin finds it in (and cites it from) Bergler, 'Zur Psychologie', pp. 409–10.

22 The entire section reads as follows: 'With the discovery of Tahiti, declares

Fourier, with an example of an order in which "large-scale industry" is compatible with erotic freedom, "conjugal slavery" has become unendurable' (O11a, 2).

23 An Indian city famed for its wealth. 'Chambers' refers to the French Parliament.

24 From *Pétition des filles publiques de Paris à MM. Le Préfet de police etc., redigée par Mlle. Pauline et apostillé par MM. les épiciers, cabaretiers, limonadiers et marchands de comestibles de la capitale . . .*, cited in Friedrich von Raumer, *Briefe aus Paris und Frankreich im Jahre 1830*, vol. 1(Leipzig: n.pub., 1831), pp. 206–7.

~

Idleness

The bourgeois have very good grounds for falsely ascribing supernatural creative power to labour, since precisely from the fact that labour depends on nature, it follows that the man who possesses no other property than his labour power must, in all conditions of society and culture, be the slave of other men who have made themselves owners of the material conditions of labour. (Karl Marx, 'Notes to the [Gotha] Programme of the German Workers' Party' (X5, 1))[1]

Benjamin's elaboration of the concept of idleness covers three key areas. First, idleness can be productive, akin to Keats's diligent indolence both as not-work and as an alternative form of creative activity. Second, idleness as a form of anti-work becomes useful rather than instrumental in the sense of use described by William Morris in his distinction between 'useful work' and 'useless toil'.[2] Third, the recognition that in all societies, excepting perhaps the semi-mythical realm of Benjamin's reconstructed primitive communism, the space and time to think have depended upon a brutal division of labour.

A note on translation[3]

Benjamin's chosen term for the concept he explores in Convolute m of the *Arcades Project* is *Müßiggang*, although the convolute also includes the more pejorative *das Indolenz* or *l'indolence*, and *Faulheit* (which is closer to laziness) and the French *l'oisiveté*. *Müßiggang* is a literary term derived from *Muße*, 'leisure', and *Gang*, 'walk, course or passage'. It might be translated literally as 'idle walk', the mode in which Benjamin's urban characters, for example, the flâneur, saunter through the arcades and the appropriate pace for thumbing through the *Arcades Project* itself. A related word is *Müßigkeit*, meaning 'futility' or 'pointlessness'. Paradoxically, *das Muße* stems from the same etymological root as *das Muß*, meaning necessity, an origin which suggests the kind of linguistic ambivalence discussed by Freud in relation to words such as *heimlich*, both 'homely', 'intimate', 'familiar' and 'secret', 'secretive', 'kept from sight'.[4] *Muße* incorporates a sense of its opposite, the necessity of work. While Benjamin never comments explicitly on this root, Convolute m is exemplary in its form as an attempt to represent a complex of political, philosophical and aesthetic problems for which the concept of *Müßiggang* stands as the starting point for critical and creative thinking.

Proverbs

Idleness is proverbial: in English 'the devil makes work for idle hands'; in German '*Müßiggang ist alle Laster Anfang*' (Idleness is the beginning of all sins). By its nature it does not lend itself to the continuity or sequence that Benjamin sees as a requirement of *Erfahrung* (see m2a, 4; we have discussed *Erfahrung* – long, considered or reflective experience – in 'Modernity/Modernism'). It is epigrammatic. Its mode has all the pleasures of uncertainty. Yet this does not mean that it is unproductive. Idleness, Benjamin suggests, is both not-work and anti-work: it involves a resistance to the Calvinist work ethic (m3a, 1) and to Taylorism (M10, 1). But idleness might also be its opposite, the possibility of a different kind of work, which would not be work as bourgeois society, or indeed the German Social Democrats, understood it. Idleness is premonitory of unalienated work, which only becomes a possibility, according to Marx in the 'Critique of the Gotha Programme':

> In a higher phase of communist society, after the enslaving subordination of the individual to the division of labor, and therewith also the antithesis between mental and physical labour, has vanished; after labor has become not only a means of life but life's chief necessity. (X5, 3)[5]

This is the kind of distinction William Morris made when he wrote: 'the ideal of the future does not point to a lessening of men's energy by the reduction of labour to a minimum, but rather to the reduction of *pain in labour* to a minimum'.[6] The theme of replacing alienated labour with pleasurable, satisfying work is part of a tradition in popular and socialist writing that runs from the medieval idea of Cockaigne through Charles Fourier, Karl Marx and George Orwell to Herbert Marcuse. It includes E. P. Thompson's work on the temporality of pre-capitalist forms of work-time and his analysis of the time discipline that is integral to industrialisation.[7] More recently the work of André Gorz and eco-socialist politics have refused to accept a bourgeois work ethic as the norm.[8] Convolute m should be read in relation to that tradition of socialist critique.

Idleness is both a temporality and a sensibility. As a temporality it can be imposed by modernity as 'enforced idleness', but as a sensibility it might be cultivated in opposition to modernity's most deadening forms. Benjamin quotes Rousseau: 'The idleness [*l'oisiveté*] of society is deadly because it is obligatory; the idleness of solitude is delightful because it is free and voluntary' (m4, 1).

Modes of idleness

Convolute m takes a long view (that of 'long experience' or *Erfahrung*), a view that requires time and leisure. Behind the collage of excerpts which gives it its form lies a historicist account that the convolute both recognizes and then supersedes. A Marxian narrative of development takes the reader through three modes of production, for which Benjamin finds corresponding modes of idleness. In the first section of the convolute (m1), excerpts on ancient, feudal and capitalist modes of idleness stand in sequence at paragraphs m1, 1, m1, 2 and m1, 3. Outside the sequence stand two alternative modes of idleness, primitive and post-capitalist, which call the historicist account into question. Unlike the first three, these two are not directly accessible. Primitive idleness is available only through its residues in the present. Future idleness can be anticipated only through the traces of possibility that exist in the present or what Benjamin elsewhere calls *Jetztzeit*, 'now-time'. Both these modes explode the antitheses of work and not-work and cannot be bound by a determinate class history.

Idleness as form

The structure of Convolute m is not and cannot be finished or complete, because such a form would be incompatible with idleness itself, the definition of which involves *Unabschließbarkeit* 'unfinishability' (which is also, for Benjamin, one of the characteristics of intellectual work) (m2a, 1). But as we have already described above in 'Method', Convolute m is, in terms of the *Arcades Project* as a whole, exemplary in its technique, in so far as it attempts to bring the concept of idleness to consciousness through its form. Each section rewrites the preceding sections often by means of a repetition that subtly changes its meaning. Thus, although short in comparison to other convolutes, it cannot be rushed. It calls for an idle pace and a high degree of distraction.

The effect of the convolute's structure offers a discrete example of one of the aims of the *Arcades Project* as a whole: to convey the relationship between a determinate and a dialectical approach to history or what might be called enforced work and productive intellectual work. The accounts of different modes of idleness, ripped from their literary and historical context then placed in the collage of the convolute, are chosen and positioned in such as way as to tease out their contradictions. The first excerpt begins with the ancient world, which is cited, apparently favourably, as a counter-example to the protestant work ethic:[9] 'Noteworthy conjunction: in ancient Greece, practical labour is branded and proscribed. Although essentially left in the hands of slaves, it is condemned not least because it betrays a base aspiration for earthly goods (riches)' (m1, 1). The ideal of 'studious leisure', valued by the Greeks, looks back to primitive idleness and forward to a future of unalienated work. But Benjamin's commentary on his source, Pierre-Maxime Schuhl, brings to light the central contradiction: ancient idleness is bought at the expense of a class of slaves. There is, in effect, no going back to a golden age of intellectual work. Its legitimation must take into account the division of labour on which it depends.

In the second excerpt, on feudal idleness, both the active and the contemplative life are bound to the wheel of fortune; but, while both lives are subject to it, idleness permits a greater freedom, bound, 'immobile' to the centre of the wheel rather than to its outer edge. The intellectual life already permits a separation from the realm of necessity. But under capitalism, as observed by Sainte-Beuve and Marx, the class of 'connoisseurs and amateurs' – who, in the *Arcades Project*, always appear as relics of an earlier time – has 'practically disappeared' (m1, 3). In bourgeois society, according to Marx, industry is victorious over 'heroic laziness [*Faulheit*]' (m1a, 1). In a scenario familiar now even to the formerly leisured professions, idleness ceases to be a privilege and exists only as a form of resistance.

Idleness under capitalism

The intervention of Marx (m1a, 1) initiates a new section in the Convolute, in which the concept of redemptive idleness is introduced, a concept found, like so many of Benjamin's critical terms, in the work of

Charles Baudelaire. Baudelaire, reinventor of a notion of the heroic for modernity, seeks to salvage idleness for the nineteenth century: 'In the figure of the Dandy, Baudelaire seeks to find some use for idleness, just as leisure once had some use' (m1a, 2). Just as Benjamin finds a dialectical conception of modernity in Baudelaire's lyric poetry, he finds a dialectical relationship between idleness and 'toil' in the process of creative work he undertakes:

> Baudelaire is familiar with the 'indolence naturelle des inspirés'; Musset – so he says – never understood how much work it takes 'to let a work of art emerge from a daydream' . . . Barrès claimed that he could recognize 'in every little word of Baudelaire a trace of the toil that helped him achieve such great things'.[10]

In Part III of 'The Paris of the Second Empire in Baudelaire', Benjamin cites 'Le Soleil' as sole example of a poem where the poet is shown at his 'labours':

> Je vais m'exercer seul à ma fantasque escrime
> Flairant dans tous les coins les hasards de la rime
> Trébuchant sur les mots comme sur les pavés
> Heurtant parfois des vers depuis longtemps rêvés
>
> (I go out alone to practise my fantastical fencing, / Scenting opportunities for rhyme òn every streetcorner, / Stumbling over words as though they were cobblestones, / Sometimes knocking up against verses dreamed long ago.)[11]

For Benjamin, Baudelaire, as heroic idler of the modern age, becomes an example of the intellectual as guerilla, fighting to reconfigure modernity in the face of the imposition of a new regime of work. The relationship between the outlaw intellectual and commodity culture is summed up in the following paragraph of Convolute m, which consists solely of the epigrammatic '*Erfahrung* is the outcome of work; *Erlebnis* is the phantasmagoria of the idler [*Die Erfahrung ist der Ertrag der Arbeit, das Erlebnis ist die Phantasmagorie des Müßiggängers*]' (m1a, 3), a sentence that condenses the Convolute down to a single phrase, but which, for that reason, needs some unpacking.[12]

Like the proverbs cited above, the epigram appears at first to oppose a positive with a negative: work, leading to full and connected experience (*Erfahrung*) is a positive; idleness, leading to the distracted and fragmented experience (*Erlebnis*) that characterizes a phantasmagoric modernity, is a negative. But the sentence reverses the expected moral opposition. *Erlebnis* is the phantasmagoria experienced by the idler, the

idler does not produce it himself or herself. Shock experience, paradoxically, is produced by work or, more precisely, alienated labour, as well as
being the fragmented experience of the city under capitalism: 'The shock
experience [*Erlebnis*] which the passer-by has in the crowd corresponds
to the isolated "experiences" of the worker at his machine.'[13] Whereas the
worker is, at least for the duration of the working day, bound to the
machine, the phantasmagoria of the city of consumption presents the
urban idler with the possibility of a new kind of work, although that very
possibility is, for the time being at least, dependent on the worker's
bondage. Two divergent outcomes are possible: Baudelaire's model of
creative idleness or a 'new field of force in the form of planning' (m1a, 4).
Against the latter is juxtaposed the idea of 'total *Erlebnis*' for which the
correlate is total war (m1a, 5).

The trace

The alternative to total *Erlebnis*, which Benjamin suggests involves an
empathy with exchange value, is a form of idleness appropriate to historical enquiry – the pursuit of the *Spur* or trace.[14] The introduction of the
trace opens a new section of the Convolute, m2, which now completes the
break with a historicist narrative. The idea of the trace offers the possibility of breaking out of the degraded experience of modernity. The traces
of the past might be found in the present, while the configurations of the
future might be found in the hidden aspects of modernity. Ironically,
the very distractedness (*Zerstreuung*) induced by *Erlebnis* might also
create the right mode to hunt and collect the traces of past and future.
The hunter, as both primitive and modern figure, must cultivate a kind of
distracted attention:

> Whoever follows traces must not only pay attention; above all, he must have
> given heed already to a great many things. (The hunter must know about the
> hoof of the animal whose trail he is on; he must know the hour when that
> animal goes to drink; he must know the course of the river to which it turns,
> and the location of the ford by which he himself can get across.) In this way
> there comes into play the peculiar configuration by dint of which *Erfahrung*
> appears translated into the language of *Erlebnis*. (m2, 1)

The figure of the hunter now appears as one who practised the earliest
mode of idleness, one which was, at the same time, unalienated work:[15]
'*Erfahrungen* can, in fact, prove invaluable to one who follows a trace –
but *Erfahrungen* of a particular sort. The hunt is the one type of work
in which they function intrinsically. And the hunt is, as work, very prim-

itive' (m2, 1). Tracing the residues of the hunt in the present – and not unusually with Benjamin the method is the same as the hoped for outcome – allows the possibility of future configurations of unalienated work:

> The experiences <*Erfahrungen*> of one who attends to a trace result only very remotely from any work activity, or are cut off from such a procedure altogether. (Not for nothing do we speak of 'fortune hunting.') They have no sequence and no system. They are a product of chance, and have about them the essential interminability that distinguishes the preferred obligations of the idler (m2, 1).

In the modern world, the hunter is replaced by the student. Study, properly conceived, represents for Benjamin the form of resistant intellectual work appropriate to his times. He connects the primitive hunter with the modern student as harbinger of the future: 'The fundamentally unfinished collection of things worth knowing, whose utility depends upon chance, has its prototype in study' (m2, 1).[16] 'The text is a forest in which the reader is hunter. Rustling in the underbrush – the idea, the skittish prey, the citation – another piece "in the bag"' (m2a, 1). Benjamin's conception of an ideal life of study goes back to an early essay written during his participation in the German student movement, 'The life of students', where intellectual work is seen as antithetical to professionalism or a vocation: 'scholarship, far from leading inexorably to a profession, may in fact preclude it. For it does not permit you to abandon it; in a way, it places the student under an obligation to become a teacher, but never to embrace the official professions of doctor, lawyer, or university professor.'[17] In opposition to the bourgeois profession, idleness has a relationship to a form of privileged decadence, where the spaces of decadence, for example the bachelor's studio, are connected to sexual libertinism or experimentation: 'the *studio* became a sort of pendant to the *boudoir*' (m2, 3).

Individual creativity, that which makes intellectual work possible, however, is at odds with the general idleness that pervades commodity culture and which is visible in journalism, the mass entertainment and the alienated experience of routine work. Section m2a introduces the modern conditions that require idleness as a 'form of work preparedness', specifically, 'the news service and nightlife' (m2a, 2). These are socially enforced forms of idleness. Reportage and the feuilleton reflect *Erlebnis*. In response, the individual idleness of the poet is anti-work as defined by the Calvinist ethic: 'Idleness seeks to avoid any sort of tie to the idler's line of work, and ultimately to the labour process in general. That distin-

guishes it from leisure' (m3, 1). In the face of the enforced 'atrophy of experience' imposed by commodity production and the phantasmagoria of the modern city, the urban idler has to resort to guerilla tactics. As Benjamin remarks in Convolute M, 'The flâneur': 'the idleness of the flâneur is a demonstration against the division of labour' (M5, 8).

Section m4 of the convolute begins the dialectical synthesis where socially enforced idleness is countered by its knowing appreciation: 'Idleness can be considered an early form of distraction or amusement. It consists in the readiness to savour, on one's own, an arbitrary succession of sensations' (m4, 1). Significantly, this is distinguished by Benjamin from mass culture: 'But as soon as the production process began to draw large masses of people into the field, those who "had the time" [*frei hatten*] came to feel a need to distinguish themselves en masse from labourers' (m4, 1). Modern idlers attempt a kind of partial transcendence – imitating the gods – that temporarily overcomes the shock experience of modernity: 'The idler's *imitatio dei*: as flâneur, he is omnipresent; as gambler, he is omnipotent; and as student, he is omniscient' (m4, 3). These are both real and ideal types. Their ambitions are for transcendence, their reality is a partial success in combating its opposite, empathy, which synchronizes itself with shock experience without challenging it. Their individual idleness, 'in a bourgeois society that knows no leisure, is the precondition of artistic production', a prefiguring of unalienated work not otherwise available under capitalism: 'idleness is the very thing that stamps that production with the traits that make its relation to the production process so drastic' (m4a, 4).

The final section of m completes the dialectic by bringing modern idleness back into relation with the historical traces that allow it to achieve its full meaning and to gesture to its potential. The limitations of the modern idler's perspective are described in terms of Hegel's 'bad infinity', a false transcendence; but there is an open-endedness, an unfinishedness, to idleness that means that it cannot be curtailed by a Hegelian dialectic:

> The student 'never stops learning'; the gambler 'never has enough'; for the flâneur 'there is always something more to see'. Idleness has in view an unlimited duration, which fundamentally distinguishes it from simple sensuous pleasure of whatever variety. (m5, 1)

The convolute ends, incompletely, in the synthesis that brings together the hunter and the idler as one: 'The spontaneity common to the student, to the gambler; to the flâneur is perhaps that of the hunter – which is to say, that of the oldest type of work, which may be intertwined closest of all with idleness' (m5, 2). It mops up with four citations that allude to the historical sense that is needed to make that connection: Flaubert on the melancholic mind set that is needed to imagine the historical past; Baudelaire on the flâneur as modern savage; Spengler on the urban poor as nomads and the modern intellectual as "*intellectual nomad* [. . .] wholly microcosmic, wholly homeless, as free intellectually as hunter and herdsman were free sensually"' (m5, 6).[18] The utopian synthesis is that outlined by Benjamin in the Exposé of 1935:

> In the dream in which each epoch entertains images of its successor, the latter appears wedded to elements of prehistory – that is, to elements of a classless society. And the experiences of such a society – as stored in the collective unconscious of the collective – engender through interpenetration with what is new, the utopia that has left its trace in a thousand configurations of life, from enduring edifices to passing fashions.[19]

Benjamin's concept of idleness offers little comfort for nostalgic and conservative thinkers. But its utopianism is preserved in the belief that intellectual work, despite the most unpromising of environments, can presage a collective engagement in fulfilling, unalienated labour.

Notes

1 Cited from Karl Marx, *Randglossen zum Programme der deutschen Arbeiterpartei*, ed. Karl Korsch (Berlin and Leipzig: n.pub., 1922), p. 22. This passage is also cited in 'Modernity', Section III of 'The Paris of the Second Empire in Baudelaire', p. 42, and in 'On the concept of history', p. 393 (Thesis XI).
2 William Morris, 'Useful work versus useless toil', in A. L. Morton (ed.), *The Political Writings* (London: Lawrence and Wishart, 1973), pp. 86–109.
3 We are grateful to Elizabeth Harvey for her help and guidance on the translation of *Müßiggang*.
4 Sigmund Freud, 'The uncanny' [1919], in *Pelican Freud Library*, vol. 14, trans. J. Strachey (Harmondsworth: Penguin, 1985), pp. 335–76 (p. 341); the German *müssen*, comparable to the English 'must', achieves a sense of compulsion only in Middle High German, before that it is closer to *können* (can) or *dürfen* (to permit or allow).
5 Cited from Marx, *Randglossen*, p. 27.
6 William Morris, 'Review of Edward Bellamy's *Looking Backward*' [1889], in A. L. Morton (ed.), *The Political Writings* (London: Lawrence and Wishart, 1984), pp. 245–53 (p. 252).
7 E. P. Thompson, *Customs in Common* (London: Merlin, 1991).
8 See André Gorz, *Farwell to the Working Class: An Essay on Post-Industrial Socialism*, trans. Michael Sonenscher (London: Pluto, 1982) and *Paths to Paradise: On the Liberation from Work* (London: Pluto, 1985).

9 Oddly, Weber is not mentioned anywhere in the *Arcades Project*. The only work of Weber's to appear in Benjamin's 'Verzeichnis der gelesenen Schriften' (a list of books he had read) is 'Wissenschaft als Beruf' ('Science as a vocation'). See the 'Verzeichnis' in Benjamin, *Gesammelte Schriften*, vol. 7: 1, ed. Rolf Tiedemann and Hermann Schweppenhäuser (Frankfurt am Main: Suhrkamp, 1989), pp. 437–76 (p. 451).

10 Benjamin, 'The Paris of the Second Empire', pp. 39–40.

11 Benjamin, 'The Paris of the Second Empire', p. 40. We have quoted only the latter half of the section of the poem quoted in the text.

12 Throughout this entry we have, as in 'Modernity/modernism', maintained the original German for *Erfahrung* and *Erlebnis* when quoting from the *Arcades* and related texts. In the translations these are generally rendered as 'long experience' (sometimes 'connected experience') and 'immediate experience' respectively.

13 Benjamin, 'On some motifs in Baudelaire', p. 329.

14 *Die Spur* means both trace and spore in German.

15 There is, of course, a major problem with this vision of primitive communism in that, in its desire to seek an image of unalienated labour, it fails to see the gendered division of labour simply because it does not include women. This failure of vision has implications for Benjamin's conception of the urban savage, the flâneur, although his masculinist perspective is not always as easy to categorize as some accounts have suggested.

16 The unfinishability (*Unabschließbarkeit*) of unalienated labour does raise a question about the unfinished status of the *Arcades Project* itself. Did its method make it unfinishable?

17 Walter Benjamin, 'The life of students' [1915], in *SW 1*, pp. 37–47 (p. 38).

18 The idea of the modern savage is expanded at length in Convolute M, 'The flâneur'. See M11a, 5 to M14, 3 and *passim*.

19 Benjamin, 'Exposé of 1935', pp. 4–5.

Night

As an inevitable by-product of his eclecticism, Walter Benjamin has been convincingly claimed by many and opposing camps. In addition to the Marxist, the theological and the surrealist Benjamin, there is Benjamin the proto-post-structuralist, Benjamin the latent Romantic. And, in spite of the paucity of evidence, commentators as diverse as Margaret Cohen, Terry Eagleton, Esther Leslie, and Susan Buck-Morss, as well as many others, assert the affinities between Benjamin and Freud.[1] The existence of this psychoanalytically inspired Benjamin has become routinely accepted but rarely justified in any detail. This may largely be because the detail reveals fairly quickly the thinness of Benjamin's familiarity with psychoanalysis in general and with Freud's writings in particular. Whether or not Benjamin's acquaintance with psychoanalysis was anything other than nodding is more than pertinent to a reading of the *Arcades Project*, which rests heavily on the concept of the 'dream collective' and its dialectical counterpart, awakening. As early as the 'First sketches' for the *Arcades*, Benjamin describes 'the new, the dialectical method of doing history' as passing through 'with the intensity of a dream [. . .] what has been, in order to experience the present as the waking world to which the dream refers',[2] and in Convolute N, 'On the theory of knowledge', he says that 'the historian takes up . . . the task of dream interpretation [*die Aufgabe der Traumdeutung*]' when faced with what he calls 'dialectical images' (N4, 1).

Clearly, it would not be possible to talk about interpreting dreams in a metropolitan European context in the 1920s and 1930s without being aware of the heavy shadow of that other *Traumdeutung* (1899/1900), but, even though Benjamin gives passing recognition to psychoanalysis in his conception of dreams, the muddled and unsatisfactory formulations on the dreaming collective in the *Arcades* bear little resemblance to the highly systematic and fully developed theory worked out by Freud at the turn of the century. It is more accurate to say that Benjamin cobbled together his dream theory from the mystical musings of Ludwig Klages and the highly selective readings of Freud undertaken by Breton and Aragon (see 'Method' for the further influence of Proust and Marx on this awkward medley). This is not to say that there are no possible links to be made between Freud and Benjamin, but that they do not exist at an explicitly conceptual level.

Benjamin without Freud

Neither the *Arcades Project* nor biographical information betrays any evidence that Benjamin carried out a serious study of Freud or psycho-analysis. References to Freud are few and far between in the *Arcades*. When, in Convolute K, Benjamin invokes the 'psychoanalytic theory of memory' (K8, 1) as well as Freud's supposed 'definition of experience' (K8, 2), his source is not Freud but a book by Theodor Reik, *Surprise and the Psycho-analyst*. The citation of secondary, expository material is symptomatic, and nothing else in the *Arcades* serves to dispel the impression that Benjamin relied on handed-down accounts for his understanding of psychoanalysis. A case in point is the series of entries in Convolute O (on the psychology of the gambler) that we discussed in '*Jeux/ Joie/ Jouissance*'. As is so often the case in the *Arcades*, we cannot tell from the transcribed quotations what Benjamin thought of either Edmund Bergler or the source he quotes in turn, Ernst Simmel. In fact, the only part of these long quotations from Simmel and Bergler that attracts Benjamin's attention is Bergler's rather innocuous if enigmatic assertion that 'according to Freud, the sexuality of human beings bears the stamp of a function that dwindles' (O11, 1). Four entries later in this convolute, Benjamin repeats Bergler's statement, but, like a lazy undergraduate, elides the source, and now attributes the position directly to Freud. It is worth citing this entry at length because it is typical of Benjamin's use of psychoanalysis as a tool of analogy:

> Apropos of Freud's conjecture that sexuality is a dwindling function 'of' the human being, Brecht remarked on how the bourgeoisie in decline differs from the feudal class at the time of its downfall: it feels itself to be in all things the quintessence of humankind in general, and hence can equate its own decline with the death of humanity. (This equation, moreover, can play a part in the unmistakable crisis of sexuality within the bourgeoisie.) (O11a, 3)

Not only is there a slippage in attribution from Bergler to Freud but it is clear that for Benjamin the psychoanalytic insight is of value only if it can be brought to bear analogically on the analysis of political economy.

Benjamin's fondness for finding such parallels manifests itself more fully in Convolute R, 'Mirrors', where he argues that the social fact of the arcades undergoes 'sublimation' in the description of a fantastic underwater city found in Friedrich Gerstäcker's *Die versunkene Stadt* (1921):

> If a work of literature, an imaginative composition, could arise from repressed economic contents in the consciousness of a collective, as Freud says it can from sexual contents in an individual consciousness, then in the above description we would have before our eyes the consummate sublimation of the arcades, with their bric-à-brac growing rankly out of their showcases. (R2, 2)

Benjamin's fervent allegorical imagination seeks out correspondences, confidently finding analogies between sexual contents and economic ones, individual and 'collective' consciousnesses. But isn't such parallelism too neat, too hasty? Can it really be borne out, or is the transposition, dazzling in rhetorical terms, unworkable at a conceptual level? Can economic and psychological categories be so readily interchanged? Evidently not, since the above examples constitute the full range of Benjamin's direct references to Freudian psychoanalysis in the whole of the *Arcades*, a dearth of material which indicates a sporadic, even abortive endeavour on Benjamin's part.

An examination of Benjamin's correspondence with Adorno confirms that his study of Freud was, rather like his move to Palestine and study of Hebrew, always planned and promised, but never carried out.[3] In the exchange of letters Benjamin generally defers to Adorno on matters relating to psychoanalysis, while Adorno offers suggestions for reading. In December 1934, he recommends that Benjamin should look into Freud's papers on analysis, and in June 1935 he writes, 'You should definitely read everything you can by Freud or the extremely important Ferenczi concerning the anal personality and the anal problematic.'[4] 'I shall be looking at Freud soon,' Benjamin replies in June 1935 to acknowledge a task not yet undertaken, and then asks whether Adorno knows of any 'psychoanalytic study of waking'.[5] In his reply, the notorious Hornberg letter, Adorno (also see 'Awakening'), now showing signs of impatience, says he knows of no such literature and proceeds remarkably to dismiss 'all this dream-interpreting and newly emergent psychoanalysis' as merely an element of *Art Nouveau*.[6] Perhaps as an olive branch, in November 1936 Adorno then offers to exercise his influence in Vienna by setting up a meeting for Benjamin with Freud, 'Although one cannot count on any fruitful results from talking to him'.[7] The meeting did not take place, but then Benjamin's record of his own reading, the 'Verzeichnis der gelesenen

Schriften', indicates that at this point his most recent reading of Freud had been *Beyond the Pleasure Principle* around 1928. This text, number 1076 in Benjamin's list, is the only one by Freud to be found there during this period, although it reappears again at number 1680, which meant that Benjamin only got round to 'looking at Freud' around 1939.[8] It is additionally worth noting that the dream theory of the arcades dates from the earliest stages of the *Arcades Project*: the 'First sketches' from the period 1927–30 already contain many of Benjamin's formulations concerning both the dreaming condition and awakening. In other words, the dream framework was established well in advance of Benjamin's exchanges with Adorno about psychoanalysis.

Even though Benjamin did not appear to have much contact with Freud during the time he was working on the arcades (1927–40), he had in fact had a more sustained, if unfruitful, encounter with psychoanalytic writings during his student days. While at the University of Berne in 1917–18 he took various courses in psychology with Paul Häberlin (1878–1960), including one on 'Psychology of suggestive, hypnotic and occult phenomena', although he apparently felt he was wasting his time writing essays on this subject, and concentrated primarily on completing his dissertation on *The Concept of Criticism in German Romanticism*.[9] Gershom Scholem confirms that Benjamin extracted little of value from his psychoanalytic studies, explaining that his friend 'produced a detailed paper on Freud's libido theory, arriving at a negative judgment'.[10] It hardly needs saying that to arrive at a negative judgment of libido theory in 1917–18 did not involve swimming upstream. The 'Verzeichnis der gelesenen Schriften' reveals that around 1918 Benjamin read *Jokes and their Relation to the Unconscious* (number 540), 'On the Introduction of Narcissism' and the Schreber case-study (number 549), and *Five Lectures on Psychoanalysis* (number 609), presumably in conjunction with his courses with Häberlin.[11] Benjamin's exposure as a student to Freud, then, was patchy, and the 'Verzeichnis' records no further ventures into this area. Even though the 'Verzeichnis' does not necessarily register all Benjamin's reading, it is safe to say in light of other evidence that his first-hand experience of Freud's writing does not extend much further.

Neither biographical data nor textual evidence from the *Arcades* suggests that Freud interested Benjamin much. What, then, is the source of his reputation as a creative interlocutor of psychoanalysis? T. J. Clark remarks that 'Benjamin learned more about the logic of capitalism from a skim of Hugo Fischer and Otto Rühle than most of us ever shall from months in the Marx-Engels archive'.[12] Does the same rule apply to

Benjamin's encounter with Freud, whose concepts and terminology achieved widespread dissemination independently of his publications? It is true that, even in the absence of a close understanding of psychoanalysis, Benjamin was proficient at incorporating basic psychoanalytic vocabulary into his aphoristic style. Perhaps the most notable and oft-cited instance of such an incorporation is found in 'Little history of photography':

> Whereas it is a commonplace that, for example, we have some idea what is involved in the act of walking (if only in general terms), we have no idea at all what happens during the fraction of a second when a person actually takes a step. Photography, with its devices of slow motion and enlargement, reveals the secret. It is through [photography] that we first discover the existence of this optical unconscious, just as we discover the instinctual unconscious through psychoanalysis [*Von diesem Optisch-Unbewussten erfährt er erst durch sie, wie vom dem Triebhaft-Unbewussten durch die Psychoanalyse*].[13]

The phrasing – reproduced virtually word-for-word in the 'Work of art' essay – is so felicitous that we can easily be distracted from the improbable violence of that 'just as', yet another instance of the Benjaminian proclivity for discovering parallels, secret correspondences, and an echo of the all too rapid equation of sexual and economic sublimation in Convolute R.[14] However, in this instance, the shortcut betrays the writer. The unconscious invoked by Benjamin here bears little resemblance to the scandalous discovery of Freud, a rupture which forever undermines the security and sovereignty of consciousness. For Benjamin, the unconscious is simply a place which 'exists' and can be revealed or can reveal hitherto unknown things, a far cry from Freud's unconscious which is accessible only through its traces. Benjamin operates within a visual model in which there is an order of the unseen or not-seen, an order simply brought to light by virtue of photography. In a psychoanalytic schema, then, he comes closer to the distinction between the preconscious and the conscious, and leaves out the unconscious altogether.[15]

There is no denying the seductiveness of Benjamin's wording, and he might productively be called the philosopher of the 'just as' (*wie . . . so*), so typical of his thinking is this sort of analogical construction.[16] He may comment wistfully (by way of Alphonse Karr) that 'no one knows how to make mirrors any more' (R1, 7), but the *Arcades Project* energetically sets out to remedy that situation. A swift and by no means complete stroll through the *Arcades* throws up the following instances of more or less extravagant '*wie . . . so*' thinking:

Just as the first factory buildings cling to the traditional form of the residential dwelling, and just as the first automobile chassis imitate carriages, so in the clothing of the cyclist the sporting expression still wrestles with the inherited pattern of elegance. (B1, 2)

just as the slopes of Vesuvius, thanks to the layers of lava that cover them, have been transformed into paradisal orchards, so the lava of revolutions provides uniquely fertile ground for the blossoming of art, festivity, fashion. (C1, 6)

Just as waiting seems to be the proper state of the impassive thinker, doubt appears to be that of the flâneur. (M4a, 1)

Just as [the flâneur's] final ambit is the department store, his last incarnation is the sandwich-man. (M17a, 2)

There are, of course, more. For the reader these startling correspondences can be intoxicating, but the analogies are also in some instances strained and at others simply showing off. However, this illustrates how the notes for the *Arcades Project* are Benjamin's little linguistic workshop, a mirror-making machine which can construe resemblances in the most improbable ways, with the understanding that only the most polished products, like the remarks on the 'optical unconscious', see the light of day. Nevertheless, in that famous sentence from 'Little history of photography' (and 'The work of art in the age of its technological reproducibility'), Benjamin's mirror-machine cannot disguise his incomplete assimilation of psychoanalytic insights.

Dreaming without Freud: Klages, surrealism

Whether or not the *Arcades Project* would have benefited from further exposure to Freud is doubtful, but it is safe to say that Benjamin's model of the dream lacks the clarity and rigour of the psychoanalytic version. Even the staunchest of Benjamin loyalists are willing to admit the weaknesses and discrepancies in his dream theory, although they generally soldier on in the hopes of salvaging its nucleus. Less sympathetic are Elizabeth Lenk and Rita Bischof, who have conducted one of the most thoroughgoing critiques of the *Arcades'* dream apparatus, concluding that it amounts to no less than a theoretical impasse in a project which ultimately fails to distinguish between dreams and the related concepts of ideology, utopia and myth, and in fact ends up with a 'vague oneiric amalgam' in which the three concepts are 'dissolved and merged'.[17] If the blame for this murkiness is to fall anywhere, then as good a place as any to begin is at the door of the mystical philosopher Ludwig Klages, who first set Benjamin on the trail of dreams. In essays such as 'On dream consciousness' (1914), Klages was less concerned with arriving at interpretations of dream contents than with assessing the dream as a form of perception differing from waking. Rolf Wiggershaus helpfully identifies three key features of the dreaming state in Klages: 1, 'perceptual passivity – an abandonment to impressions only made possible by shedding, or bursting out of, customary forms of perception', 2, 'a sense of being far away . . ., even to things close at hand', and 3, 'the feeling of fleetingness'.[18] It should be obvious why Klages is more amenable to Benjamin than Freud, for dreams here are not the disguised expressions of unconscious wishes but something more akin to the experience of the flâneur, that dreamer of the streets: 'Nowhere, unless perhaps in dreams, can the phenomenon of the boundary be experienced in a more originary way than in cities' (C3, 3). The influence of Klages is even more evident in Benjamin's characterisation of another key type in the *Arcades Project*, the collector:

> At bottom, we may say, the collector lives a piece of dream life. For in the dream, too, the rhythm of perception and experience is altered in such a way that everything – even the most seemingly neutral – comes to strike us; everything concerns us. In order to understand the arcades from the ground up, we sink them into the deepest stratum of the dream; we speak of them as though they had struck us. (H1a, 5)

While this passage, with its emphasis on the special sort of receptivity supposedly at work in dreaming, illustrates well Benjamin's debt to Klages, it also underlines the sort of problems raised by Bischof and Lenk. In many places in the *Arcades*, the 'dream' – not quite ideological mystification, not quite illusion – is precisely what must be overcome, if we are to awaken from the nineteenth century. And yet in this formulation, an understanding of the arcades is made possible only by sinking 'into the deepest stratum of the dream'. The only way out of the dream is to go back into the dream.

This paradoxical attitude can be partly explained by turning to the other main source for Benjamin's understanding of dreams, the surrealists.[19] In the first *Manifesto of Surrealism*, Breton credits Freud for shedding light on dream life: [20]

> Under the pretense of civilization and progress, we have managed to banish from the mind everything that may rightly or wrongly be termed superstition, or fancy; forbidden is any kind of search for truth which is not in

conformance with accepted practices. It was, apparently, by pure chance that a part of our mental world which we pretended not to be concerned with any longer – and, in my opinion by far the most important part – has been brought back to light. For this we must give thanks to the discoveries of Sigmund Freud. On the basis of these discoveries a current of opinion is finally forming by means of which the human explorer will be able to carry his investigations much further, authorized as he will henceforth be not to confine himself solely to the most summary realities. The imagination is perhaps on the point of reasserting itself, of reclaiming its rights . . . Freud very rightly brought his critical faculties to bear upon the dream. It is, in fact, inadmissible that this considerable portion of psychic activity . . . has still today been grossly neglected.[21]

To Freud go the plaudits, but, as this excerpt and the subsequent *contretemps* between Breton and Freud demonstrate, the surrealist and the psychoanalytic understanding of dreams had very little in common.[22] Beyond a shared assumption that dreams emanate from the unconscious and that they bear witness to something other than civilizing forces, they could not be further apart on the fundamental issues. Invoking the 'imagination', Breton emphasizes the liberatory qualities of dreams in their raw state, suggesting that here already consciousness and rationality have been defeated, whereas for Freud the remembered dream in its 'raw' state has already been worked upon and modified by consciousness to disguise or distort the unconscious wishes that lie on the other side of a process of displacement and condensation known as the dream-work. The task of the psychoanalytic interpretation of dreams is the unraveling of the dream-work through a painstaking process of association; the surrealist in contrast delights in the *undeciphered* dream, which acts as a prototype for automatic writing. The ultimate goal for Breton is 'the future resolution of [. . .] dream and reality [. . .] into a kind of absolute reality, a *surreality*'.[23]

Richard Wolin argues that Benjamin was drawn to the surrealist version of the dream rather than the Freudian one because of the former's utopian impulses:

The dream, for Benjamin, becomes an autonomous source of experience and knowledge, a hidden key to the secrets and mysteries of waking life. Dreams become the *repositories of the utopian visions of mankind*; they serve as the refuge of the aspirations and desires that are denied to humanity in the sphere of material life.[24]

Indeed, while for Freud disguised wishes *always* lie at the base of a dream, those wishes are disguised precisely because they are prohibited or destructive impulses. The surrealists' idealization of dreams was much more suited to Benjamin's perspective, in which the dreams of the collective are simultaneously illusions *and* utopian wishes. The architectural forms which Benjamin designates 'dream houses of the collective' – 'arcades, winter gardens, panoramas, factories, wax museums, casinos, railroad stations' (L1, 3) – are already the embodiment of bourgeois wishes and will gain nothing from being analysed as the products of a work of displacement and condensation or secondary elaboration. This is why Benjamin's analogy in Convolute R between 'repressed economic contents' and repressed sexual ones does not work: his theory of the dream does not really require a notion of repression.

Benjamin acknowledges in Convolute I ('The interior, the trace') (I1, 3) that the unconscious is not ultimately his prey. Adorno, who eventually rejected Benjamin's dream theory, at first endorsed this view. Commenting on Breton's *Les Vases communicants*, he writes, 'It too counters the psychological interpretation of dreaming and defends an approach in terms of objective images; and it also seems to ascribe a crucial historical character to such images'.[25] It was this 'non-psychological' approach which attracted Benjamin to Louis Aragon's *Paris Peasant*, which gave a trance-like glimpse into the world of things, making visible what was otherwise imperceptible to the quotidian gaze. Through an intoxicated, non-rational, mode of perception, the surrealists were able to reveal the mythical basis of the modern city. As Susan Buck-Morss puts it, 'Aragon is recording a fact that the theory of instrumental rationality represses: Modern reality in this still-primitive stage of industrialism *is* mythic, and to bring this to consciousness in no way eliminates the possibility of a critique'.[26] Although Benjamin objected that the surrealists were too content to remain in the realm of dreams, they did offer a lesson in seizing the object by seeing it other than in its everyday functionality. They demonstrated that things can in fact be seen historically only if we remove them from their supposed 'natural' environment, an environment which of course is not natural at all but the field of alienated social relations.

Dreaming, then, is but one strategy among several for generating dialectical images, that is, for generating a new kind of historical knowledge. It was not really necessary for Benjamin to privilege the dream as a mode of knowing when it was in fact simply part of a repertoire of such methods he had been progressively assembling. That repertoire includes collecting, intoxication, so-called 'children's cognition' and new technologies of representation such as photography and film.[27] In each case, the object is subjected to a mode of apprehension distinct from the dumbly empirical: the collector removes the commodity from the marketplace and establishes it in the new constellation divorced from all utility; the 'trance' of the hashish eater 'cuts itself off from everyday reality with fine, prismatic edges';[28] children 'are irresistibly drawn by the detritus generated by building, gardening, housework, tailoring, or carpentry';[29] and photography allows us to dissect movement in hitherto impossible ways.[30]

This assemblage of modes of perception, like so many prisms held up to the everyday, transforms the world of things which is Benjamin's quarry. At the same time, these various strategies suffer from the same shortcomings as Benjamin's theory of dreams. Buck-Morss inadvertently puts her finger on the problem by imposing the Piagetian term 'cognition' on Benjamin's notion of childhood perception.[31] Benjamin seeks out ways of seeing or kinds of knowledge that are not governed by traditional forms of reasoning, but in the person who does this perceiving does he not reinstate the sovereignty of reason? At different points he compares the collector, the hashish eater and the actions of the photograph with the physiognomist, a paradigm for perception which indicates that he had in mind a single, even para-scientific consciousness for this new mode of apprehending the world of things.[32] The perspective adopted may change (child, addict, dreamer, film spectator, collector), but is it not in each case ultimately the same perceiver, who, to use Lacanian phraseology, issues, inevitably, from the *cogito*? Like the surrealists who rushed headlong to embrace what they mistook for Freud's promotion of irrationalism, but never truly took on board the implications of the unconscious, Benjamin fails to question the coherence or unity of the subject who collects, adopts the standpoint of a child, eats hashish, watches a film. This ultimately centred consciousness, presumably the subject of a new kind of historiography, becomes all the greater a liability when the malign influence of Jung intervenes with the notion of a perceiving 'collective'. Of all the modes of 'tracking' and reconfiguring 'things', perhaps only collecting is not hamstrung by an ill-defined notion of the perceiving subject, because it is the *practice* of collecting and the resulting collection which are key rather than the subjectivity of the collector.

Freud, too, was a collector. Just as Benjamin accumulated rare books, Freud assembled around him an array of idols and animal-shaped gods, an archaeological menagerie that overlooked his work-space. In this shared activity, the two gave expression to a form of bourgeois acquisitiveness that from within its own conservative procedures contained a radical impulse. Benjamin would not deny that the habit marks both out as anachronistic: 'this passion is behind the times' he writes in 'Unpacking my library'.[33] And yet, just as 'revolutionary energies [...] appear in the "outmoded", in [...] objects that have begun to be extinct',[34] so 'Only in extinction is the collector comprehended'.[35] An unfashionable nineteenth-century passion exemplified by the pathos of Balzac's doomed hoarder, Cousin Pons, is reborn in the twentieth century as a form of rescue and rearrangement of things whose resale value is negligible. For, rather than aesthetic objects, Benjamin and Freud collect rubbish, remainders, detritus, to put together the modern, post-bourgeois collection. What are the early, heroic texts of psychoanalysis – *The Interpretation of Dreams*, *The Psychopathology of Everyday Life*, *Jokes and their Relation to the Unconscious* – if not the proud and obsessive collector laying out on display his lovingly gathered waste products of psychic life: dreams, slips of the tongue, acts of forgetting, bungled actions, jokes? Freud often remarked that psychoanalysis was interested in details considered meaningless by others: 'It [psychoanalysis] is accustomed to divine secret and concealed things from despised or unnoticed features, from the rubbish-heap, as it were, of our observations.'[36] The protean nature of *The Interpretation of Dreams* (enlarged and revised five times by Freud) and the *Psychopathology* (enlarged seven times) bears witness to the obsession of the collector whose collection is always one item short of completion, of victory in 'the struggle against dispersion' (H4a, 1). At the risk of succumbing to an overly Benjaminian taste for correspondences, might it not be possible to identify a homologous relation between Benjamin's approach to material things and Freud's to psychical ones? Benjamin writes, 'We need only recall what importance a particular collector attaches not only to his object, but also to its entire past, whether this concerns the origin and objective characteristics of the thing or the details of its ostensibly external history: previous owners, price of purchase, current value, and so on' (H2, 7; H2a, 1). By the same token, for Freud, a dream, a slip of the tongue, a forgotten name, a symptom, a joke, are all meaningless until their pedigrees have been investigated, their histories thoroughly excavated, a search which often goes as far back as the childhoods of their originators.

In both Benjamin and Freud there are countervailing impulses at work – the micrological and the system-building. In Benjamin the former wins out easily, with fidelity to the singularity of the object by far eclipsing any attempts on his part to synthesize, to arrive at a totalizing theory. The weakness of his dream theory, supposedly the conceptual armature of the entire *Arcades*, attests to this triumph of the irreducible over the system in the work of a highly accomplished rag-picker but indifferent dialectician. In Freud, so the story goes, it is the opposite, with all roads leading to Oedipus. Any resistant data or dissident voice is suppressed, or sacrificed to the larger theory, or partially contained by Freud's slyly bracketed doubts and prevaricating footnotes. And yet, in spite of this Freud who relentlessly finds the same story wherever he looks, the constant revision and enlarging of his great collections points to another conclusion, to the perpetually unfinished, incomplete state of the psychoanalytical enterprise. As latter-day feminist and post-structuralist readers have been eager to point out, the gaps that Freud leaves in his totalizing edifice are so large and so numerous that they positively invite the reader to prise them further open. It remains to be seen whether it is more rewarding to seek out the fissures and faults in one of the great conceptual edifices of modernity, or to piece together the rubble from one of its many incomplete projects.

Notes

1 Cohen argues this case most fully, claiming that the *Arcades Project* is influenced throughout by psychoanalysis (Cohen, *Profane Illumination*, p. 6). Her argument is based mainly on Benjamin's dialogue with Breton and surrealism, which, as we shall see, is hardly the same as conducting a dialogue with Freud. In a review of volumes 3 and 4 of the *Selected Writings*, Eagleton writes of Benjamin that, 'In a single paragraph of sober, scintillating prose, he can weave together Freud's theory of the unconscious, Kabbalistic ideas of interpretation, Marx's concept of the productive forces, and the ragpickers of Paris', although he does not identify the paragraph (Terry Eagleton, 'A Visionary at the Crossroads', *Times Higher Education Supplement*, 11 July 2003). Buck-Morss admits that 'Benjamin's direct references to Freudian theory remained limited and quite general', but argues that 'even if direct indebtedness cannot be proven, there was a clear consensus' (Buck-Morss, *Dialectics of Seeing*, p. 282). She goes on to compare Freud's theory of wish-fulfilment with Benjamin's analysis of bourgeois dreams. Comparing Trotsky and Benjamin, Leslie asserts that 'Both men were extremely interested in Freud and the relationship of Marxism to psychoanalysis' (Leslie, *Overpowering Conformism*, p. 233).
2 Benjamin, 'First sketches', p. 838 (Convolute F°, 6).
3 These prevarications are chronicled by the editors of Volume 2 of the *Selected Writings*; see 'Chronology, 1927–1934', in *SW 2*, pp. 823–56 (pp. 827–37).

4 Letter 25, from Adorno to Benjamin, 5 December 1934, and Letter 33, from Adorno to Benjamin, 5 June 1935, in *Adorno–Benjamin Correspondence*, pp. 60–5 (p. 62) and pp. 92–5 (p. 93), respectively. Around this time the Frankfurt School in exile, and Erich Fromm in particular, were using Freud's theory of anality as a way of accounting for the psychology of fascism (see Rolf Wiggershaus, *The Frankfurt School: Its History, Theories and Political Significance*, trans. Michael Robertson (Cambridge, Polity Press, 1994), pp. 151–3, 164).

5 Letter 35, from Benjamin to Adorno, 10 June 1935, in *Adorno–Benjamin Correspondence*, pp. 98–101 (p. 99). Although Adorno answered in the negative, an obvious place to start would have been chapter 7 of *The Interpretation of Dreams* (vol. 4, The Pelican Freud Library, trans. James Strachey (Harmondsworth: Penguin Books, 1976)) and the dream of the burning child, which was subsequently taken up by Jacques Lacan (*The Four Fundamental Concepts of Psychoanalysis*, trans. Alan Sheridan (Harmondsworth: Penguin Books, 1977), pp. 57–60), and Slavoj Žižek (*The Sublime Object of Ideology* (London: Verso, 1989), pp. 44–7).

6 Letter 39, from Adorno and Gretel Karplus to Benjamin, 2–4 and 5 August 1935, in *Adorno–Benjamin Correspondence*, pp. 104–16 (p. 112).

7 Letter 62, from Adorno to Benjamin, 7 November 1936, in *Adorno–Benjamin Correspondence*, pp. 158–61 (p. 160).

8 See Benjamin, 'Verzeichnis', pp. 460, 475.

9 Broderson, *Walter Benjamin*, p. 101.

10 Scholem, *Walter Benjamin: The Story of a Friendship*, p. 57.

11 Benjamin, 'Verzeichnis', pp. 440–1.

12 T. J. Clark, 'Should Benjamin have read Marx?', *boundary 2*, 30: 1 (2003), 31–49 (p. 41).

13 Benjamin, 'Little history of photography', pp. 510–12; 'Kleine Geschichte der Photographie', in *Gesammelte Schriften*, vol. 2, ed. Rolf Tiedemann and Herbert Schweppenhäuser (Frankfurt am Main: Suhrkamp, 1977), pp. 368–85 (p. 371).

14 Benjamin, 'The work of art (third version)', p. 266.

15 Rosalind Krauss, who borrows the term 'optical unconscious' for the title of a book, goes along with Benjamin's analogy in so far as 'hitherto unseen visual data can operate as a parallel to . . . slips of the tongue or pen', but wonders 'Can the optical field . . . have an *unconscious*?' She goes on to explain that her use of the term is 'at an angle to Benjamin's', because she uses it to argue that 'human vision can be thought to be less than master of all it surveys, in conflict as it is with what is internal to the organism that houses it'; *The Optical Unconscious* (Cambridge, Mass.: MIT Press, 1993), pp. 178–80. Although Benjamin does not use the term again, he suggests that just as *The Psychopathology of Everyday Life* 'made analyzable things which had previously floated unnoticed on the broad stream of perception', so 'A similar deepening

of apperception [. . .] has been accomplished by film' ('The work of art (third version)', p. 265). By reducing unconscious 'phenomena' to the level of perception alone, he repeats here the traduction of psychoanalysis carried out in the 'photography' essay.

16 In the sentence from 'Little history of photography', only the *wie* to indicate similarity is present in an abbreviated construction where the *so* is implied. Thanks to Rainer Emig, who pointed out that the '*so* . . . *wie*' structure is very common in German, but Benjamin's preferred '*wie* . . . *so*' is much less so. A survey of several German dictionaries yielded only one example of this usage, which occurs mainly in proverbial constructions.

17 Elizabeth Lenk and Rita Bischof, 'L'Intrication surréelle du rêve et de l'histoire dans les Passages de Benjamin', in Wismann, *Walter Benjamin et Paris*, pp. 179–99 (p. 183).

18 Wiggershaus, *Frankfurt School*, p. 198.

19 Bischof and Lenk explain that reading Aragon's *Une vague de rêves* led Benjamin to transcribe his dreams ('L'Intrication', p. 180). Ten of these were subsequently published in Ignaz Jezower's *Der Buch der Träume* (Berlin: Rowohlt, 1928).

20 The *Manifesto* appears at number 990 on Benjamin's 'Verzeichnis', meaning that he read it around 1925–6 ('Verzeichnis', p. 457).

21 André Breton, 'Manifesto of Surrealism', *Manifestoes of Surrealism*, trans. Richard Seaver and Helen R. Lane (Ann Arbor: University of Michigan Press, 1969), pp. 1–47 (pp. 10–11).

22 In *Communicating Vessels* Breton accused Freud of failing to acknowledge one of his predecessors in dream theory. Freud gave Breton the curtest of brush-offs by writing back, 'I do not know what surrealism wants'. The exchange of letters can be found in André Breton, *Communicating Vessels*, trans. Mary Ann Caws and Geoffrey T. Harris (Lincoln, NE: University of Nebraska Press, 1990).

23 Breton, 'Manifesto of Surrealism', p. 14.

24 Richard Wolin, *Walter Benjamin: An Aesthetic of Redemption* (New York: Columbia University Press, 1982), p. 127.

25 Letter 23, from Adorno to Benjamin, 6 November 1934, in *Adorno–Benjamin Correspondence*, pp. 52–9 (p. 54).

26 Buck-Morss, *Dialectics of Seeing*, p. 260.

27 The term 'children's cognition' is Susan Buck-Morss's, who explores this topic at length (*Dialectics of Seeing*, pp. 262–6).

28 Walter Benjamin, 'Hashish in Marseilles' [1932], in *SW 2*, pp. 673–9 (p. 676).

29 Benjamin, 'One-way street', p. 449.

30 Benjamin, 'Little history of photography', pp. 510–12.

31 Philip Rosen, introducing a special issue of *boundary 2* devoted to the new translation of the *Arcades Project*, also uses this slightly un-Benjaminian term to describe the working of Benjamin's *Jetztzeit* ('Introduction' to *Ben-*

jamin Now: Critical Encounters with The Arcades Project, *boundary 2*, 30: 1 (2003), 1–15 (p. 2). In an extraordinary act of omission, there is not a single reference in the entire special issue to Susan Buck-Morss, who was instrumental in bringing the *Arcades Project* to the attention of an anglophone audience.

32 'collectors are physiognomists of the world of things' (H2, 7; H2a, 1); 'For [hashish] made me into a physiognomist' ('Hashish in Marseilles', p. 675); 'photography reveals in this material physiognomic aspects, image worlds, which dwell in the smallest things' ('Little history of photography', p. 512).

33 Walter Benjamin, 'Unpacking my library: a talk about collecting' [1931], in *SW 2*, pp. 486–93 (p. 491).

34 Benjamin, 'Surrealism', p. 210.

35 Benjamin, 'Unpacking my library', p. 492.

36 Sigmund Freud, 'The Moses of Michelangelo', in *Art and Literature, Penguin Freud Library*, vol. 14, trans. James Strachey (Harmondsworth: Penguin Books, 1985), pp. 249–82 (p. 265).

Nazis

The relationship of Nazism to the author of the *Arcades Project* could not be simpler or more brutal. Nazism was directly responsible for Benjamin's persecution, exile and death. Although Benjamin made much of his own unworldliness (and commentators tend to take him at his word), he was far more alert than many other German Jews to the likely consequences of the Nazi seizure of power. Already in the summer of 1932 he noted, in letters to his closest friend Gershom Scholem, that his commissions from Berlin Radio had dried up and the *Franfurter Zeitung* was no longer printing his work.[1] The Nazi takeover the following year manifested itself in the 'almost mathematical simultaneity with which every conceivable office returned manuscripts, broke off negotiations either in progress or in the final stages, and left inquiries unanswered'. 'Under such conditions', Benjamin concluded, 'the utmost political reserve, such as I have long and with good reason practised, may protect the person in question from systematic persecution, but not from starvation.'[2] He therefore left for Paris in March 1933, where he remained in exile until the noose began to tighten there as well. Shortly before the German occupation of his adopted city, Benjamin fled south, first to Lourdes, then to Marseilles, from which he made his failed attempt to cross into Spain.[3] Nazi politics, and the mass slaughter to which they led inexorably, were the decisive historical experiences in Benjamin's short life.

But what is the relationship of Nazism to the *text* of the *Arcades*? That is a different question. Ironically, research for the *Arcades Project*, which had stalled after 1929, was given renewed impetus by Benjamin's enforced move to Paris. Not only did he find himself replanted in the *Project*'s natural habitat, the Bibliothèque Nationale, but his first commission from a French publication was a contract to compose a piece on Haussmann – who would eventually merit his own chapter heading in the two exposés – for *Le Monde*.[4] In the course of Benjamin's fresh studies for the *Project* in 1934, it assumed a new and different shape, both conceptually (in so far as Benjamin was bent on securing a solid Marxist orientation for it) and compositionally, for this was the period in which the mass of notes was arranged into convolutes, the sheaths that would constitute its ultimate structure. But perhaps most importantly, from this point onwards it would become 'the actual, if not the only, reason not to lose courage in the struggle for existence'.[5]

If the dialectical images that populate the *Arcades* are, therefore, unique constellations of the 'what has been' with the 'now', then the rise of Fascism surely makes its presence felt; it would be the most burdensome of the 'few heavy, massive weights' (N6, 5) one balances in the scales of historical knowledge. Yet for all that, Nazism is mentioned explicitly only once in all the notes and one looks in vain for evidence that the gamblers, flâneurs and advertisements of the nineteenth century are related to the Fascism of the twentieth.

This was not because Benjamin was averse to the topic in general. In the final section of his 1936 essay, 'The work of art in the age of its technological reproducibility', he argued that the Fascist appropriation of the technologies of art (presumably film and radio in particular) led inexorably to 'an aestheticizing of political life', a tendency that would culminate in the fetishization of war.[6] In itself this represented a more concise and direct formulation of an analysis of fascism first proposed in a review of a collection of articles bemoaning the decline of war and the soldierly virtues, edited by the right-wing theorist Ernst Jünger. In 'Theories of German Fascism' Benjamin locked on to two central, intertwined features of Fascist consciousness: the cult of war and heroic death in battle, and a distinctive, distorted relationship with technology and nature.[7] The German right had attempted 'to pervert the German defeat into an inner victory by means of confessions of guilt', which would ironically make Germany the witness and prophet of the 'decline of the West'.[8] They were still fighting a war Germany had not fought correctly, in so far as it had allowed the 'despised rational element', in the form of machines and civilian leadership, to destroy war itself.[9] This was, Benjamin argued, ludicrous self-deception, a mystification of war that relied secretly on the massive forces unleashed by military hardware. 'War, in the metaphysical abstraction in which the new nationalism believes, is nothing other than the attempt to redeem, mystically and without mediation, the secret of nature, understood idealistically, through technology.'[10] In fact, the only war that counted would be 'the one, fearful last chance to correct the incapacity of peoples to order their relationships to one another in accord with the relationship they possess to nature through their technology'.[11] Only those 'who possess in technology not a fetish of doom, but a key to happiness' could win that war.[12]

It is perhaps surprising that in the very same year Benjamin wrote the above he sent a copy of his book *The Origin of the German Mourning Play* to Carl Schmitt – legal theorist, relentless critic of Weimar's parliamentary democracy and future apologist for the Third Reich – with an adulatory note, which made clear 'how much my book is indebted to you'.[13] Schmitt had published a series of works during the 1920s and 1930s attacking parliamentary government and providing justification for Presidential rule by emergency decree.[14] The Weimar Constitution provided for parliamentary government, but it combined this with a directly elected President who, by recourse to article 48 of the constitution, could invoke emergency powers and rule by decree. For Schmitt, contemporary Germany offered concrete proof that democracy and liberalism were incompatible, and that the latter, with its insistence on resolving public issues through reasoned debate, led to paralysis when state action was desperately needed. In the words which open his manifesto, *Political Theology*, the sovereign was 'he who decides the exception', the individual with the authority to determine when law and constitutional procedure had to be suspended to save the state itself. In the event, article 48 became a popular resource for a series of German interwar Presidents, increasing in use through the early 1930s until Hitler's Enabling Act of 1933 allowed him to do away with the *Reichstag* once and for all.

Benjamin read *Political Theology* and plundered its concept of sovereignty for his analysis of the German Baroque, with the appropriate footnote.[15] That his letter of 1930 was not merely an attempt to gain favour with a possible intellectual patron – Benjamin was hardly above that sort of thing – is demonstrated by Benjamin's curriculum vitae of 1928, in which the two crucial intellectual influences named are the aesthetician Alois Riegl and Schmitt, praised for the way in which his studies in political theory drew freely on the intellectual universe, incorporating theology and aesthetics when necessary.[16] Nor did his interest and attention go unrequited. Many years later, Schmitt apparently claimed that his study of Hobbes's *Leviathan* in 1938 was meant as a reply to Benjamin.[17] More explicitly, he addressed Benjamin's comments on Shakespeare at some length in an appendix to one chapter of his book *Hamlet or Hecuba* (1956).[18]

When Benjamin's association with Schmitt was first revealed, it was considered somewhat scandalous: how could a man of the left and a Jew consort with a writer whose far right commitments were clear even before he became a public defender of the Fascist regime and its anti-Semitic campaigns? Benjamin's interest in a figure like Schmitt was, however, typical rather than exceptional. His first dip in the choppy waters of political theory had involved a liaison with that most ambiguous of political thinkers, George Sorel, whose *Reflections on Violence* and *The Illusion of Progress* Benjamin read in 1919 (along with a series of other anarchist writers such as Bakunin and Landauer).[19] Sorel shared with Schmitt a distrust of parliament, which he regarded as a reformist talking shop which only dulled the enthusiasm of the labour movement. In opposition to parliament Sorel offered the great myth of the general strike, in which grand insurrectionary theatre replaced organization and argument (Schmitt would devote a chapter of his essay on 'the crisis of parliamentary democracy' to Sorel's case). In the 'Critique of violence' that followed this reading, Benjamin used Sorel's argument to draw a distinction between the violence of revolutions and the law-making and law-preserving violence of the state.[20] Sorel became a source for both left and right: his hostility to constitutional procedures was, to say the least, double-edged. For Benjamin's purposes, however, he was ideal.

For what Sorel and Schmitt offered was 'a critique of a liberalism lacking in seriousness, extremity and depth'.[21] Benjamin has a reputation as a political *Luftmensch*: it is probably revealing that, when he heard of the proclamation of the Bavarian Republic, his only comment on it in a letter to his friend Ernest Schoen was to note that it meant that a book auction at which he intended to bid would probably be cancelled.[22] The theoretical manifestation of this unworldliness was an emphasis on the metaphysics of politics, rather than the details of political structures and action. Although committed to the causes of the left throughout his life (his decisive friendship with Scholem was cemented by their shared opposition to the First World War), he was drawn to theorists such as Schmitt, who refused to reduce politics to the mutually conditioning behaviour of actors or sever it from religious considerations. When Benjamin went to work on a three-part *Politics* in 1921, it was to be composed of a critique of Bloch, and chapters entitled 'The dismantling of power' and 'Teleology without ultimate goal'. To this extent, he seems to have shared the preference for *Kultur* over politics so typical of the German intelligentsia in the early part of the century.

Although Benjamin was well aware of the social forces behind Fascism, the phenomenon itself was analysed in metaphysical rather than political-scientific terms. Fascism was not a structure emerging from the conjuncture of mass democracy and continuing bourgeois rule, nor was it the outcome of particular struggles after the death of liberal Europe: it was a way of relating humanity, technology and nature in the moment of modernity. In two critical respects it is the counterpoint for Benjamin's nineteenth-century melodies: it structures the treatment of technology, and it evokes the contrast between the archaic and the dialectical image.

If there is one image we associate with the arcades it is the 'world of secret affinities' Benjamin evokes when enumerating the bizarre objects found juxtaposed within: 'palm tree and feather duster, hairdryer and Venus de Milo, prostheses and letter writing manuals'. If commodity fetishism and the phantasmagoria to which it gives rise is the crucial motif, then the central scene is Balzac's 'great poem of display', the disposition of commodities whose strange logic justifies the claim that surrealism is the nineteenth century's hidden truth. But if we read carefully, there is another motif that, although related, has an equal claim to centrality. On those occasions when Benjamin paused to draw his thoughts together (usually at the request of Adorno), it was not the commodities inside the arcade but the arcade itself that drew his attention. In this respect it's worth recalling the opening of the first pieces emerging from the project, 'The ring of Saturn, or some remarks on iron construction':

> The beginning of the nineteenth century witnessed those initial experiments in iron construction whose results, in conjunction with those obtained from experiments with the steam engine, would so thoroughly transform the face of Europe by the end of the century.[23]

Likewise, the exposés of 1935 and 1939 immediately point to iron construction, based on the 'first artificial building material', as a decisive moment, before turning to world exhibitions, panoramas, Haussmann, the barricades, that is, to structures made possible by the new technologies of glass, iron and gaslight (and, in the case of the barricades, some older technology). In the project itself, the arcades are, for sure, explored as unique spaces, 'temples of commodity capital' (A2, 2), which become the nodal point for a web or network of themes. But below the music of the arcades one can hear the low hum of technology, embodied in iron and glass, lighting and mirrors, Grandville's fantasies and Fourier's utopias, Haussmann's city planning and the new railways. All of which might remind us that the commodities on display were often handicraft or small manufactures: the true lifting-off point for capitalism is the creation of heavy industry.

At the beginning of the nineteenth century 'the possibility now arises that art will no longer find time to adapt somehow to technological processes' (G1, 1). What strikes Benjamin about the architectural forms and structures that suddenly assault Paris is the confluence of technology and dream: 'the infant prodigies' he finds within the arcades – 'the brief-case with interior lighting, the metre-long pocket knife' (H1, 1) – find their complement in grand palaces built of 'glass before its time, prema-ture iron' (F3, 2). Sigfried Giedion already quoted comment that 'in the nineteenth construction plays the role of the subconscious' (K1a, 7) pro-vided him with the catalyst he needs to bond the sphere of dreams with hard surfaces of bridges and buildings. There is no need, however, to stop with architecture: 'the peculiar and unmistakeable dream world' that attaches to railroad tracks, at first glance the most mundane and utilitar-ian of structures, illustrates 'just how great the natural symbolic power of technological innovation can be' (F3, 4).

Where art cannot 'adapt', it uses its material to dream, producing bizarre concatenations of the most ancient and the most modern. The arcades themselves exemplify this principle, embodying a space which is simultaneously street and bourgeois interior, a dream synthesis made possible by glass, gas and iron. That it depends on these technologies is not 'hidden', not a weakness, but is flaunted. The wonder which every arcade should inspire depends on full consciousness of what the technol-ogy can do: it is, so to speak, wonder not at the space itself, but at the fact that technologies exist that can create it. Benjamin describes this as the formal prerogative of nature, which, in solving a problem objectively, creates form:

> When the wheel was invented, enabling continuous forward motion over the ground, wouldn't someone there have been able to say, with a certain justification, 'And now, into the bargain, it's round – it's in the *form of a wheel*? Are not all great conquests in the field of forms ultimately a matter of technical discoveries? (F2a, 5)

'Only now are we beginning to guess', Benjamin concludes, 'what forms lie hidden in machines' (F2a, 5). The contemporary equivalent to this wonderment is surely the science fiction film, in which the special effects not only produce a pseudo-realistic representation of extraordinary events (cosmic explosions, time travel etc.) but also function as a stun-ning display of modern technical prowess.[24] Like the arcades, they inspire wonder at the power of technology itself.

All this dreaming has a price, though. Benjamin notes that 'construc-tions in which the expert recognises anticipations of contemporary building fashion' seem distinctly 'old-fashioned and dreamlike' rather than modern (K1a, 3). The bourgeois overinvestment in new technologies creates structures that are prey to the modern dynamic of fashion and liable to become kitsch. The lack of sobriety evident in the 'dream houses of the collective' (L1, 3), the bourgeois tendency to treat technology as a toy for the creation of wonders, leaves Paris full of strange creations. In her famous 'Notes on "camp"', Susan Sontag, focusing on many of the same objects that entranced Benjamin, argues that the essence of the naively camp object is 'a seriousness that fails', but which, in its failure, maintains 'the proper mixture of the exaggerated, the fantastic, the passionate and the naive'.[25] Just as dreams sound ridiculous once you have woken up, so the arcades and their kin look 'past it' once technology finally finds its feet. 'At one blow, they become the hollow mold from which the image of "modernity" was cast' (S1a, 6). The surrealist fascination with the outmoded depends on empathy with the kitsch and camp of the past.

'When and how', Benjamin asks, 'will the worlds of form which, without our assistance, have arisen, for example, in mechanics, in film, in machine construction, in the new physics, and which have subjugated us, make it clear for us what manner of nature they contain?' (K3a, 2). But surely Benjamin could not have thought it was simply a matter of waiting for the news? As other sections of the *Arcades* make clear, there are different paths to take, perhaps even a struggle to be waged over the relationship we have with new technical forms, and through this, with inner and outer nature. This might explain one of the *Project*'s more striking judgements: Benjamin's clear preference for the crazed Fourier over the 'scientific' Saint-Simon. Although each has a convolute devoted to his Utopian project, Saint-Simon is cast as forerunner of the modern technocrats, while Fourier's outlandish architecture and technologizing of happiness generates thirty pages of quotations. Saint-Simon hopes merely to use technology and imagines it as mere means; Fourier's phalanstery, by contrast, 'can be characterised as human machinery' (W4, 4). But in designing a 'machine made of human beings', Fourier effects a dialectical switch, in which technology appears less as the bending of nature to human ends (and therefore something eternally alien) than as the very organisation of complex human happiness. Fourier is a dreamer, to be sure, but rather than fill technology with fantasy, he allows technology to fill out a vision of human community.

The path that leads to the First World War and mechanized slaughter is less clearly marked. But one can discern a battered signpost in Benjamin's account of *Jugendstil*, the modernism by which Germany hoped to avoid coming to grips with the changing situation. If the early nineteenth century used technology to dream, in *Jugendstil* 'the problem as such was already prey to repression' (S8a, 1). In so far as it does not real-ize it is competing with technology, it reacts to it all the more aggressively, stylizing its forms, betraying a guilty conscience in its knowingness. For Benjamin this kind of decadence reveals only that 'the bourgeoisie senses that its days are numbered; all the more it wishes to stay young' (S9a, 4). In a review of a study of Stefan George's poetry written while working on the *Arcades*, Benjamin expressed himself with a little more candour:

> What is expressed in its [*Jugendstil*'s] formal idiom is the will to evade imminent developments and the presentiments that rise up to confront it. The same may be said of that 'spiritual movement' that aspired to the renewal of existence without paying heed to politics. It, too, amounted to a retrospective transformation of societal contradictions into those hopeless, tragic tensions and convulsions that are so typical of the life of small con-venticles.[26]

The spectacular displays of the Nazis, their cult of national will and power, reduce technology to a means for obliterating nature, rather than a force that might alter it. The hope Benjamin nurtured for film, that it could 'establish equilibrium between human beings and the apparatus' and 'assure us of a vast and unsuspected field of action' is dashed in Fascism, which wants to use the medium to artificially enhance its pseudo-tragic heroics.[27] The *Arcades* shows us the dreamworld of the nineteenth-century bourgeoisie precisely at its crisis point, when every dream is guaranteed to be a nightmare, and the dream-form itself has become dangerous.

If the danger is a Fascist renewal that revives past glories industrially, its formal embodiment is the archaic, as opposed to the dialectical, image. Benjamin explicitly wages a war over the past – for '*even the dead* will not be safe if the enemy is victorious' – but the war is over the form in which we retrieve the past, not just the substance of our interpretation of it.[28] In this case, however, Benjamin found a distinct target at which to aim. In a letter to Scholem, he announces his intention 'to safeguard certain foun-dations of "Paris Arcades" methodologically by waging an onslaught on the doctrines of Jung, especially those concerning archaic images and the collective unconscious'.[29] This onslaught has political as well as method-ological significance, for Jung's theory renders 'auxiliary services to National Socialism'.

In Jung the archaic image has an 'unequivocally regressive function' (N8, 2): it maintains the past in dream-like form (in notes for his 1935 précis, Benjamin claims that Jung 'wants to distance awakening from the dream').[30] The archaic image inherits the dreams of the past, modifying or refitting them for use in the crisis situation of the present. But the contrast Benjamin draws is not with debate and argument, the heritage of the parliamentary tradition, but with a different kind of image, the 'dialectical' one that doesn't dismiss the dreamed-of past but seeks to harness its energy. The point is not to disenchant technology, for it is indeed magical, in Benjamin's eyes. The point is to key that magic to the pursuit of a new relationship to nature. The entire symbology of National Socialism is bent on a re-enchantment of the German national past. Its refusal to wake up is, for Benjamin, coterminous with its refusal of politics, politics not as the moment of decision or the state of emergency but as the reordering of relationships aimed at happiness.

The massive weight of Fascism tugs the scales in the *Arcades*, but interestingly enough, not as a political phenomenon. Instead, we encounter Fascism as metaphysics and as art, a reactionary modernism of the ruling class. Schmitt had urged his readers not to dilute politics by imaging it as intellectual debate or economic competition. It was a struggle between 'friend' and 'enemy', a struggle over ways of life and metaphysically defined world-views. Benjamin's warm words for Schmitt ceased after 1930, and he conducted a not-so-subtle polemic with him in 'On the concept of history'.[31] But to the end he carried through Schmitt's belief that liberalism, with its rationalism and its instrumentality, demeaned politics, and that only metaphysics could save us.

Notes

1 See Letters 6 (24 August 1932) and 7 (September 1932), in *Scholem–Benjamin Correspondence*, pp. 17–18. Benjamin had worked as a writer and presenter for radio stations in Frankfurt and Berlin since 1929, benefiting from the patronage of his longtime friend Ernst Schoen (see Brodersen, *Walter Benjamin*, pp. 191–4). Schoen was arrested and removed from his post at the station in early 1933.

2 Letter 14, from Benjamin to Scholem, 20 March 1933, in *Scholem–Benjamin Correspondence*, pp. 33–5 (p. 34).

3 See Lisa Fittko's moving account of the attempt, 'The story of old Benjamin', in *AP*, pp. 946–54.

4 See Letter 229, from Benjamin to Gretel Adorno, 30 December 1933, in *Correspondence*, pp. 431–2 (p. 432). In the end, Benjamin seems to have decided not to write the article, although the research for it made its way into the *Arcades*.

5 Letter 260, from Benjamin to Theodor Adorno, 31 May 1935, in *Correspondence*, pp. 488–91 (p. 490).

6 Walter Benjamin, 'The work of art in the age of its technological reproducibility (Second Version)' [1936], in *SW 3*, pp. 101–33 (p. 121).

7 Walter Benjamin, 'Theories of German Fascism' [1930], in *SW 2*, pp. 312–21.

8 Benjamin, 'Theories of German Fascism', p. 315.

9 Benjamin, 'Theories of German Fascism', p. 316.

10 Benjamin, 'Theories of German Fascism', p. 319.

11 Benjamin, 'Theories of German Fascism', p. 320.

12 Benjamin, 'Theories of German Fascism', p. 321

13 Letter from Benjamin to Schmitt, December 1930, quoted from Horst Bredekamp, 'From Walter Benjamin to Carl Schmitt, via Thomas Hobbes', *Critical Inquiry*, 25: 2 (1999), 247–66. To seal the irony of this gesture, Schmitt would eventually be the editor of Jünger's correspondence.

14 See Schmitt, *The Crisis of Parliamentary Democracy* [1923], trans. Ellen Kennedy (Cambridge, Mass.: MIT Press, 1988); *Political Theology: Four Chapters on the Concept of Sovereignty* [1922], trans. George Schwab (Cambridge, Mass.: MIT Press, 1985); *The Concept of the Political* [1931], trans. George Schwab (New Brunswick, NJ: Rutgers University Press, 1976).

15 Benjamin, *Origin*, pp. 65, 238 n14. Benjamin, however, modified Schmitt's arguments in a critical manner; see Samuel Weber, 'Taking exception to decision: Walter Benjamin and Carl Schmitt', *Diacritics*, 22: 3–4 (1992), 5–18.

16 Benjamin, 'Curriculum vitae III', pp. 77–8.

17 Bredekamp, 'Benjamin to Schmitt', p. 253.

18 See Carl Schmitt, 'The source of the tragic', *Telos*, 72 (1987), 133–51, a translation of the relevant chapter of Schmitt's book.

19 Benjamin, 'Verzeichnis', p. 447. The works listed are Bakunin, *Dieu et l'état*, Landauer, *Aufruf zum Sozialismus*, and also Rudolf Stammler, *Die Theorie des Anarchismus*.

20 Walter Benjamin, 'Critique of violence' [1921], in *SW 1*, pp. 236–51.

21 Bredekamp, 'Benjamin to Schmitt', p. 248.

22 Letter 72, from Benjamin to Ernst Schoen, 8 November 1918, in *Correspondence*, pp. 135–7 (p. 136).

23 Benjamin, 'The ring of Saturn or some remarks on iron construction', p. 885.

24 See Scott Bukatman, 'The artificial infinite: on special effects and the sublime', in Annette Kuhn (ed.), *Alien Zone II: The Spaces of Science Fiction Cinema* (London: Verso, 1999), pp. 249–75.

25 Susan Sontag, 'Notes on "camp"' [1964], in *Against Interpretation and Other Essays* (New York: Dell, 1969), pp. 277–93 (p. 285).

26 Walter Benjamin, 'Stefan George in retrospect' [1933], in *SW 2*, pp. 706–11 (pp. 707–8).

27 Benjamin, 'The work of art (second version)', p. 117.

28 Benjamin, 'On the concept of history', p. 391 (Thesis VI).

29 Letter 93, from Benjamin to Scholem, 2 July 1937, in *Scholem–Benjamin Correpsondence*, pp. 197–9 (p. 197).

30 'Materials for the exposé of 1935', p. 906.
31 Benjamin, 'On the concept of history', p. 392 (Thesis VIII). At stake is Schmitt's concept of the 'state of emergency', which Benjamin pointedly argues is 'not the exception but the rule'. See Bredekamp, 'Benjamin to Schmitt'.

Ending

We have left a few things out of this book. The interested reader might have hoped for entries on Boredom, Collecting, Fashion, the Flâneur, Gender, Haussmann, Marx, Photography, Streets . . . By way of explanation, we could point out that we have played to our strengths, that we touch on all these topics at some point or other, that this was meant to be a little book about a big one and that every commentary on the *Arcades* is doomed to appear incomplete. We were, in addition, working under a self-imposed constraint, which explains why this is an 'Ending' and not a 'Conclusion'. We didn't choose our topics randomly – they seem to us central to the *Project* – but we decided at the outset that we would try to produce a multi-pronged commentary, which could be read as a consecutive argument or dipped into in more scattershot fashion. This decision, and a little onomastic legerdemain, allowed us to narrow down our entries to a manageable sixteen. Someone else, then, will have to write those missing entries; someone else is undoubtedly doing so.

Perhaps what is needed, though, is not more entries to the *Arcades* but a few exits. Readers of the *Project* have freely confessed they find the book not only exhilarating but also frustrating, and anyone aiming at a total exegesis must realize sooner or later that the whole thing doesn't quite hang together (there would be no point in deconstruction: it would fall apart in your hands). Irving Wohlfarth reminds us that, according to Benjamin's own philosophy of history, the *Arcades Project* has to be radically 'incomplete', lacking the fullness of meaning its very ambition promises.[1] For if, as Benjamin put it in 'On the concept of history', 'only for a redeemed mankind has its past becomes citable in all its moments', any work produced before that moment will at best be able to evoke the synthesis and plenitude it strives for.[2] In a critical climate that luxuriates in ruins and enjoys nothing better than leaping over a textual crevasse, it is natural that many critics regard this lack of conclusive argument as a virtue rather than a weakness. Susan Buck-Morss, one of the first and still most compelling commentators on the *Arcades* in English, warns against the temptation of academic hermeneutics when faced with the challenging opacity of Benjamin's writing.[3] She rejects as sterile the study of Benjamin's intellectual influences and antecedents, and favours imitation of his methods over faithful explication of them.

We don't go quite that far. It is impossible to know whether the *Arcades Project* is exactly the kind of work Benjamin intended or only preparation for something a little more discursive, but we were always interested in writing a book about Benjamin and not a Benjaminian book. For that reason, we have thought it worthwhile discussing the history of arcades in Europe, contextualizing Benjamin's account of the modern and mapping the intellectual heredity of the *Project* itself. The form of the *Arcades* is beguiling, the practice of montage a stimulus, the one-liners on display often a pleasure: but one derives maximum benefit from it by establishing a critical distance that is formal as well as substantive. In its style and structure the *Arcades* remains faithful to the claim that 'knowledge comes only in lightning flashes' (N1, 1), but behind each dialectical image lay years of pedantic research, and the illumination on offer should be a spur to further work, not a signal that the end is nigh. In this spirit we have aimed to provide, to use a word of Benjamin's, a prolegomenon to future research. Future research on fashion and consumerism, the structure of historical knowledge, urban space and politics, the culture of insurrections and so on. Most importantly, future research that fans the messianic spark with the utmost sobriety, accepting that knowledge of the past, however dialectical, doesn't come cheap. But then, what is the *Arcades Project* itself if not proleptic, in its unpublished state acting as seed-bed for all the published work of the 1930s? Already we find the methods and insights of the *Arcades* infiltrating the work we do independently of each other.

To read all the way through a thousand-page book, one needs some considerable incentives. For us, the author's name on the cover was the main guarantee of the value of the exercise, and the rewards, we hope we have shown, were ample. However, the *Arcades* has its share of theoretical confusions and historical omissions, and we have aimed to be fair but unsparing in our assessment of them (a moment's glance at Benjamin's own reviewing practice reveals this is no less than he deserves). In the illustrious gallery of influential theorists, Benjamin has perhaps come in for less open chastisement than most. Like Adorno, Derrida, Foucault, Lacan, he has his full complement of ardent admirers, but has remained relatively immune to the virulent detraction that accompanies theoretical importance. If anything, the harshest critics have been what Bobby Fischer would have called his 'frenemies', those closest to him such as Adorno, Horkheimer and Scholem. We've been dazzled, too, but in each case we have stepped out of the light for a moment to get a better look at what was on offer. While the insights are real and enduring, the blindspots are striking in their own way, and we have strived throughout to do more than merely note them. At times we have allowed ourselves space to make clear what's missing or needs to be done, but we've often been able only to indicate a possible route out or trace the lineaments of a problem.

Benjamin's other works, and perhaps his *oeuvre* as a whole, have substantial, overarching claims on which one can offer a final assessment, if not a final verdict. The *Arcades*, intentionally or no, is not like that: there are many arguments, and even more exemplification, and evidence, but the end result is a network or web of connected claims, without a clear hierarchical patterning. To that extent it's been impossible for us to go beyond the structure of the text under discussion, unless we wanted to provide something other than a commentary. Certainly, if you seek a Benjaminian handbook, the *Arcades* is a rather discouraging place to start. But for those who want to find in it a programme for future work, it does offer an eccentric set of imperatives: Collect. Stroll. Gamble. Redeem. But make sure to reserve yourself a good place in the library as well.

Notes

1   Wohlfarth, 'Re-fusing theology', pp. 5–6.
2   Benjamin, 'On the concept of history', p. 390 (Thesis III); Wohlfarth, 'Re-fusing Theology', pp. 5–6.
3   Buck-Morss, *Dialectics of Seeing*, p. 6.

Bibliography

Abdy, Jane, *The French Poster: Chéret to Cappiello*, London, Studio Vista, 1969.

Adorno, Theodor W., 'A portrait of Walter Benjamin', in *Prisms*, trans. Samuel and Shierry Weber, Cambridge, Mass., MIT Press, 1981, pp. 227–41.

——, *Minima Moralia: Reflections from Damaged Life* [1951], trans. E. F. N. Jephcott, London, Verso, 1981.

Adorno, T. W. et al., *Aesthetics and Politics*, London, Verso, 1980.

Aragon, Louis, *Paris Peasant*, trans. Simon Watson Taylor, London, Pan, 1980.

Barnicoat, John, *Posters: A Concise History*, New York, Thames and Hudson, 1972.

Barre, Josette, *La Colline de la Croix Rousse, histoire et géographie urbaine*, Lyon, Privat, 1993.

Barrès, Maurice, *La Terre et les morts, sur quelles réalités fonder la conscience française*, Paris, Bureau de la Patrie Française, 1900.

Barrows, Susanna, *Distorting Mirrors: Visions of the Crowd in Late Nineteenth-Century France*, New Haven, Yale University Press, 1981.

Bataille, Georges, *Visions of Excess: Selected Writings, 1927–1939*, trans. and ed. Allan Stoekl, Minneapolis, University of Minnesota Press, 1985.

Baudelaire, Charles, 'The painter of modern life', in *Selected Writings on Art and Artists*, Harmondsworth, Penguin, 1972.

——, *Complete Poems*, trans. Walter Martin, Manchester, Carcanet, 1997.

——, *The Flowers of Evil: A New Translation with Parallel French Text*, trans. James McGowan, Oxford, Oxford University Press, 1998.

——, *Oeuvres complètes*, Paris: Robert Laffont, 1980.

Beck, Ulrich, 'The cosmopolitan society and its enemies', *Theory, Culture and Society*, 19: 1–2, (2002), 17–44.

Bellina, A., *Les Polonais et la Commune de Paris*, n.p., 1871.

Bellman, H., *Architects of the New Age: Bright, Kossuth, Lincoln, Mazzini and Tolstoy; with an Introductory Essay*, London: S. Low, Marston, 1929.

Benjamin, Andrew (ed.), *The Problems of Modernity: Adorno and Benjamin*, London, Routledge, 1989.

Benjamin, Walter, *Œuvres de Walter Benjamin*, 2 vols, ed. Maurice de Gandillac, Paris, Les Lettres Nouvelles, Denoël, 1971.

——, *Gesammelte Schriften*, 7 vols, ed. Rolf Tiedemann and Hermann Schweppenhäuser, Frankfurt am Main, Suhrkamp, 1972–89.

——, *Understanding Brecht*, trans. Anna Bostock, London, NLB, 1973.

——, *The Origin of German Tragic Drama*, trans. John Osborne, London, New Left Books, 1977.

——, 'Conversations with Brecht', in T. W. Adorno and others *Aesthetics and Politics*, London, Verso, 1980.

——, *Das Passagen-Werk*, Vols 1 and 2, ed. Rolf Tiedemann, Frankfurt am Main, Suhrkamp, 1982.

——, *Charles Baudelaire: A Lyric Poet in the Era of High Capitalism*, London, Verso, 1983.

——, *The Correspondence of Walter Benjamin*, ed. Theodor Adorno and Gershom Scholem, trans. Manfred R. Jacobson and Evelyn M. Jacobson, Chicago and London, University of Chicago Press, 1994.

——, *Selected Writings, Volume 1, 1913–1926*, ed. Marcus Bullock and Michael W. Jennings, Cambridge, Mass. and London, Belknap Press, 1996.

——, *Selected Writings, Volume 2, 1927–1934*, ed. Michael W. Jennings, Howard Eiland and Gary Smith, trans. Rodney Livingstone and others, Cambridge, Mass. and London, Belknap Press, 1999.

——, *The Arcades Project*, ed. Rolf Tiedemann, trans. Howard Eiland and Kevin McLaughlin, Cambridge, Mass. and London, Belknap Press, 1999.

——, *Selected Writings, Volume 3, 1935–1938*, ed. Howard Eiland and Michael W. Jennings, trans. Edmund Jephcott, Howard Eiland and others, Cambridge, Mass. and London, Belknap Press, 2002.

——, *Selected Writings, Volume 4, 1938–1940*, ed. Howard Eiland and Michael W. Jennings, trans. Edmund Jephcott and others, Cambridge, Mass. and London, Belknap Press, 2003.

Benjamin, Walter and Theodor Adorno, *The Complete Correspondence 1928–1940*, ed. Henri Lonitz, trans. Nicholas Walker, Cambridge, Polity Press, 1999.

Benjamin, Walter and Gershom Scholem, *The Correspondence of Walter Benjamin and Gershom Scholem, 1932–1940*, ed. Gershom Scholem, trans. Gary Smith and Andre Lefevere, Cambridge, Mass., Harvard University Press, 1992.

Bensaude-Vincent, Bernadette and Christine Blondel (eds.), *Des Savants face à l'occulte, 1870–1940*, Paris, La Découverte, 2002.

Béraud, F. F. A., *Les Filles publiques de Paris et la police qui les régit*, Paris and Leipzig, 1839.

Biale, David, *Gershom Scholem: Kabbalah and Counter-History*, 2nd edn, Cambridge, Mass. and London, Harvard University Press, 1982.

Blanqui, [Louis-] Auguste, *Textes choisis*, Les Classiques du Peuple, Moscow, Éditions Sociales, 1955.

——, *L'Éternité par les astres* [1872], ed. Lisa Block de Behar, Geneva, Fleuron, 1996.

——, *Science et foi*, Conflans-Sainte-Honorine, Édition de la Revue L'Idée Libre, 1925.

——, *Instructions pour une prise d'armes; L'Éternité par les astres, hypothèse astronomique et autres texts*, ed. Miguel Abensour & Valentin Pelosse, Paris, Société encyclopédique française, Éditions de la Tête de feuilles, 1973.

Bloch, Ernst, *The Principle of Hope*, Oxford, Blackwell, [1959] 1986.

Bonnell, Victoria E., *Iconography of Power: Soviet Political Posters under Lenin and Stalin*, Berkeley, California University Press, 1997.

Bosc, Ernest, *Dictionnaire de l'art, de la curiosité et du bibelot*, Paris, 1883.

Un bourgeois républicain, *Histoire de l'internationale, (1862–1872)*, London, Paris and Brussels, n.p., Combe et Vande Weghe, 1873

Brecht, Bertolt, *Brecht on Theatre: The Development of an Aesthetic*, 2nd edn, trans. and ed. John Willett, London, Methuen, 1974.

—— , *Poems, Part 2, 1929–1938*, ed. John Willett and Ralph Manheim, London, Methuen, 1976.

——, *Plays: One*, London, Methuen, 1987.

Bredekamp, Horst, 'From Walter Benjamin to Carl Schmitt, via Thomas Hobbes', *Critical Inquiry*, 25: 2 (1999), 247–66.

Breton, André, *Manifestoes of Surrealism*, trans. Richard Seaver and Helen R. Lane, Ann Arbor, University of Michigan Press, 1969.

——, *Communicating Vessels*, trans. Mary Ann Caws and Geoffrey T. Harris, Lincoln, NE, University of Nebraska Press, 1990.

Britzolakis, Christina, 'Phantasmagoria: Walter Benjamin and the poetics of urban modernism', in Peter Buse and Andrew Stott (eds), *Ghosts: Deconstruction, Psychoanalysis, History*, Basingstoke, Macmillan, 1999, pp. 72–91.

Brodersen, Momme, *Walter Benjamin: A Biography*, trans. Malcolm R. Green and Ingrida Ligers, London, Verso, 1997.

Brubaker, R., *Citizenship and Nationhood in France and Germany*, Cambridge, Mass., Harvard University Press, 1992

Bruckner, Pascal, *Le Vertige de Babel*, Paris, Arléa, 2000.

Buber, Martin, *Drei Reden über das Judentum*, Frankfurt am Main, Rütten and Loening, 1911.

——, *On Judaism*, New York, Schocken, 1967.

Buck-Morss, Susan, *The Dialectics of Seeing: Walter Benjamin and the Arcades Project*, Cambridge, Mass. and London, MIT Press, 1989.

Bukatman, Scott, 'The artificial infinite: on special effects and the sublime', in Annette Kuhn (ed.), *Alien Zone II: The Spaces of Science Fiction Cinema*, London, Verso, 1999, pp. 249–75.

Burton, Richard, *Baudelaire and the Second Republic: Writing and Revolution*, Oxford, Clarendon Press, 1991.

Burton, Richard D. E., *The Flaneur and His City: Patterns of Daily Life in Paris, 1815–1851*, Durham, University of Durham, 1994.

Caceres, Béatrice and Yannick Le Boulicaut, *Les Écrivains de l'Exil: Cosmopolitisme ou ethnicité*, Paris, L'Harmattan, 2002.

Camp, Maxime du, *Les Ancêtres de la Commune, l'attentat Fieschi*, Paris, Charpentier, 1877.

Caron, Vicki, *Uneasy Asylum: France and the Jewish Refugee Crisis 1933–1942*, Palo Alto, CA, Stanford University Press, 1999.

Certeau, Michel de, *Heterologies: Discourses on the Other*, Manchester, Manchester University Press, 1986.

Chevalier, Louis, *Classes laborieuses et classes dangereuses*, Paris, Plon, 1958.

——, *Montmartre des plaisirs et du crime*, Paris, Robert Laffont, 1980.

Clark, T. J., 'Reservations of the marvellous', *London Review of Books*, 22 June 2000, 3–9.

——, 'Should Benjamin have read Marx?', *boundary 2*, 30: 1 (2003), 31–49.

Cohen, Margaret, *Profane Illumination: Walter Benjamin and the Paris of Surrealist Revolution*, Berkeley and London, University of California Press, 1993.

Daudet, Léon, *Le Stupide XIXe Siècle: exposé des insanités meutrières qui se sont abattues sur la France depuis 130 ans, 1789–1919*, Paris, Nouvelle Librairie Nationale, 1922

Deleuze, Gilles and Félix Guattari, *A Thousand Plateaus*, London, Continuum, 2002.

Delorme, Jean-Claude and Anne-Marie Dubois, *Les Passages couverts parisiens*, Paris, Parigramme, 1996.

Derrida, Jacques, *Spectres of Marx: The State of the Debt, the Work of Mourning, and the New International*, trans. Peggy Kamuf, London and New York, Routledge, 1994.

Doisneau, Robert, *Passages et galleries du xixème siècle*, texte Bernard Delveille, Paris, ACE, 1981.

Dommanget, Maurice, *Auguste Blanqui à Belle Ile*, Paris, Librarie du Travail, 1935.

——, *Un Drame politique en 1848: Blanqui et le document Taschereau*, Paris, Les Deux Sirènes, 1948.

——, *Auguste Blanqui au début de la Troisième République, 1871–1880, dernière prison et ultimes combats*, Paris, La Haye: Mouton, 1971.

Drumont, Édouard, *La France juive: essai d'histoire contemporaine*, Paris, C. Marpon & E. Flammarion, 1886.

Dufour-El Maleh, Marie-Cécile, *La Nuit Sauvée: Walter Benjamin et la pensée de l'histoire*, Brussels, Ousia, 1993.

Dyer, Gillian, *Advertising as Communication*, London, Methuen, 1982.

Eagleton, Terry, 'A Visionary at the Crossroads', *Times Higher Education Supplement*, 11 July 2003.

Ferguson, Priscilla Parkhurst, *Paris as Revolution: Writing the Nineteenth Century City*, Berkeley, University of California Press, 1994.

Fife, John (ed.), *Manual of the Turkish Bath: Heat a Mode of Cure and a Source of Strength for Men and Animals*, London, Mr. Urquhart, 1865.

Flaubert, Gustave, *The Letters of Gustave Flaubert, 1857–1880*, trans. Francis Steegmuller, Cambridge, Mass., Harvard University Press, 1982.

Fleming, Marie, *The Anarchist Way to Socialism: Elisée Reclus and Nineteenth-century Europe*, London, Croom Helm, 1979.

Forth, Christopher, *Zarathustra in Paris: The Nietzsche Vogue in France*,

1891–1918, DeKalb, Northern Illinois University Press, 2001.

Freud, Sigmund, *The Interpretation of Dreams* [1900], *Pelican Freud Library*, vol. 4, trans. James Strachey, Harmondsworth, Penguin Books, 1976.

——, *Jokes and their Relation to the Unconscious* [1905], *Pelican Freud Library*, vol. 6, Harmondsworth, Penguin Books, 1976.

——, 'The uncanny', in *Art and Literature*, *Pelican Freud Library*, vol. 14, trans. James Strachey, Harmondsworth, Penguin Books, 1985, pp. 335–76.

——, 'The Moses of Michelangelo', in *Art and Literature*, *Pelican Freud Library*, vol. 14, trans. James Strachey, Harmondsworth, Penguin Books, 1985, pp. 249–82.

Frisby, David, *Fragments of Modernity: Social Theories of Modernity in the Works of Georg Simmel, Siegfried Kracauer and Walter Benjamin*, Cambridge, Polity Press, 1986.

Gagnebin, J.-M., *Histoire et narration chez Walter Benjamin*, Paris, L'Harmattan, 1994.

Gaillard, Jeanne, *Paris, la Ville 1852–1870*, Lille, Champion, 1976.

Gavagna, Riccardo, *Benjamin in Italia, bibliographica italiana, 1956–1980*, Florence, Sansoni, 1982.

Geffroy, Gustave, *L'enfermé*, Paris, Charpentier, 1897.

Geist, Johann Friedrich, *Arcades: The History of a Building Type*, Cambridge, Mass., MIT Press, 1983.

Gilloch, Graeme, *Myth and Modernity*, Cambridge, Polity Press, 1996.

Goldstein, Robert Justin, *Censorship of Political Caricature in Nineteenth-Century France*, Kent, Ohio, Kent State University Press, 1989.

Gratry, R. P., *La Crise de la foi*, Paris, C. Douniol, 1863.

Greenhalgh, Paul, *Ephemeral Vistas: The* Expositions Universelles, *Great Exhibitions and World's Fairs, 1851–1939*, Manchester, Manchester University Press, 1988.

Gunnell, Doris, *Stendhal et l'Angleterre*, Paris, Charles Bosse, 1909.

Habermas, Jürgen, 'Consciousness-raising or rescuing critique', in *Philosophico-Political Profiles*, trans. Frederick G. Lawrence, Cambridge, Polity Press, 1983.

Haine, W. Scott, *The World of the Paris Café: Sociability among the French Working Class, 1789–1914*, Baltimore and London, Johns Hopkins University Press, 1996.

Hannerz, Ulf, 'Cosmopolitans and locals in world culture', *Theory Culture & Society*, 7: 2 (1990), 237–51.

Hansen, Miriam, 'Foreword', in Oskar Negt and Alexander Kluge, *Public Sphere and Experience: Towards an Analysis of the Bourgeois and Proletarian Public Sphere*, Minneapolis, University of Minnesota Press, [1972] 1993, pp. xvi–xvii.

——, 'Benjamin, cinema and experience: "the blue flower in the land of technology"', *New German Critique*, 40 (1987), 179–224.

——, 'Room-for-play: Benjamin's gamble with cinema', *October*, 109 (2004), 3–45.

Harvey, David, *Consciousness and the Urban Experience: Studies in the History and Theory of Capitalist Urbanization*, Oxford, Blackwell, 1985.

——, *Paris: Capital of Modernity*, London, Routledge, 2003.

Hill, Christopher, *Society and Puritanism in Pre-revolutionary England*, London, Secker & Warburg, 1964.

Hillier, Bevis, *Posters*, London, Spring Books, 1974.

Hutton, Patrick H., *The Cult of the Revolutionary Tradition: The Blanquists in French Politics, 1864–1893*, Berkeley, University of California Press, 1981.

Iliasu, A. A., 'The Cobden–Chevalier commercial treaty of 1860', *The Historical Journal*, 14: 1 (1971), 67–98.

Ingram, David, 'Between political liberalism and postnational cosmopolitanism: toward an alternative theory of human rights', *Political Theory*, 31: 3 (2003), 359–91.

Jameson, Fredric, 'Beyond the cave: demystifying the ideology of modernism', in Francis Mulhern (ed.), *Contemporary Marxist Literary Criticism*, London, Longman, 1992, pp. 168–87.

——, 'The theoretical hesitation: Benjamin's sociological predecessor', *Critical Inquiry*, 25: 2 (1999), 267–88.

Jankowski, Paul, *Stavisky: A Confidence Man in the Republic of Virtue*, Ithaca and London: Cornell University Press, 2002.

Jenner, Mark and Bertrand Taithe, 'The historiographical body', in John Pickstone and Roger Cooter (eds), *History of Medicine in the Twentieth Century*, New York, Harwood Publishing, 1999, pp. 187–200.

Jezower, Ignaz, *Des Buch der Träume*, Berlin, Rowohlt, 1928.

Joyce, Patrick, *Visions of the People*, Cambridge, Cambridge University Press, 1991.

Kahn, Robert, *Images, passages: Marcel Proust et Walter Benjamin*, Paris, Kiné, 1998.

Kamenka, Eugene, *Paradigm for Revolution? The Paris Commune, 1871–1971*, Canberra, Australian National University Press, 1972.

Kittsteiner, H. D., 'Walter Benjamin's historicism', *New German Critique*, 39 (1986), 179–215.

Koepnick, Lutz P., 'The spectacle, the *Trauerspiel*, and the politics of resolution: Benjamin reading the Baroque reading Weimar', *Critical Inquiry*, 22:2 (1996), 268–91.

Krauss, Rosalind, *The Optical Unconscious*, Cambridge, Mass., MIT Press, 1993.

Kristeva, Julia, *Le Temps sensible: Proust et l'expérience littéraire*, Paris, Gallimard, 1994.

Kropotkine, Petr, *Anarchistes en exil: correspondance inédite de Pierre Kropotkine*, Paris, Institut d'études slaves, 1995.

Lacan, Jacques, *The Four Fundamental Concepts of Psychoanalysis*, trans. Alan Sheridan, Harmondsworth, Penguin Books, 1977.

Langford, Rachael, *Jules Vallès and the Narration of History: Contesting the French Third Republic in the Jacques Vingtras Trilogy*, Bern, Peter Lang, 1999.

Laqueur, T. W., 'Sexual desire and the market economy during the industrial revolution', in D. C. Stanton (ed.), *Discourses of Sexuality: From Aristotle to AIDS*,

Ann Arbor, University of Michigan Press, 1992, pp. 185–215.

Le Bon, Gustave, *The Crowd: A Study of the Popular Mind*, London, T. Fisher Unwin, 1896.

Lehning, James R., *To Be a Citizen: The Political Culture of the Early French Third Republic*, Ithaca, Cornell University Press, 2001.

Lejuif, Bernard, 'Les Apatrides' (Thèse de doctorat, université de Caen, 1939).

Lemoine, Bertrand, *Les Passages couverts en France*, Paris, Délégation à l'Action Artistique de la Ville de Paris, 1989.

Leslie, Esther, 'Telescoping the microscopic object: Benjamin the collector', in Alex Coles (ed.), *The Optic of Walter Benjamin*, London, Black Dog, 1999, pp. 58–93.

——, *Walter Benjamin: Overpowering Conformism*, London, Pluto, 2000.

——, 'Stars, phosphor and chemical colours: extraterrestiality in *The Arcades*', *new formations*, 54 (2004/5), 13–27.

Lipovano, I. P., *L'Apatridie*, Paris, Les Éditions Internationales, 1935.

Loyer, François, *Paris XIXe siècle: L'Immeuble et l'espace urbain*, Paris, Imprimerie de l'APUR, 1982.

Lukács, Georg, *History and Class Consciousness*, trans. Rodney Livingstone, Cambridge Mass., MIT Press, 1971.

Mack Smith, D., *Mazzini*, New Haven, Yale University Press, 1994.

McLaughlin, Kevin and Philip Rosen (eds), *Benjamin Now: Critical Encounters with* The Arcades Project, *boundary 2*, 30:1 (2003).

Maitron, Jean, *Le Mouvement anarchiste en France*, vol. 1, Paris, Gallimard, 1975.

Mallgrave, Harry Francis and Eleftherios Ikonomou (eds), *Empathy, Form, and Space: Problems in German Aesthetics 1873–1893*, Chicago, University of Chicago Press, 1994.

Marcus, Sharon, *Apartment Stories: City and Home in Nineteenth-century Paris and London*, Berkeley, University of California Press, 1999.

Marx, Karl, *Die Frühschriften*, Stuttgart, Alfred Kröner, 1953.

——, *Early Writings*, trans. Rodney Livingstone and Gregor Benton, Harmondsworth: Penguin, 1975.

——, *Capital*, vol.1, trans. Ben Fowkes, London, Lawrence and Wishart, 1977.

Mayer, Hans, *Der Zeitgenosse Walter Benjamin*, Frankfurt am Main, Jüdischer Verlag, 1992.

Mertens, Bram, '*The Arcades Project*: a Talmud for our time', *new formations*, 54 (2005).

Milner, John, *Art, War and Revolution in France 1870–1871, Myth Reportage and Reality*, New Haven and London, Yale University Press, 2000.

Moncan, Patrice de, *Les Passages de Paris*, Paris, Seesan, 1990.

——, *Le Guide des passages de Paris*, Paris, Seesan, 1991.

——, *Les Passages en Europe*, Paris, Edn du Mécène, 1993.

——, *Les Passages couverts de Paris*, Paris, Edn du Mécène, 1995.

——, *Guide littéraire des passages de Paris*, Paris, Hermé, 1996.

Monnoyer, Jean-Maurice (ed.), *Walter Benjamin*, avec les témoignages d'Adrienne Monnier, de Gisèle Freund et de Jean Seltz, Paris, Gallimard, 1991.

Benjamin's *Arcades*

Morris, William, 'Useful work versus useless toil', in A. L. Morton (ed.), *The Political Writings*, London, Lawrence and Wishart, 1973, pp. 86–109.
——, 'Review of Edward Bellamy's *Looking Backward*' [1889], in A. L. Morton (ed.), *The Political Writings*, London, Lawrence and Wishart, 1984, pp. 245–53.
Münster, Arno *Progrès et catastrophe, Walter Benjamin et l'histoire: Réflexion sur l'itinéraire philosophique d'un Marxisme mélancolique*, Paris, Kiné, 1996
Muray, Philippe, *Le Dix-neuvième siècle à travers les âges*, 2nd edn, Paris, Gallimard, 1999.
Nava, Mica, Andrew Blake, Iain MacRury and Barry Richards (eds), *Buy this Book: Studies in Advertising and Consumption*, London, Routledge, 1997.
Niethammer, Lutz, 'The blown-away angel: on the posthistory of a historical epistemology of danger', in *Posthistoire: Has History Come to an End?*, trans. Patrick Camiller, London, Verso, 1992, pp. 101–34.
Nora, Pierre (ed.), *Realms of Memory,* 3 vols., New York, Columbia University Press, 1996–8.
Nussbaum, Martha, et al., *For Love of Country: Debating the Limits of Patriotism*, Boston, Beacon Press, 1996.
Nye, Robert, *The Origins of Crowd Psychology: Gustave Le Bon and the Crisis of Mass Democracy in the Third Republic*, London, Sage, 1975.
——, *Crime, Madness and Politics in Modern France: The Medical Concept of National Decline*, Princeton, NJ, Princeton University Press, 1984.
Oettermann, Stephan, *The Panorama: History of a Mass Medium*, New York, Zone Books, 1997.
Oppenheim, Janet, *The Other World: Spiritualism and Psychical Research in England, 1850–1914*, Cambridge, Cambridge University Press, 1985.
Osborne, Peter, *The Politics of Time: Modernity and Avant-Garde*, London, Verso, 1995.
——, 'Small-scale victories, large-scale defeats: Walter Benjamin's politics of time', in Andrew Benjamin and Peter Osborne (eds), *Walter Benjamin's Philosophy: Destruction and Experience*, 2nd edn, Manchester, Clinamen Press, 2000, pp. 55–107.
'Passages de Paris', Géo, 274 (Juin 2001).
Paz, Maurice, *Un Révolutionnaire professionnel: Auguste Blanqui*, Paris, Fayard, 1984.
Pilbeam, Pam, *Madame Tussaud and the History of Waxworks*, London, Hambledon, 2002.
Poole, Brian 'From phenomenology to dialogue: Max Scheler's phenomenological tradition and Mikhail Bakhtin's development from "Toward a philosophy of the act" to his study of Dostoevsky', in Ken Hirschkop and David Shepherd (eds.), *Bakhtin and Cultural Theory*, 2nd edn, Manchester, Manchester University Press, 2001, pp. 109–35.
Proust, Marcel, *In Search of Lost Time*, vol. 1, *Swann's Way*, trans. C. K. Scott-Moncrieff and Terence Kilmartin, rev. D. J. Enright, London, Vintage, 1996.

Rabinach, Anson, 'Between enlightenment and apocalypse: Benjamin, Bloch and modern Jewish messianism', *New German Critique*, 34 (1985), 78–124.

Raulet, G., 'Citizenship, otherness and cosmopolitism in Kant', *Social Science Information — Sur Les Sciences Sociales*, 35: 3 (September 1996), 437–46.

Remarque, E. M., *Liebe Deinen Nächsten*, Munich, Desch, 1953.

Rifkin, Adrian and Roger Thomas (eds), *Voices of the People: The Politics and Life of 'La Sociale' at the End of the Second Empire*, London, Routledge & Kegan Paul, 1987.

Rochlitz, Rainer, *Le Désenchantement de l'art: la philosophie de Walter Benjamin*, Paris, Gallimard, 1992.

Rorty, Richard, *Achieveing Our Country: Leftist Thought in Twentieth-century America*, Cambridge, Mass., Harvard University Press, 1998.

Rose, Gillian, 'Walter Benjamin – out of the sources of modern Judaism', *new formations*, 20 (1993), 59–81.

Rosen, Philip, 'Introduction' to *Benjamin Now: Critical Encounters with* The Arcades Project, *boundary 2*, 30: 1 (2003), 1–15.

Rude, Fernand, *L'Insurrection Lyonnaise de novembre 1832: Le Mouvement ouvrier à Lyon de 1827–1832*, Paris, Anthropos, 1969.

Sabatier, P., *Histoire de la législation sur les femmes publiques et les lieux de débauches*, Paris, 1828.

Samuel, Raphael, 'Reading the signs', I and II, *History Workshop Journal*, 32 (1991), 88–109; 33 (1992), 220–51.

——, *Theatres of Memory: Past and Present in Contemporary Culture*, London, Verso, 1992.

——, *Island Stories: Unravelling Britain*, London, Verso, 1998.

Sartre, Jean-Paul, *Baudelaire*, Paris, Gallimard, 1947.

Schmitt, Carl, *The Concept of the Political* [1931], trans. George Schwab, New Brunswick, NJ, Rutgers University Press, 1976.

——, *Political Theology: Four Chapters on the Concept of Sovereignty* [1922], trans. George Schwab, Cambridge, Mass., MIT Press, 1985.

——, 'The source of the tragic', *Telos*, 72 (1987), 133–51.

——, *The Crisis of Parliamentary Democracy* [1923], trans. Ellen Kennedy, Cambridge, Mass., MIT Press, 1988.

Scholem, Gershom, *The Messianic Idea in Judaism*, London, Allen & Unwin, 1971.

——, 'Walter Benjamin and his angel', in *On Jews and Judaism in Crisis*, New York: Schocken Books, 1976, pp. 198–236.

——, *Walter Benjamin: The Story of a Friendship* (London: Faber & Faber, 1982).

Schor, Ralph, *L'Opinion française et les Étrangers 1919–1939*, Paris, Publication de la Sorbonne, 1985.

Schwartz, Vanessa, *Early Mass Culture in Fin-de-siècle Paris*, Berkeley, University of California Press, 1998.

Schulkind, Eugene, *The Paris Commune of 1871: The View from the Left*, New York, Grove Press, 1974.

Simmel, Georg, 'The metropolis and mental life', in D. Levine (ed.), *Individuality and Social Forms*, Chicago, University of Chicago Press, 1974.

Smith, Roger, *Inhibition: History and Meaning in the Science of Mind and Brain*, Berkeley, University of California Press, 1992.

Sontag, Susan, 'Notes on "camp"' [1964], in *Against Interpretation*, New York, Dell, 1969, pp. 277–93.

Steedman, Carolyn, *Dust*, Manchester, Manchester University Press, 2001.

Stendhal, *Souvenirs d'égotisme*, Paris, Le Divan, 1927.

Surya, Michel, *Georges Bataille: An Intellectual Biography* (1992), trans. Krzysztof Fijalkowski and Michael Richardson, London and New York, Verso, 2002.

Taithe, Bertrand, '*Monuments aux Morts*? Reading Nora's *Realms of Memory* and Samuel's *Theatres of Memory*', *History of the Human Sciences*, 12:2 (1999), 123–39.

——, *Citizenship and Wars: France in Turmoil, 1870–1*, London, Routledge, 2001.

Thomas, Brook, *The New Historicism: And Other Old-fashioned Topics*, Princeton, NJ, Princeton University Press, 1991.

Thomas, Keith, *Religion and the Decline of Magic: Studies in Popular Beliefs in Sixteenth and Seventeenth-century England*, Harmondsworth, Penguin, 1973.

Thompson, E. P., *William Morris*, New York, Pantheon Books, 1976.

——, *Customs in Common*, London, Merlin, 1991.

Thompson, Victoria E., *The Virtuous Marketplace: Money and Politics in Paris, 1830–1870*, Baltimore and London, Johns Hopkins University Press, 2000.

Tiedemann, Rolf, *Études sur la philosophie de Walter Benjamin*, revised edition of 1973, Arles, Actes Sud, 1987.

——, 'Dialectics at a standstill: approaches to the *Passagen-Werk*', in Walter Benjamin, *The Arcades Project*, ed. Rolf Tiedemann, trans. Howard Eiland and Kevin McLaughlin, Cambridge, Mass. and London, Belknap Press, 1999. pp. 929–45.

Tisa, John (ed.) *The Palette and the Flame: Posters of the Spanish Civil War*, Wellingborough, Collett's, 1980.

Tombs, Robert, 'Prudent rebels: the Second Arrondissement during the Paris Commune of 1871', *French History*, 5: 4 (1991), 393–413.

——, '"Les Communeux dans la ville": des analyses récentes à l'étranger', *Le Mouvement Social*, 179 (1997), 93–104.

Turner, Bryan S., 'Cosmopolitan virtue, globalization and patriotism', *Theory, Culture and Society*, 19:1–2 (2002), 45–63.

Turner, E. S. *The Shocking History of Advertising!*, Harmondsworth, Penguin, 1965.

Vallès, Jules, *Oeuvres complètes: Souvenirs d'un étudiant pauvre, le candidat des pauvres, lettre à Jules Mirès*, Paris, Éditeurs Français Réunis, 1972.

Varouxakis, G., *Mill on Nationality*, London, Routledge, 2002.

Vignier, Philippe, *Blanqui et les Blanquistes*, Paris, SEDES, 1986.

Viroli, Maurizio, *For Love of Country: An Essay on Patriotism and Nationalism*, Oxford, Oxford University Press, 1995.

Wahnich, Sophie, *L'Impossible Citoyen, l'étranger dans le discours de la Révolution française,* Paris, Albin Michel, 1997.

Walton, Whitney, *France at the Crystal Palace: Bourgeois Taste and Artisan Manufacture in the Nineteenth Century,* Berkeley, University of California Press, 1992.

Wassermann, Suzanne, *Les Clubs de Barbès et de Blanqui en 1848,* Paris, E. Cornély, 1913.

Weber, Max, *The Protestant Ethic and the Spirit of Capitalism,* London, Allen and Unwin, 1930.

——, *General Economic History,* trans. F. H. Knight, New York, Collier Books, 1961.

Weber, Samuel, 'Taking exception to decision: Walter Benjamin and Carl Schmitt', *Diacritics* 22: 3–4 (1992), 5–18.

Weigel, Sigrid, *Body- and Image-space: Rereading Walter Benjamin,* trans. G. Paul, London and New York, Routledge, 1996.

Weil, Patrick, *The transformation of Immigration Policies: Immigration Control and Nationality Laws in Europe: A Comparative Approach,* Series, EUI working paper EUF; no. 98/5, San Domenico, European University Institute, European Forum, c. 1998

Weil, Simone, *L'Enracinement,* Paris, Gallimard NRF, [1943] 1949.

Weingrad, Michael, 'The College of Sociology and the Institute of Social Research', *New German Critique,* 84 (2001), 130–61.

Weisberg, Gabriel P. (ed.), *Montmartre and the Making of Mass Culture,* New Brunswick, NJ, Rutgers University Press, 2001.

Werckmeister, O. K., 'Walter Benjamin's angel of history, or the transfiguration of the revolutionary into the historian', *Critical Inquiry,* 22:2 (Winter 1996), 239–67.

White, Stephen, *The Bolshevik Poster,* New Haven, Yale University Press, 1988.

Wiggershaus, Rolf, *The Frankfurt School: Its History, Theories and Political Significance,* trans. Michael Robertson, Cambridge, Polity, 1994.

Williamson, Judith, *Decoding Advertisements: Ideology and Meaning in Advertising,* London, Marion Boyars, 1978.

Wischermann, Clemens and Elliot Shore (eds), *Advertising and the Modern European City: Historical Perspectives,* Aldershot, Ashgate, 2000.

Wismann, Heinz, *Walter Benjamin et Paris,* Paris, CERF, 1986.

Wismann, Heinz, interview by Lionel Richard, *Magazine Littéraire,* 408 (April, 2002).

Witte, Bernd, *Walter Benjamin: An Intellectual Biography,* trans. James Rolleston, Detriot: Wayne State University Press, 1991.

Wohlfarth, Irving, 'On the messianic structure of Walter Benjamin's last reflections', *Glyph,* 3 (1978), 148–212.

——, 'Re-fusing theology: some first responses to Walter Benjamin's Arcades Project', *New German Critique* 39 (1986), 3–24.

——, 'The measure of the possible, the weight of the real and the heat of the moment: Benjamin's actuality today', *new formations,* 20 (1993), 1–20.

Wolin, Richard, *Walter Benjamin: An Aesthetic of Redemption*, New York, Columbia University Press, 1982.

Woolf, Stuart (ed.), *Nationalism in Europe, 1815 to the Present: A Reader*, London, Routledge, 1996.

Zévaès, Alexandre, *Auguste Blanqui, patriote et socialiste français*, Paris, Marcel Rivière, 1920.

——, 'Une Révolution manquée', *Nouvelle Revue Critique*, 17 (1933), 89–95.

Žižek, Slavoj, *The Sublime Object of Ideology*, London, Verso, 1989.

Zola, E., *Nana*, Paris, Bibliopolis, [1880] 1999.

——, *Au bonheur des dames*, Paris, Bibliopolis, [1883] 1999.

——, *L'Argent*, Paris, Bibliopolis, [1891] 1999).

~

Index